Aging Consciously, Dying Awake

...a path forward

Roz Bound

Aging Consciously, Dying Awake

Copy Editor and Design: Jane Churchill

ISBN: 978-0-9881407-3-8

rozwriter@hotmail.com

Helen Harvey
Goddess Conference 2023.
Glastonbury.

To Vicki, my beloved partner who ages with me so gracefully.

With much gratitude to Jim Garrison and the faculty of the Wisdom Graduate School of Ubiquity University for offering such a unique and transforming Doctoral programme that changed my life at such an important time; to Judith Yost (1943~2021) for walking with me through my dissertation journey with such patience; to my dearest children and their children - I love you all so much and am so proud of you; and to my friends far and wide who are so encouraging and supportive. All of you, including Open Floor, the Evolutionaries, Dead Group, Write of Passage, and Death Café, have kept me focussed, and with Jane Churchill's confidence and technical knowledge while evolving my dissertation into this book, have been my inspiration and support. Thank you from the bottom of my heart.

Contents

Prologue, 2021

We do not receive wisdom.
We must discover it for ourselves after a journey through the wilderness which no one else can make for us, which no one else can spare us.
For our wisdom is the point of view from which we come, at last, to regard the world.

Marcel Proust

I am exploring aging in a chaotic world from the perspective of an ordinary woman with a limited income but unlimited dreams, whose several lives in this one lifetime have been lived in very different circumstances all over our planet, and whose environment and society is undergoing fearful changes. At 80, I still play many roles but besides the more recognizable ones, like partner, mother, and writer, those of information-gatherer, energy-holder, wanna-be activist, and ritual-maker now underline my life. Behind each role spiral life stories, both personal and collective, that affect them in very different ways, causing them to play out differently now than they did 40, 20, even five years ago. The umbrella over them all is called tightrope-walker: she who is trying to walk in balance with all states of being in our modern zeitgeist, along with all the factors of aging. We are in a far more fragile place than our new-born selves ever expected. Or maybe they did, and that is why they chose to be born into this time. How can I leave behind a soul legacy to strengthen younger souls as they age into their own uncertain future? As Charles Hugh

Smith writes: 'Who has the time and motivation to comprehend the mess we're in? Almost nobody.'[1]

A huge change is upon us, both in the collective, where institutions as we know them are breaking down, and personally, as my body's time on earth approaches its end. I wrote this at 75, but five years later, I am still wondering what 'old' feels like and it is still very relevant. I am searching my life to see how my thoughts and values about aging and death have evolved and find that tying off threads of connection are a crucial part of Proust's wild journey. Aging in itself has become a practice – actually, a practice in preparation for dying.

Aging with grace is at the centre of the spiral. For me, aging with grace means dispelling the illusions that have accompanied my life thus far, assimilating grief and sorrow that are always in the shadows, trying to 'stay sane in a suicidal culture'[2] as Joanna Macy says. I have reached a point in my life where I have nothing to lose as I peel away the illusions I have grown up with, try to understand the paradigms that surround us, to believe that I can change the world by changing myself, and dig deep to find out who I really am before I die. It's a labour of love.

Aging with grace is trying to discover what consciousness means from an aging perspective, when death is not too far away. Also Macy: 'The most radical thing any one of us can do at this time is to be fully present to what is happening in the world.'[3] Surely this means living in the world as it is today, witnessing the pain of Mother Earth and Her creatures, fitting shock and horror into daily existence without being overwhelmed. It means trying to walk a fine line between light and dark, to find balance in the everyday life I yearn to lead with family, friends, and community in cooperation, gratitude and love, accepting my body changes and its deterioration. The link between aging and dying is organic; I envision them as seamless and cannot visit one without addressing the other.

How would the past me want to be living right now? Certainly not by regretting or wishing, not by pretending or feeling sorry for myself, not by separating myself from the real world and living in denial of what is happening around me. My future self would want me to have witnessed what goes on around me, alert to what affects me. Aging is no pity-party. It is a fact of life, as real as babyhood. Programmed to see babies as adorable in their vulnerability, our culture's response to aging is usually one of distaste and dismissal. This is the old story I need to re-write as a 'new story,' so my way of thinking will naturally carry me forward, maybe even as a template for those coming after me.

My spirituality is earth-based, fairly eclectic. I believe we are all one body with Mother Earth, as above, so below, as within so without, a dance between science and spirituality. I study and work with the Goddess movement while trying to walk the path of Zen wisdom. I grew up with Bible stories told by my beloved grandfather who made sure I always tended the light burning within me and I am beginning to understand that the Cosmic Christ is an archetype. But, like most people, if a truck is bearing down on me on the highway I call out to God for help.

I do believe that the Divine speaks through us, and as I have a female form in this lifetime, I call the Divine She. And I listen to Her. She has no hands, no voice. What greater way can She communicate other than speaking through us, through our words, our art, our music – through our creative process? It is through writing that I find healing, truth, answers, in communication with the Divine.

When I wrote this, as part of a doctoral dissertation, pre-covid, I could not pretend to know what my life would be like at 80 or 90, certainly not dreaming up a pandemic. Still fortunate in health and attitude, though beginning to feel and see differences in my body, mind, and spirit, I am actually excited about reaching 80. My life has definitely not proceeded in a linear fashion, and I have never succeeded in making five- or ten-year plans, though many years ago, I would fantasize about a make-believe future. Then I would wipe away tears for my imagined funeral, but now, ignoring Hollywood's manipulating fantasies, I can coolly plan it out. And I don't fall into the commercial trap that tells me to take the medication that allows frantic games with grandchildren, as the second mortgage makes me and my handsome husband oh so happy. I do not create imaginary dramas any more.

Old life stories have no hold on me, but I use them in story-telling because they have lessons, punch-lines, hidden angels or tricksters, reminders that there is so much more in life than that which we take in with our five senses. I am not my story so I can tell it objectively. And now we need new stories fit for a new paradigm. As I reach aging milestones, and all the daily ones in between, I want to live my life with some measure of peace, self-acceptance and love. I must look at strengthening the whole me, body, mind, spirit and soul, so when my last days arrive, whether by design or circumstance, I will be as ready as can be to leave this land for whatever comes after my last breath.

Birth and death can be counted on to begin and end life as we know it. Animals, humans, fish, birds, plants, minerals, rocks, all have a beginning and an ending. Rocks began multi-millennia ago from crystals that were formed by gases: Birth. Once I took a rock from the ocean and placed it in a bonfire burning on the shore. Three days later, my rock had cracked in the smouldering fire, some of it was reduced to flakes. I brought it home and since then it has continued powdering to a fine dust. It died to its life as a rock: Death. Both are journeys. In one we are welcomed, in the other we are missed - on this planet. Are we missed somewhere when we are born? Are we welcomed somewhere after death?

The older I become, the more I regard the world with an overwhelming depth of appreciation and gratitude for what is real, with an urge to freeze certain moments, to experience them for as long as I can. I used to anticipate mourning their absence in my life after death, although intellectually I know that after I die there won't be 'a life' with sensations enough to feel 'absence' as I now understand it. When we die, activity on our planet will flow like water through the space left by our bodies, and we, or what we think of as 'we,' will be no more. That time seems closer now. This body has breathed for over 80 years; does it know its days are numbered? Is there a cell deep in my reptilian brain that believes in the 'three score years and ten' life span (quite likely absorbed from my father's words, which seemed challenging when he said them), a cell that silently counts off the time I have left before that previously imagined funeral?

If, as Proust says in the epigraph, 'our wisdom is the point of view from which we come, at last, to regard the world,' I wonder if that includes seeing beyond the illusions with a sense of betrayal that everything is not as I thought it was, having been taught by others to see through their eyes instead of learning through my own heart, hypnotized by their images as if staring at the back of Plato's cave. Surely understanding and forgiving the perpetrators of illusions, so-called traditions that I have believed in all my life, and re-framing them a different way could heal the past and create a spiritually sustainable future? And is wisdom for me the grief at loss - loss of people and places, of activities and things, and of innocence? Is it the guilt I feel in my collusion with the pain acted out on Mother Earth by willingly collaborating with the corporate giants who tell me how to survive in a narcissistic world for their gain? It has taken all this time to even know that I could see things as they really are, while sad to lose what I thought was the 'right way,' everything I believed in – or was told to believe in. I wonder if this is the normal preparation process before death, a separation that everyone goes through in these so-called golden years? Does wisdom try to balance it all - in body, mind, spirit and soul? Is that what aging in these times of world chaos is all about?

Strange things make me cry. The trigger has always been the crumbling of illusion, discoveries that nothing is as it has seemed, hypocrisy, the lack of justice. And loss, little dyings, one after the other. Unexpected joy and exuberance in flash-mobs or earnest choirs, a new-born sentient being, also make me tear up. Behind the tears is awe at the depth of feeling, of spirit. I smile readily too: at hopeful inventions, funny emoticons in family tweets, unlikely animal pairs cuddling together in videos, at love expressed. Poignant in their brevity and serendipity, these moments stir something deep - the strength of human spirit.

Change is a certainty, a test of the human spirit. My parents had to adjust to bank machines and computers. Their parents marveled at automobiles, learned how to work with electricity, telephones. My grandparents wouldn't allow a telephone in their house, no letting an intruder into their home. None of my grandparents owned a car. They survived world wars and depressions and could not have imagined the present-day culture of instant communication and surveillance, witnessing insidious drone wars fought like video games. Every morning brings more news of death, destruction, and collapse. Worries about food, finance, and climate change infiltrate decisions and choices. Global terrorists creep into my dreams. My body feels the world's anxiety. When my heart pounds, I know something disastrous is happening somewhere and people are in fear. The insecurity is frightening. But I must not contemplate complacency or ignorance, or revert to the positivity the younger me espoused. We are living in an unprecedented time. I must wake up before I die; I must learn the true meaning of 'waking up.' Once one wakes up to truth, one cannot go back to sleep.

For years, I have read many books and articles about aging, about befriending our emotions, adapting to change, the dangers of the next extinction, positive thinking, stages of dying, and I follow, share, and discuss them all eagerly. But every time, there comes a point in my reading about aging where I feel a disconnect. The answers I am looking for are not found in new hobbies or challenging exercises or cruise ships. Intentions behind them are very important to give everyday life a balance, but not enough for a full, authentic life, especially today. My inner crone tells me not to be satisfied with these messages, and not to join the ranks of deniers, or aging cheerleaders. I want my aging to somehow benefit the collective. I need to dig deeper within and provide what it is I am searching for. I need to go into the darkness, not always be looking for the light. Quoting Lilian Frey-Rohn: 'Without the conscious inclusion of the shadow in daily life, there cannot be a positive relationship to other people, or...an individual relationship to the Divine.'[4] Both are very important as we age.

Books may address aging in body, mind and spirit, but fail to mention the factors we have to deal with in the real world, fears often engendered in the media about civilization's very survival, our family's survival, our own survival. Today, we live under a 'evolve or die' mandate. How does that apply to someone who is becoming more frail and fearful? I am not there yet, but I see others who are, and who live in fear. I need to assimilate what I am learning into my life situation, and, hopefully, exponentially into that of many others. The personal is the universal. There are many others out there who also do not want to deny the truth of what's happening, but do not have a lot of time left to truly understand how we got here and how to leave the planet with grace. I would not be speaking my truth if I did not bring these aspects of life, of my energy field, into any conversation about aging.

Apparently, an anti-aging drug can extend a healthy life span to 120 years - to 'slow down aging...because aging is not an inevitable part of life.' The theory is that if biological aging is slowed down, the health span can be increased and therapy would prevent age-related problems like falling, dementia, etc. 'People could be older (but still) feel young'.[5] The drug is being used on a trial group of 3000. The ripple effect of something like this could be huge. Would the maximum working age be extended? Can governments and corporations afford to pay pensions for longer lives? Would poor people get poorer? And what about the emotional aspect? I hear many older people say that they have heard enough, seen enough, they are ready to die.

Would the fact that they maybe would be more active change that attitude? Not wanting to stand in the way of scientific progress, I doubt if this is the answer.

Overheard yesterday in the supermarket: 'Forget about the golden years. They stink.' And spoken by a bitter-in-life friend, who died alone soon after: 'They say that older women are so valued because they are wise. That's hogwash. Nobody cares about our so-called wisdom. There's no such thing.' There are hundreds of thousands of rooms full of hundreds of thousands of lonely old people living out their lives, for one reason or another, in isolation. How would a life-prolonging pill help them? They could be me. The best of intentions get buried in the morass of despair over illness and finances, loneliness at the end of a life. Where is there room for soul-work in the void that lies ahead of them, each day blending into the next with monotony and fear? Will I get to a certain point when the emphasis will be on my sheer survival day by day? Curiosity about the next meal, absorbed with bodily functions, disparaging the younger generation, fears of falling - will they eclipse my aspirations of grace and a sharp mind, as I have seen in many elders who earlier claimed the same hopes and desires as I do today?

How will I age emotionally and soulfully while the ground constantly shifts beneath my feet? Ideally, I want the process to be positive, holistic, full of grace. How can I move into elderhood with joy and grace, trying to accept a new paradigm and the turbulent changes it brings, without resorting to the clichéd patterns of a so-called senior's attitude? How can I embrace my feelings of guilt, betrayal, and grief without compromising my confidence and integrity? How have my life events come together to prepare me for this moment in time? In documenting an evolving consciousness that has brought me to this moment, I want to create a flexible framework in which to live out my life, true to my soul's path, not caught up in manipulated distractions aimed at hiding the real truth. That is my search.

Often when elderly people get together, their only topics of conversation are grandchildren, cruises, and medications. While not discounting the place of family, holidays, and health in balancing life roles – and we do need to support each other - I sometimes feel disappointed at myself when I join in, hypocritical, as if colluding with Martha Stewart's Good Housekeeping myth. Yes, our discussion groups still chat briefly about recipes and gossip while the tea is brewing. Then we delve in passionate talk about the economy, climate change, and the way each social institution is collapsing in front of our eyes, pondering the existence of democracy in the world, and our own community. We mourn the fact that our age and financial situations prevent us from living as off-the-grid as we would like to, but we still try to blend simple living into our suburban homes.

When we talk about dying, we not only share a common desire to be aware of death by exploring every aspect, but we also see the possibility of a future where our pensions might die before we do, our bank accounts raided, our community under fear of attack, looters stealing our food. I do not read about that in books and articles about aging. In fact, I only read about crisis planning on the websites of survival preppers, some of whom advocate storing guns and ammunition which does not apply to my lifestyle. Though mainstream media did talk about bug-out bags a while ago – briefly. We have even mused over the nightmare of a cleansing where old people are culled, biological trash like stray dogs in Russia, recognizing that science-fiction Mad Max, crazy not so long ago, dares to be a possibility in our lifetime. We also talk about looking after each other in creating our own end-of-life should the need arise, and pledge to support each other in our choices.

This is not intended to be a practical list of skills necessary for sustainabilty and survival, or a diatribe on the state of the world as it stands today. Those observations will soon be obsolete, we can count on that. And this will not be a gathering of elderly musings, or a comparison of what is with what was, wishing myself back in the past. Definitely not. The past is why we are here now. I must remember to learn from it, not wish it back again.

As I practice aging with grace, I am conscious of living in sacred space as Mother Earth turns Her wheel from season to season, honouring the elements. This manuscript travels through the circle of Her year - from the spring air of East's child, new beginnings, new breath, new ideas, to the passionate fire of youth, of summer's South; water's emotional maturing of autumn's West leads to winter's North, darkness and death - ending in the centre where Spirit's regeneration, hope, and love unites heaven and earth. Roots and wings, where magic begins. This container is familiar home for me.

Following this framework, I examine what aging and dying consciously means to me, through essays and memoir, story-telling and theory, metaphor and poetry. The signposts and synchronicities that have led me on my way offer elder wisdom through a personal and collective point of view, wisdom that is accessible to all of us if we are consciously aware of what we are truly seeing, hearing, and feeling. My inner crone was at my shoulder as I wrote, in all her aggravation, encouragement and unconditional love. I invite you in.

... it takes hard digging to get to the roots of one's own convictions...
if you are unwilling to write from the honest, though perhaps far
from final, point of view that represents your present state,
you may come to your deathbed with your contribution to the
world still unmade.

Dorothy Allison

Waking Up

Compared to what we ought to be, we are half awake.

William James

Two photos remain by my computer to remind me of our transitory life. Both are of Homs in Syria: one taken in 2011 shows a wide tree-lined boulevard, low balconied buildings, patio cafes, sun's shadows flickering through bushes. The other Homs photo was taken from the same vantage point in 2014. This one showed bombed-out skeletal buildings, destruction.

Twenty years ago I lived in an apartment north of Toronto, on an avenue eerily similar to the first Homs photo - taller buildings, but the view of the wide street from my window was almost exactly the same. One day, in a news story from Beirut, a video camera followed a woman and a little boy clutching water jugs, hiding from gunfire behind an army tank. They ran from one tank to another to get home. Home was a shell of a building standing in a pile of rubble that looked just like Homs. As I stood, warm and safe, in my tenth-floor apartment, the view before my eyes suddenly transformed into that of a bombed-out neighbourhood, scaffolding instead of apartments, roads blocked by rubble, military vehicles, terror in the air. I watched that scene as if it were right in front of me, and at that moment I knew what a very fine line I walk between my soft carpeted, pantry-filled home, and my Syrian sister's life of fear and struggle. I saw, without seeing, how much I took for granted and how different my life could be in a second. These two photos are a symbol of the moment that another veil shifted for me, the reminder that we are all One had never been more real. And I woke up just a little bit more.

waking up

laid open bare   cut wide heart
    guts osmosing air
no choice how to feel any more
    so this is what happens
beyond free will   when walls
break down   barriers part
love pours in easier   but so does despair
tears flow faster
    you feel so much deeper
        it hurts so much more

you don't understand

remember why you built walls in the first place?
ten Berlin walls thick   no-man's land
    and when the dust cleared
how you found your voice
        through your tears?
    you don't want to live
        behind stone walls again
    the balance will swing
  til it settles the pain
though trembling still   you'll be strong

pray it won't take too long

for now: set no limits
the answer's beyond any thought
you try to stop crying
  get on with your life
    naked and fraught

but they see who you are

you must try to find you in all that new space
and sometimes   get lost
as the boundaries blur

you are not as you were

Elemental Partnering

At play are the images of the great round of life, the cycle of the seasons, the cycle of the day - these images portray the irrepressible laws of the natural world. The human personality, like any living thing, moves through times of growth and times of decay, periods of ascent and descent. Our passages from one stage of development to another will be marked by some degree of sacrifice. These transitional points dissolve our established orientation to make way for new growth. Refusing this, we become something other than who were meant to be.

M. S. Costello

To understand how I am aging, and to discover how to do it well, I need to understand how I got to this point at all. The path was not linear, ending with a graduation, no sudden exposure to senior status. And yet, yes, a surprise that old age is really here. It has been a gradual evolution, with maybe some denial or even forgetting. I have never had a 'favourite age' – I have never been able to say the age I 'feel inside.' People say they feel like fifteen or forty; I always feel the age I am at the time. I don't know how to feel any other way. I'm not sure why.

When I was young, I was never encouraged to explore and wander; my family of three did not spend much time in woods or fields. Our only venture into the natural world seemed to be at the seaside for two weeks a year. But I have always felt very close to the earth. I remember clearly the rare times I ran through long grass or thrilled to the sounds and feels of spring through open windows. I believed that I was part of the world around me and I was kept from knowing it. Not allowed to be barefoot on the earth.

Older, I would ride my bicycle through empty country lanes waving like a princess to whatever, whoever, I knew was watching me: crows, rabbits, cows - God? 'God sees the little sparrow fall...He sees me too' has been running through my head recently. I hadn't thought of it for years. My beloved grandfather would sing to me at night as he sat on the deep sill in my bedroom. I identified with the sparrow. In fact, the little sparrow was me; I knew that I wasn't just a 'too.' God saw me fall - and it appeared that I fell often, or so I was told by my father. Many reflective years later, I have come to the conclusion that I am the sparrow, the grass blade, the tree, and the witness. We are all one body - what affects one, affects all.

I have always been curious about the body I call 'me,' about the effect 'me' has on the world, and that the world has on me. And as I get older, this has become more important in that I need to know how I can work, not against or with, but as the collective one that we all are. Years ago, I read a book called *Zen Driving* at a time when I was doing much challenging highway travelling in between meetings. I enjoyed merging into the traffic as part of the one 'snake' it described, envisioning all the cars and trucks moving as one rippling set of reptilian muscles, stopping together, moving off again together. It made my patience level somewhat easier, but unfortunately other drivers' different reflexes didn't always create the snake effect I was yearning for.

The latest exciting studies in modern fields of science, molecular biology, cosmic ecology, cosmology, astrobiology, show that our bodies are made up of the same elements as the stars. Life developed from Earth's primordial atmosphere, emerging from a myriad of elements within the five basic elements in alchemical processes. In one of my most cherished books, *The Stardust Revolution*: 'The four most common atoms that make up you and me - oxygen, carbon, nitrogen, and hydrogen - are four of...the most common elements in the cosmos...96.2% of you...The magnificent story of the origin of life on earth only becomes accessible when viewed in a cosmic context.'[6] The fact that I am made of stardust instantly connects me with the cosmos and gives me clues to my beginning, ending, and returning. And as these atoms make up the original elements - air, fire, water, earth, ether - believed in the time of Ancient Greece to be included in all matter, then the elements are part of me too, not isolated out there, separately existing and often inconveniently disturbing our everyday lives within the language of weather or environmental disasters. A Goddess chant I often sing is 'Earth my body, Water my blood, Air my breath, and Fire my spirit.' Mother Earth's lungs are Her trees; rivers and seas are Her water; Her fire is the sun and the magma in Her core; and the earth is Her precious ground beneath our feet. We are but a microcosm of the macrocosm, and the latest cosmic discoveries make this a more spectacular story, a new story which helps me understand aging and dying.

Earth-based spirituality celebrates the passage of the seasons as Mother Earth turns the wheel, making and fulfilling Her promises of harvest sowing and reaping, birth and death, dark and light. On Solstices and Equinoxes, we invite the five elements to join us in our circle to begin our ritual: air from the East, fire from the South, water from West, earth from the North, and ether/Spirit in the Centre. In doing so, we acknowledge and honour their valuable presence in our lives and ask for their wisdom in our work. At the end, we symbolically let them go with a 'stay if you will, go if you must,' though knowing they are always with us. The basic elements are as essential to my spiritual survival as to my physical survival; daily they remind me of their vital presence, often shocking enough to emphasize their important participation in our lives. Put very simply, they provide our life's nourishment and we depend on them for our survival. Along with human choice and free will, we have combined them in different ways to create the catalyst for our industrial progression to the technological age we live in today, which has led in turn, to a rising pollution that could eventually destroy us.

Why is this important to me now, as someone who quite likely won't be alive when forecasted climate disasters might overcome civilization as we know it? Practically, I want to keep abreast of new scientific discoveries, finally know if I really am a hologram of the big picture before I join it. Spiritually, I am grateful for the space in the cosmos that I occupy, and, as these elements are within my body, as well as without, my consciousness demands an awareness of how my body responds to the world 'out there', and vice versa.

As the ocean tides swell at full moon time, so the water in my own body shifts, sets me off-balance, re-settles; essential water refreshes my body, cools my emotions. Walking on the earth in bare feet grounds me, brings me closer to my core, and to Her core; the smell of damp earth revives the primal in me; kneeling in mud and planting seeds unites my matter and the matter of our planet. As the barometric pressure in the air changes, my nerves jangle, bones ache; strong winds agitate my body, gentle air calms me down. Dancing flames inspire new ideas, solutions appear in imaginative energy; pictures in the fire bring deep reflection, revive fantasies, stories, excite creation; fire cooks my food, keeps me warm. While the atoms of my body will be received by the elements on my death, my spirit will remain. That won't die. Maybe I will experience evolution or destruction in a form I cannot even imagine now, or I may experience it in what could be called another lifetime. So I cannot ignore science or spirit. This life-gift is mine to experience, to learn, to grow through, to appreciate, to emulate, to share, however old I am.

So on reflecting on the elements, I go back into this lifetime, to remember how they have affected my personal evolution, emotionally and spiritually, providing experiences for me that have proved to be valuable for learning and practising wisdom. This introspection has shown me how my resilience has grown; I will need that as I get older. These experiences taught me to trust, I will need that too. They have taught me not to ignore the value of the elements in my life, and to be grateful for them.

Air has given back to me: in Jamaica, nurses sat on my knees and refused to let me give birth to my third child until the doctor arrived, using colonial protocol to control what would have been a quick natural birth. My panting breaths expelled curses and pleas that they let my baby be born, let her breathe. Get off my body! Free my baby! Finally the doctor made his presence known, and she slid out, blue and limp, no breath, released from the prison that my body had become, my thighs capturing her against my will. She was rushed over to an adult oxygen mask and I heard her cry almost before it dawned on me that impossibly she was dead. That cry-song was a miracle. Grateful for her breath and her perfection, the horror of her birth did not manifest in accusations and court cases, difficult in a foreign country and forgotten in the emotion of receiving her. But her own fear remains today in her social anxiety, claustrophobia. Denied air at birth, now her adult self gasps for air in so many ways. But the power of air gave her life. For that I am grateful.

Water has given back to me: my baby boy almost drowned in the ocean after he was wrenched out of his father's arms by a rogue wave, which also stole the glasses my husband needed to see with when he surfaced. From the shore, I screamed and pointed as I saw the baby's white styrofoam bubble float out fast on the wave's powerful ebb. Through his myopic, watery vision, my husband flailed out and miraculously grabbed the white bubble. A heartbeat later my son was spread-eagled in the air like a starfish, his tiny ankle caught in the strap, sputtering when he saw my panic. I was twenty-eight, my first Saturn return. Life in Venezuela was carefree: two babies, one a newborn, then sleeping under a palm tree on the deserted beach, an exciting life ahead. When I saw my husband rise from the ocean like a dripping monster with empty arms, the bottom fell out of that world. When I saw the bubble rushing out to sea taking my baby to the source of the monster wave, I went crazy. Then water gave me back my son. That day sobered me. Life wasn't like a Hollywood movie any more. Life wasn't just looking like the cutest family. Life was damn serious and had better be respected. As we drove home in silence, the first wedge of doubt insinuated itself between us, words of accusation hovering but remaining unspoken. But the power of water gave my son back to me. For that I am grateful.

Earth has given back to me: moving to Brazil from Jamaica was a swift transition from green to brown, from leafy trees to towers and highways, from fecund dark soil to dry disease-carrying dust. Hearing screeching brakes instead of birdsong was shocking on our first Sunday in Sao Paulo, as we walked our dogs along strange city streets. No Sunday gospel-singing calm. Trying to make it fun for the children, my throat ached as we sang our walking song, looking for signs of nature to sing about. Instead of breathing green, we inhaled endless fumes. Mother Earth was choking here. Then our five year old daughter ran away as she often did since she first climbed over the sides of her playpen at nine months old. She veered to the left and, unaware of these strange surroundings, it wasn't until I saw the road arc upward that I realized we were on an overpass. She was running as fast as her little legs could carry her up the curved side towards the unguarded edge. Ahead of her was a free-fall to the highway below. As I held back our dogs and her two siblings, my husband chased after her which only encouraged her game more. I heard her joyous giggle and I could sense her preparing to jump - to fly? - just as her father grabbed her jacket. Forty-five years later, my heart still pounds when I think of that paralyzing moment: her laughter, the arcing pavement, the traffic roaring underneath us, an image of her already in flight. But earth held on to her, it did not reject her. I learned to gain respect for this cemented city we had moved to, not to compare and despise it, but try to find some evidence of beauty. Earth could be honoured in different ways there: sculptures teased from solid pieces of granite, innovative architecture where murals and buildings are carved from marble and wood. The power of earth enclosed my child and saved her life. For that I am grateful.

Fire has given back to me: in 1968, the Rockefellers owned many business interests in Venezuela and national sentiment had turned against American intervention. Living in Valencia, a dormitory town an hour outside Caracas, we ex-pats wore Canadian pins on our lapels, softening initial aggression to us as suspect 'Yankees.' I was driving home after shopping, my one-year-old son beside me in his car seat, and quite likely singing something like Itsy Bitsy Spider. In a millisecond, the parked truck right in front of me exploded several times, blowing up in smoke and flames. Boom, boom, boom. The truck belonged to the Rockefellers' supermarket chain. When I slammed on my brakes, the passenger seat fell forward, towards the dashboard. In the first Mustang models, Ford did not anchor the front seats well, so my son's car-seat went with it, his head hitting the glove compartment. Car-seats in the '60s were made so children could see out of the car window, no safety codes, no strong seatbelts holding them back.

As soon as the explosion entered my consciousness, I looked for an exit, swerving into a laneway ahead on my right, one hand trying to wrench back the heavy seat and my son. The laneway turned into a road, and thanks to the Mustang's horsepower, I sped for a few blocks until the flames were way behind us before stopping to soothe him. Amazingly he only had a small bump. I didn't dare think of what could have happened had I panicked or been a bit closer, or even been recognized as American near such explosive emotion. Today we read of car bombs, suicide bombers, strewn bodies; we have become immune to blood savagely spilled in the marketplace. It happens 'over there.' Until now, I hadn't drawn comparisons between my Venezuelan experience and today's headlines. But when I focus on the similarity, I see how I am part of it all. I respect the fire that burned that awareness into my soul, ashes to be discovered so much later in my life. And the power of that fire did not take my son's life. For that I am grateful.

So many transitions in my life have been marked by the elements. They wake me up, tell me to keep my eyes and ears open, be aware, to respect the passage of life. Signs tell me to become more conscious. A feather presents itself on my deck at a sad time or a breeze ruffles my hair when I have a brainwave; sun's rays gleam through a dot in a stained glass window and shine on to a certain page. Now I am older, I look at the elements around me and see how they enrich my life every day. I see how they intertwine with my life, supporting me, growing me.

At my dear friend Koko's funeral in Glastonbury, England, we called in the elements to protect her on her journey to Avalon. Earth was scattered from a shell onto her coffin, earth her body; candles were lit, fire her spirit; water was sprinkled on the hundreds gathered there, water her blood; and air was wafted by large feathers and wings, air her breath. The congregation held not only priestesses and pagans, but also business men and women, mayors and town councillors, people from every walk of life. Later many of them spoke of how significant the ritual was to them, how it made them think about death in a different way.

As I call the elements into my life circle, I am calling in those that have been part of my journey, creating valuable learning experiences for me, given me immeasurable gifts, supporting me. And I am calling myself into the circle, to be present and awake. I can continue to connect with the elements every day, in every way. I need this practice, no matter how old I am, no matter how close I am to death, hopefully on my deathbed. It unites me with everything there is, to where I shall return. How very comforting.

May the air carry your spirit gently
May the fire release your soul,
May the water wash you clean of pain and sorrow and suffering
May the earth receive you
May the wheel turn again and bring you to rebirth

Starhawk [7]

Air

I face the East: I welcome Air into the circle of my life.

Sunrise glows on smoky hills, blends land and sky horizon deep
or shines in city windows, wakes night workers trying to sleep;

moon shadows fade away when first birdsong of day
brings all the news I need to know - for now.

Air breathes Her gift of life, billows sails,
blows away the cobwebs in my mind, Her play of spiralled air reminds me of a dream...

...where energy can paint a song, a symphony, an ode to joy.
Ideas blow in the morning breeze: awake, I relish the day ahead.

Girl-child turns the wheel to spring, fulfills Her winter vow,
makes Her pledge of plenty to the summer fields.

Air begins the day as inspiration began my life - all lives.

When air no longer fills my lungs I'll walk the sunrise path
with East into an unknown day,
unknown re-birth, unknown destiny.

With gratitude, I hail East. I welcome Air.

Blessed Be.

Footsteps towards Aging

We do not grow absolutely, chronologically. We grow sometimes in one dimension, and not in another, unevenly. We grow partially. We are relative. We are mature in one realm, childish in another. The past, present and future mingle and pull us backward, forward, or fix us in the present. We are made up of layers, cells, constellations.

Anaïs Nin

Early morning, on awakening, I invite in the spirits of the East, calling in Air, all aspects of air: breath, birth, gestation, music, new ideas and creativity, sunrise, a new day, springtime, listening to Her in birdsong and breezes. When I bring aging into breath and consciousness, I naturally think of spirit. The word 'spirituality' seems to be bandied round a lot these days as an answer or a reason or an excuse for a multitude of issues, as if it is a separate 'thing' that can be called on at will. By my definition of practising spirituality, it is everything, not an isolated few moments a day, or a prayer morning and night, or a church sermon one day a week. On the blog GaiamLife, David Steindl-Rast says this better than I: 'Sometimes people get the mistaken notion that spirituality is a separate department of life, the penthouse of existence. But rightly understood, it is a vital awareness that pervades all realms of our being.'[8] I try to live by this.

Centering myself is calling in spirit through breath. Peeling potatoes is calling in spirit through earth; participating in a work meeting is calling in spirit through service. Walking by the lake is calling in spirit of place; taking soup to a neighbour is spirit in community. Even awareness of basic bodily functions is spirit through body. All call forth gratitude. Not one act can be separate from spirit.

I believe we are all one body with Mother Earth. Inner and outer journeys are mirrors for each other. I am grateful for signs and synchronicities that tell me I am on the right path, asking me to look and listen. As children we are taught how to cross the road, to be aware of traffic coming. We are told that this is a lesson never to be forgotten, the consequences could be dire. The mantra 'look and listen' can apply to so much more than attention to traffic. We can look and listen no matter where we are, and in whatever circumstance, for it is in what we see and hear that we can understand our place in the universe. The Divine can be understood in many ways. I wonder if that is why 'look and listen' is one of the first messages we are taught? Maybe 'see and hear' should come next.

Air brings change on the wings of the bird, the winds in the trees, the spout-song of a whale. Change calls for trust, trust that an idea will take root, trust that a new move will bring success, trust that the new baby will thrive. I inhale with trust that breath will enliven my body, and in turn will lead to an exhale. We live with trust far more that we realize. Of course we rely on trust when we sign a contract, shake hands on an agreement, elect a public figure, pledge devotion to a sweetheart. When we drive, we trust that everyone on the road is alert and capable; we take our toddlers to kindergarten and trust that they will be cared for and heard; we trust that the food we buy is fresh and nutritious, that the medication the doctor prescribes will make us feel better. The older we get, more trust is needed. We want to trust in our health provider, our ability to function and remember appointments, to call on facts. As we age, we need to trust the people around us. Aging brings a lot of changes, we trust that we will adapt with change, that we are where we are supposed to be.

So much today calls for us not to trust. Trust is oft belied. Every day, we learn more about institutional corruption, police brutality, sexual violations by people we once admired, government controls, church betrayals. Often we are taught not to trust; overcoming that can take a lifetime. Trust becomes more elusive, for to trust means that we have to surrender to the outcome, much harder to do when there is so much information arriving faster than the speed of sound. What to believe? I can understand how older people can become complacent and set in their ways - wading through all the options can seem confusing. But when we don't trust, we become fearful and anxious, cynical, suspicious of others, of offers to help, of new ideas.

Years ago, I led study groups through the books of Eckhart Tolle; his *Power of Now* was the catalyst for a turning point in my life. Tolle suggests that we do not pre-suppose an action's outcome. Instead we say 'Maybe yes, maybe no.' Eventually we'll see the answer, maybe not for years. 'The wise man's 'maybe' signifies a refusal to judge anything that happens. Instead of judging what is, he accepts it and so enters into conscious alignment with the higher order. He knows that often it is impossible for the mind to understand what place or purpose a seemingly random event has in the tapestry of the whole. But there are no random events, nor are there events or things that exist by and for themselves, in isolation.' [9]

I continue to use my Maybe reaction, for it helps me surrender to the outcome being the way it is meant to be, even though we cannot see it at the time. Not knowing is very liberating. Trust is about taking a risk, making a choice, surrendering to the outcome even if it means sacrifice and oh, how hard it is to remember that sometimes. Trust is about surrendering to your own truth.

Bringing my past to the present: as a child, I imagined that I was protected by something so much bigger than I could language. Maybe that was because I learned very early not to trust reactions of most of those around me, not to believe their words. I must have been living with betrayal for a long time, as most things I trusted in ended up hurting me. Favourite teachers wrote critical report cards which evoked anger at home - home, where my father taught me that nobody was to be trusted, everything was a secret to be kept within my family of three. Friends, who I wanted to like me, teased and taunted. I still went through life naïvely trusting, so betrayal was a familiar feeling, manifested as hurt and deep loss. I see that now. Institutions I have always trusted as 'being there' - banks, schools, government, even food sources and medical care - I now see as not having the firm foundations I believed in. Another betrayal. I think that this must be why many elderly people settle into a non-challenging way of life because it all gets 'too much,' as I hear many times. I don't think I could give up; once one knows something that important, one can't go back and forget. Once you see, you cannot un-see. I think of Jimmy Carter and Joanna Macy and know that I could not settle into an armchair for the rest of my life either.

I remember at ten, when I was finally allowed to walk into town by myself, I was able to walk at my own direction, pondering my place in this big scheme of things. I stopped on one crowded corner and watched a man walk towards me. I suddenly knew that he and I were going to pass for a reason - not knowing the reason, but somehow knowing how important everyone and everything in this world was to each other, how our presence depended on each other. How we shared and somehow influenced the space we found ourselves in. I held my breath as he went by; I have never forgotten his face to this day. As children we unquestioningly accept these thoughts. We celebrate our magic places, our connection with something bigger than ourselves, our place in the world. But when we eagerly share our innocent stories, we often receive the cold stares of judgment that stitch our lips shut and bind our feet. So we either ignore our mystical, magical thoughts, thinking them as 'bad' as they are deemed, or we tuck them away in secret places, not sharing them again, which is what I did.

Older, I discovered my support in a stranger's smile of recognition, the ocean's roar, in moonlit frozen branch-music. A quote from the Buddha on my Zen calendar today reads: 'If you wish to know the Divine, feel the wind on your face and the warm sun on your hand.' Not long ago, my partner and I visited Mary, a wheelchair-bound friend, at her long term care home. We took her outside where the morning sun was so strong we needed the old hats stored in the car. Because of a massive stroke, Mary was unable to speak, but when we popped a frayed cowboy hat on her head, and similar atrocities on our own, she let out a huge guffaw. Then she laid her head back and closed her eyes, letting the sun rest on her face, breathing it in, as if knowing it would be the last time. Time stopped for a moment; the Divine was there. However old we are, She is there for us. But we are imperfect human beings with vulnerable egos and we forget. That's where the practice comes in. When I imagine Her as my inner crone, I have a companion who offers me Her cane to lean on, Her sense of play to relax with, Her faith in my dealing with the next problem that comes along as they regularly do.

She sends me signs, I just have to see and hear them. Elisabeth Kübler-Ross's name for them is 'Divine manipulations.'[10] Signs like the birth of my daughter when she looked wisely into my eyes at one hour of age, and I actually heard her words out loud, 'Oh no, here we go again.' Through spirit, she was telling me that we'd been together before and that this journey would be a challenging one. Signs like a Christmas tree planted in the sandy beach outside my English flat, decorated with foil ornaments, discovered early Christmas morning. No-one knew where it came from. Signs like a car crash when I was at a crossroads in my life. If we don't notice, the signs get more and more obvious, until we finally stop and listen. 9/11 was an example of such a collective wake-up call. Was it heard by the right people? I fear not.

When I first began to write about trust, I immediately thought of risk, because it is a risk to trust. Maybe one becomes afraid of taking a risk when one becomes older, maybe it is easier to be safe, on steady ground. As I wrote, my words became a list, a list of times that I stared down risk when I was in threatening situations, almost on impulse, not even thinking about trust. Was it innocence? Naiveté – described as 'lack of wisdom'? What I wrote surprised me. It could be read as a list of betrayals of a way of life I had obediently followed, a life created for me. But while not of my own design, each day was now of my own making, one that provided opportunities for growth, learning and wisdom. These risky situations, coming after a restricted youth, gave me the opportunities I needed to firm up my courage in the face of danger, to take charge of myself, to become stronger than I had been, or was allowed to be, and to take much bigger risks, those leading to difficult decisions that would affect me and my children in the future. I could eventually say 'If I could withstand all of that, I can do this.'

My journey made me the person I am today. I was practising 'Maybe yes, maybe no,' before Eckhart Tolle sat on his bench and imagined *The Power of Now*, and I refused to be afraid. Here is my list, it's basically a list poem.

Young and pregnant with my first child, I faced the barrels of three machine guns.
I refused to pay bribes so I lost my driver's license.
A truck blew up in front of me, exploding in flames.
I ducked in the path of gun shots.
An angry mob chased me, banging sticks on the road yelling 'Go Home Yankee.'
I drove through a protest, burning tires, and rioting.
I broke military curfews to take my children swimming.
I survived hurricanes and earthquakes.
I protected my children from epidemic, tropical disease, being lost in a ghetto.
I was threatened with being thrown over the cliff to sharks.

I was threatened to death by a policeman.
I drove away from a policeman after he let go my arm - he kept my driver's license.

No, I wasn't in the army and I didn't grow up as a tomboy or a wild child who jumped in without looking. I grew into an unprepared adulthood as a frightened only child, smothered and protected in the name of love, not allowed to experience life or make mistakes in the name of safety, never trusted. All of the above came from my life as a corporate wife in South America and the Caribbean, living as regular a life as one could. At first, I was so shy that I would hide behind a palm tree if my husband left the room during a party. But I grew into someone who moved through fear, conquering that innate desire to say 'No I can't,' often in personal attack and danger, because I still trusted in something watching over me, not named yet, and had complete faith that I would survive. I didn't question it. This trust, which developed in a child who had to be her own protection and form her own values early on, held me in good stead in the latter part of my life, through disappointments and panic. And I trust that it continues as I age.

Sometimes the universe presents us with many challenges, such uncertainty and despair, that we doubt, chewing at anxieties like a puppy worrying a slipper. But it is the challenge that is the risk. We are asked to put our trust and faith on the line, that what is happening to us is happening for the right reasons, not expecting everything to make sense. No longer needing to know why. Maybe yes, maybe no. That's where surrendering control comes in and that's what is so hard. Not only trusting the process but surrendering to the outcome. Letting go.

Signs are found wherever we look in the landscape. They tell me that I am on the right path. Once on a cliff hike, I found a stone with a rune mark naturally etched into it by nature and time. Aha, I thought, a sign! I planned on looking up the meaning of the rune later, but the stone fell from my pocket and could not be found in the long grass. In late afternoon, a few miles along, I lay on the grass to watch the insects in the undergrowth. (Have you ever watched them really closely, scurrying about their day, just like us?) And right in front of my eyes, at ground level, there was another stone with exactly the same rune mark on it. I was meant to see that sign. The rune meant warrior. That day I was on the right path, in more ways than one.

Kahlil Gibran wrote: 'The most beautiful thing in life is that our souls remain hovering over the places where we most enjoyed ourselves'[11] My soul-place is Lyme Regis, a seaside village in England, known as the film setting for John Fowles' *The French Lieutenant's Woman*. It was my summer place of childhood peace. At 60, I took a risk in the form of a 'gap year.' After renting out my Ontario home, I moved there on a one-way ticket. A tiny flat by the sea became my retreat for sixteen months; leaving to fly back to Canada was like exiting a monastery. Every morning, the end of the ancient harbour wall, the Cobb, was where I would call in the directions to begin my day, let the sea do its magical work, the sound of her healing tides wash through me. To my left were high cliffs full of fossils - the past. To my right, fishing boats chugged towards the sunrise on the misty horizon - the future. But straight ahead lay the little town, full of life and energy. The Now. All we have is Now, and the trust that listens to that small voice inside or even follows one's body in response to words we don't even hear - Now.

One stormy day, a pink glow attracted me to a rock pool left by the ebbing tide. A small rock lit up the dancing shadows with its pink aura in the water. I reached for it, a sign of hope in the threat of war hanging over that rainy day in March, 2003 - a reminder of beauty within, of trust in hope. Of faith. The rock has become a talisman for the years past, for now, and for the years ahead as I age, a reminder to trust.

Sometimes, Something

Sometimes, something shines hope in the fog:
a rock caught in a pool left by moon's ebbing tide.
It gleams pink in the sea, like the tea-rosy cheeks
of your grand-daughter's joy, her trust in a life
yet to come, like silk rustle of secrets, frilled
peony petals. Brief moments but full.

Sometimes, that something reminds you to breathe
after wind and the rain dull the spaces where words
try to be. Air dares not intrude so you choke,
afraid breath should escape, lest none can return.

You catch up the glow, wrap its warmth to your body.
Up the steps of new promise, climb out
of the storm to the warm and the dry, where
away from the water the rock looks like others.

It's grey and it's dull, yet you'll always remember

your grand-daughter's laughter, sweet music of love,
gifts from the earth. And you'll give it back
to the sea in good time, for others to find
on their search for new hope and a light in their lives.

Sometimes, something shines bright in the fog,
and, if hope is finding a light in the dark,
then faith is knowing it will always be there. And
trust is as simple as letting your breath fly away
with the wind, believing that even when love shifts
its shape, it will always return to your heart.

Consciousness: life's impulse

Because I am aware of death and afraid, I lean my shoulder into living not automatically and reactively like an animal, nor passively and pleadingly like a child pretending he has a father watching over him, but with conscious choice and decision of what will constitute each fleeting moment of my life.

Paul Fleischman

Before I can search into what aging consciously means to me, I need to ask: how does consciousness apply to me, at this time of tying off ends, finding meaning in past, present and future, connecting the dots? Kathleen Dowling Singh in *The Grace of Dying* beautifully describes the unfolding of human consciousness as 'a progression from the prepersonal to the personal to the transpersonal,' the latter she describes as a state of being to which we aspire, '...by expanding beyond one's personal mind, body and emotions.'[12] Expand I must.

As a younger adult, building a family empire, then in midlife juggling a career, late-in-life education, and single motherhood while alert to aging parents, I only had time to re-act from my ego, rarely pro-acting unless task-oriented, always on the run, my mind so occupied there wasn't time to witness the bigger picture, 'lost in my own drama.'[13] Feelings of uneasiness and sadness crept in, I felt alienated and alone. Much later diagnosed as depression and fibromyalgia, the feelings were then blamed on genetics, or circumstance or relationship – all crutches, with no perspective other than the traditional. Living the old collective story of unconsciously moving through the stages of maiden and mother, mythological messages in the media demanding to be obeyed. Then post-menopause brought reassessment, a need for rebalancing. Retirement offered time to reflect, to synthesize facts, to discriminate, to connect, to relish in the Aha! To wake up. To try to become more conscious. Is this cronehood?

In my youth, I would have associated the word 'consciousness' with someone recovering from unconsciousness, as in a fainting spell or a coma. Little thought was given to its opposite, assuming that, as I was interacting with life - eyes open, lips moving - I was therefore conscious. I see now how I blundered into experiences, driven by emotion and ego. Now, with the luxury of time for introspection, I can explore in more depth, to the point that I often question what I mean by my own consciousness in all kinds of interactions, including those with myself. In her essay '*Conscious Aging as a Spiritual Path*', Melanie Starr Costello describes unconscious aging as marked by the 'absence of reflection...vulnerable to stereotypes that envision aging in terms of loss.'[14] A more conscious living will lead to a more conscious old age and a conscious dying.

Consciousness, to the older me now, is paying attention, being aware of my motives in everything I think, do, and say, understanding how I affect the big picture, knowing my responsibility to the big picture - that I am the bigger picture. I strive to be wide awake in dealing with emotions, in communication, relationships, community, with setbacks and disappointments. I try to be fully aware of my connection with the elements, with Mother Earth Herself.

Consciousness is peeling back the layers of my life, breaking through the veils of illusion, looking at the why behind traditions and the what that triggers emotional reactions, thinking outside the box to create new habits - or not. Consciousness for me is integrating the feelings of grief, guilt and betrayal that come from seeing through the illusions I have grown up with, not denying them, but understanding them. Consciousness is knowing I am one with the larger body of humanity, and need to ask for forgiveness and forgiving in return to heal the past. Consciousness is being awake to the present moment for that is all we have, not creating drama around what may never be, or never was.

To add aging into that mix means adding the dimension of time and experience. It also means that the finality of my life, as I know it, is closer than it ever has been. It means recognizing the inevitability of change, and the need to adapt to change, to accept loss with grace. Aging means understanding the part that the past plays in the present, but not dwelling there, using wisdom gained through experience to move into the future. My search into aging consciously is not one of how not to age, but a search into the truth behind how I reached my 76th year so quickly, what were my supports and hindrances, the messages I gleaned along the way to make me who I am today? And especially what can I learn from all of that to help me move forward in my journey? There is no time to dawdle or put off the practice; it is still necessary to take time for reflection and dreaming. Balance.

Consciousness is recognizing the synchronicities and signs sent by the universe to show me I am on the right path, because the universe meets us halfway if we are prepared to put in the effort. I see signs in headlines, billboards, shapes of branches, animals, overheard conversations. My son said once, 'Mom, you see signs in everything!' I have always been aware that there is more operating in our energy field than meets the eye, and if I am truly open and awake I know that I am never alone. I interpret a sign as sometimes showing me that my choice is a conscious one, offering incredible reflection and insight into my own soul. Sometimes a sign is a warning, or a pause. Maybe that was all I had to count on when I was a child.

In his book *Quantum Mind*, Arthur Mindell describes such signs and synchronicities as 'quantum flirts.'[15] By dense mathematical processes, Mindell demonstrates how the signal from the object takes place before the observation, how one is intending to observe and the other is wanting to be seen. We don't need Mindell's scientific background to experience a friend phoning at the same time that we are thinking of them, or to catch sight of someone in a crowd just as they turn around to look directly at us. In my forties, I had three very strange experiences spread out over a few years, when I saw three women falling before they fell, two in the street and one from a ladder, with no time to warn them. I saw the fall and then it happened for real. After the third time, these 'visions' frightened me. Once I felt fear, the experiences stopped.

Mindell writes that being aware of quantum flirts involves deep attention. '... awareness practice connects you not only to yourself, but also to quantum physics, psychology, the future of science and to the whole universe.'[16] This gives significance to the crow who led me up the path to the sacred Glastonbury Tor for my first time, and the injured raccoon that held my eyes for thirty minutes one morning when he clung to a tree trunk near my porch. While my neighbours discussed shooting him, I sat in the line of fire, and finally he limped away when I distracted them in conversation.

Consciousness is all about awareness of surroundings, of what goes into my body, of relationships, world events. 'Using your awareness at any moment seems to have an unlimited number of benefits, and no known side effects except greater certainty.'[17] To age with 'greater certainty' sounds so much more beneficial and life-enhancing than moving towards the end of life in fear and doubt.

Consciousness for me is being very aware of dualities, of life's opposites that are becoming even more polarized today. In *The Origin of Consciousness*, Julian Jaynes describes dualism as 'that central difficulty in this problem of consciousness.' [18] He also writes that 'the observation of difference may be the origin of the analog space of consciousness.' [19] When reflecting back into when consciousness first developed in me, one of my first memories is that of comparing the words of love I heard with the behaviour in expressing that same 'love,' unable to reconcile the two, wrestling with a childish perspective of true honesty.

Today I find it hard to enjoy a photo of a luxurious spa or hotel when I see local employees in the background sweeping the beach. I appreciate the benefits a regular salary brings them, but I also know that their people's land was exploited to build the fancy spa, and their ancestors survived on their fishing skills before our industrial age emptied the sea of healthy fish. Living in the Dominican Republic in the '70s and early '80s, I witnessed tourism merchants discovering that natural beauty could buy them a fortune, so my friends lost their farms to hoteliers who hired them back as waiters. Once I started exploring back-stories, it became more obvious that we are bombarded with these polarities from every direction: media, movies, world events, sports. While positive and holistic changes are struggling in our culture, a cruel, judgmental divisiveness is growing in strength, trying to gain balance. I just wonder how far the scales can tilt before both sides come crashing down and hopefully, a new paradigm will rise.

Often media headlines conflict with each other, maybe unknowingly by the publisher - or are they manipulated? Two news stories clashed on the front page of a popular British newspaper: a photo of terrified African girls, wailing as they waited in line for their turn at the knife in a genital mutilation tent, was directly beside a publicity photo of a self-created celebrity Kardashian's very round and over-oiled buttocks emerging from a draped sequined gown. The self-satisfied smirk on the face of the second woman as she claimed to 'break the internet,' contrasted fiercely with the tear-stained faces of the pre-pubescent girls as they awaited a future of pain and submission. This is a clear example of dualism, the virgin and the whore, only here the virgin girls are considered soiled goods unless cruelly violated, while their opposite archetype is scrubbed shiny clean to be worshipped.

Similar dualistic synchronicities appear on my Twitter feed. There is no tweeting guru who decides the order of news items and photos, yet random news headlines present obvious paradoxes, offering opportunity for deep reflection on the meaning of their seemingly synchronistic connection and the tightrope balance between them. As an example, William Blake's painting of Dante's Divine Comedy was tweeted immediately above a photograph of the construction of the Berlin Wall in Germany, 1961, surely the beginning of another form of a modern purgatory in itself. Dante described exactly the emotion roused by the barrier to freedom for the East Germans. And then I think of the story of Sleeping Beauty and the thorny forest that rescuers had to hack through to wake her up. When teaching disenfranchised adults who often lived in crisis as they tried to change their lives for the better, I shared this story often during problem-solving sessions, pondering over whether it is wise to rescue people too soon. In our journey through the dark night, each one of us has to claw through our own wall of thorns to get to the other side, however painful it is to witness. Maybe the Berlin Wall represented an opportunity of growth, of waking up. The speaker of platitudes would say that you wouldn't see the light if it wasn't for the darkness. The wall between East and West Berlin certainly presented a dark night for Germany, and the world's soul.

My reverie on consciousness from a simple instigator like Twitter, leads me to ask: What walls do I construct around me? How do I create my own 'unbreachable purgatory?' If I had nothing to lose, how far would I go? On my Zen calendar, the Buddha is quoted as asking, 'How fully did you live? How deeply did you let go?' The older I become, the more willing I am to stand firm, stake my claim. In my life, I have climbed through plenty of thorny bushes, clawing my way to the other side, only to find another forest. But if someone had plucked me out, brushed me off, rescued me, and handed me my goal as a prize without an iota of effort on my part, would I be as strong as I am now, or I would always feel entitled to being saved? Where does the need for rescue begin and end?

Another Twitter contrast: under a photograph of burning tires where gas-masked protesters feed dense smoke and flames, is an advertisement for a clothing line, introduced with the phrase: 'You've been so good! Get up to 70% off!' Adding even more irony, sandwiched between the two tweets is another from a site that sends inspiring messages. This one implores 'Listen with your whole heart, work for the common good, love well.' These two photos show where we are in the world today, their polarities so far apart, capitalism and its response happening anywhere in the world. The mantra in between applies to both - a sardonic message. The connection of overt consumerism is obvious but I remind myself to stop another rant against the government. Instead, I must look at myself. How does my shopping relate to the massacre of the earth's resources and the grief of Her people? How do I collude with the 'death-machine' as Andrew Harvey named it in one of his university lectures? If I search for sales as good as 70% off, do I add to the need for more slave labour? more oil, and more raping of Mother Earth? I have created an 'us' and 'them' with my need for stuff. The protester has nothing to lose, he stakes his peril against his family's survival. Or maybe they haven't survived and so he truly does have nothing to live for, except his rage. Have I contributed to his pain with my eagerness to get 70% off yet another blouse made in Bangladesh? I represent everything that displaces him.

This anger is familiar. As a new mother in my 20s, I lived in Valencia, Venezuela, in the mountains outside Caracas, on the Equator, in retrospect balancing between the polarities of North and South. I and other ex-pat wives often played bridge; university students were often protesting rising fees. Young adults of the same age, we walked very different paths. On this particular humid day, I drove to a friend's apartment within university limits, on a street with fiery scenes like the one I just saw on Twitter. I tried to take a circuitous route to get there, but couldn't avoid the burning tires and students, their faces covered with scarves. They waved me through. But then we young women would hang over the balcony railing watching the progress of stone-throwing students and teargas-tossing police below. It was a dance of advance and retreat. When teargas reached the fourth floor, we retreated indoors to play a few hands of bridge. Then, with our china plates and silver forks, we went out again to watch the action while we commented on our hostess's coffeecake. Remembering through older eyes now, I - we - viewed the scene below as entertainment. It had nothing to do with us. When the tear gas irritated our eyes, we re-entered our entitled life, chattering about parties and recipes and babies.

I see now how unconscious I was, how I did not truly witness what was happening, or try to understand each side. I did not see dysfunction in systems that allow control and power to dominate personal freedoms. I did not see an ironic connection between my cake and the students' deprivation, or my need for distracting entertainment and their need for justice and understanding. I did not connect this with the rebellion that was beginning to fire inside of me. In 1968, I didn't associate 'them' with me. My life was peaceful and comfortable. The students' protest only affected an inconvenient driving route, the irritation of my eyes. I felt grateful for - and entitled to - my yellow Ford Mustang cocoon as I sped back through the troubled area to the safety of my suburban home, where my napping baby was watched over by the family maid. Sometimes the company put a guard at our gate if there was trouble in town. We were safe. That was all that mattered. The rest was a play happening out there. I didn't realize that out there was in here, in me, too. It had nothing to do with me. That was unconsciousness.

But years of such experiences, in different manifestations, led me to delve into my growing uneasiness about my role as the wife of a multinational corporate executive living in third-world countries. The perks were good: meeting airport customs with only a nod after Christmas shopping in Miami, well-staffed private schools where a company driver could pick the children up if I was busy elsewhere. My babies were birthed in well-appointed clinics, not sharing a stained bed for a few hours in the over-crowded public hospital. But I didn't see the connection. I felt that this was my due because of my husband's job. So I didn't understand my depression and uneasiness that grew as the years went by. Away from North America for 15 years, I knew little of the women's movement, or any movement come to that, not having the opportunity to learn these new memes. Not often was there news of Canada or even in English, and of course then, no social media. Instead, my feelings of restlessness were translated as a personal flaw in character. It wasn't until much later that I realized I shared the frustrations of millions, a universal pain, and I learned that what happens to all, happens to each one.

Unknowingly, I was one of all women striving for equality although I did not march with them, and I was one of the university students in Venezuela, although I did not throw stones. The distraction they provided from an otherwise mundane day was for the entitled person I was, not the more conscious one that I hope I am now. Their efforts were not for naught if I have learned that.

Many years later, long after I brought my family back to Canada as a single parent, I had a mind-blowing epiphany, staring into a puddle in a bus station one day. In that transformative moment, I realized that by playing the role of a 'good' wife and mother, social hostess, respectable face in the ex-pat community, I too was working for 'the company,' and therefore was also responsible for the exploitation of the countries I lived in. I too was part of the corporate machine. How can I decry the horror that multi-national companies wreak when I actually colluded with them? I remembered occasions when I was literally bought by the company with a holiday or a car, and was appropriately grateful, not realizing that these 'gifts' were meant to keep me from distracting my husband from his work with mere problems at home. And then I realized that my family's lifestyle had actually depended on money earned from the polluting of local resources, cheap offshore labour, non-ethical practices. I was no different from the New York CEOs who came for a state visit every year at budget time.

For 15 years, I lived an elitist life. I enjoyed having a maid so I could go to parties and act in amateur plays, teach, and serve on committees. Although I rationalized that we paid her very well and she was like part of the family, her pay was still ridiculously low and she worked six days a week. I bought her a television so she could watch her novellas; fake drama in exchange for a life of servitude? Yes, we gave her work which helped support her own family, but I was part of the corporate mindset that had bought her family's land for next to nothing to build polluting factories with cheap labour, while we expats lived it up by the pool, trading paradise for profit. I lived off those profits. I was complicit in the industrial age plot to conquer the so-called third world, tempting with toxic treats. I was no different from Columbus' sailors who gifted measles to the Arawak natives and slaughtered them after they built his brother's mansion by the stone wall I used to sit on with friends, drinking too many Cuba Librés at Drake's Pub, while barefoot boys watched over our cars for a peso and a pat on the head.

Staring into that puddle, I felt a huge wave of guilt at my collusion with the injustices done in third-world countries, working for monster corporations empire-built in the name of progress. My donations to 'the poor,' the fact that we chose not to live in gated communities like many other ex-pats so my children could play with the barrio kids down the road, were all rationalizations that made me feel 'good,' that maybe assuaged a guilt so deep inside I didn't know it was there. I remember the old Dominican flower lady I befriended and how we cried when I said goodbye before I left. The danger to my soul must have been obvious to me by then. I must have finally understood that my gracious life had depended on her poverty. Instead of looking after her grandchildren in the countryside, she was forced to enter our unbalanced marketplace and, as best she could, serve those who had destroyed her home, to survive.

It is very easy to say 'But that wasn't me! I didn't build those hotels, I didn't buy her acre of land for a few pesos.' No, none of us wives forced her children to work in sweat-shops for twelve hours a day sewing T-shirts and designer jeans, or sat her on a bucket to sell wilting flowers every day. No, my physical body did not enter into those transactions. But the one body to which we all belong did. I am part of that. I was part of why she was there. To ignore the macrocosm is like saying 'I (as microcosm) walked to town today but my elbow stayed home and my pancreas went to the beach instead.' Impossible. As is withdrawing my responsibility in third world disenfranchisement. Rights bring responsibilities. We are all one body, we all have to be responsible; we all have to change our behaviour to create a more harmonious world. I am part of the 'we,' and, as such, I do stay in hotels, buy designer jeans and cheap T-shirts, pass by a homeless person without a glance. I may righteously point the accusing finger at corporations when their sweatshops burn down and dozens of seamstresses are burned to death, but I, as part of the whole, as a consumer of their products, create the market that needs to be swiftly fed, and, as such, feeds the flames - Andrew Harvey's death-machine.

Now I can see that my behaviour, which I thought was so 'good' at the time, was unconscious, toxic. I was sleepwalking. Do I behave differently now? Again, I look at the two photos of the raging protester and the primping model and I ask forgiveness for my lack of understanding, trying to have empathy for both of them. Both are prisoners of modern society. Life in the sunshine was at a cost, a cost I created unconsciously. There is no rationale that can change that, other than I didn't know better. I couldn't have seen any connection because I was so wrapped up in my own little bubble. But now I see how I contributed, and still contribute, to the imbalance of power we see today. Entitlement is devastating. So unconscious. So easy on the surface.

I cannot remedy those years. But I can be more aware now that my vote at the cash register counts. Being more careful where my clothes are made, I try not to buy an outfit from Vietnam or Bangladesh. Phones and computers and cars do not need to be replaced on a whim; those huge piles of technological waste shipped to Asia are testament to our disposable society. A holiday at a luxury resort with an infinity pool would not be as enjoyable, knowing the pain of the locals who owned the land it sits on. My practice must be to examine any sense of entitlement I may act on today, for it will still slip in. Practising compassion and empathy will move me out of my tiny self and expand into the world around me. The realist in me knows that it isn't easy or automatic. It needs constant work and awareness.

Understanding the growth of consciousness in my life has made it easier to see the importance of striving to reach that transpersonal stage, moving towards unity. Practising consciousness is necessary now. Slipping back into old habits, especially when one is facing old age, appears easy. But it is not. Once you know, you can't go back. Kathleen Dowling Singh writes in *The Grace of Dying* that 'consciousness characterizes the life impulse,'[20] demonstrating for me its vital necessity. The latest trends of designer pajamas for the street, fleecy pants and onesies, online shopping from one's comfy sofa, and zombie movies, constantly appear to be telling us to fall asleep, stay asleep, resist the 'Wake up!' message. So the work is even harder to remember deep awareness of thought, word, and action. Mindell's message about quantum flirts remains important, demonstrating the connection that we have with the universe. We need to rediscover that everything we see, hear, and feel, is significant. Our awareness is needed. That is the least I can do if I want to wake up. The entire universe depends on it.

Recognition: Santo Domingo, 1976-1982.

She sat outside the supermarket every single day
    same dirty dress, hair wild and gray, selling flowers.
Her one big rotting tooth grinned at me
quite wickedly, and we became sort-of-friends.
I called her Hag-tooth Lady to myself, forget
her real name now. Maybe I never knew.

After buying groceries, I'd stop
for lilies or calendula, pass the time of day.
She'd recognize my car and wave her bent-up hand
as I rushed by - a Yankee woman's urgency
she'd never understand. Now I know why.

Her life was sitting on a bucket, flashing goofy grins,
stuffing pesos in her pocket
    not too many, her flowers lilted in the sun.
Sometimes her head would loll and she'd wilt too.
So many beggars, people didn't see her: aging
dirty woman fading by the wall.

As years went by we chatted more and more,
giggled over oddities, strange personalities,
almost conspirators. We'd commiserate about the heat,
I gave her an umbrella for shade and rain,
old sweaters, loose change. She brought my children
sugar-cane, soothed my baby while I bought her coffee
at the check-out. She liked her coffee thick and sweet.

And when she cried with toothache, I fed her
aspirin for a week. She called me her sympatica,
paid me daily 'for my trouble' with a rose. I kept them all,
set in my mother's crystal vase until they dried.
And after hurricanes that blew our two worlds apart,
she was still outside the store amid the rubble,

blessing harried shoppers
with a lisping Vaya con Dios, mi amor.

She told me of her loneliness and I shared mine
with her in broken Spanish. Divorce she found hard
to comprehend but Yo voy manana - I go tomorrow -
that she understood.

Before I left I gave her aspirin, afraid she'd take it
all at once without me there to monitor the dose.
We hugged and held each other close. She smelled
so strong of urine and other fragrances I didn't want to place.
Tears rolled down her face and mixed with mine.

Yankee women rushing in the sunshine
with their shopping bags and lists must have thought it strange,
Hag-tooth and I crying in the street.
But I knew we had to meet - she was sent
in place of one I missed
and in that moment
in the busy steamy noisy crazy smelly heat,
she was my mother in a different life
and I loved her.

A Metaphor on Consciousness

We must struggle for a life of consciousness, and this consciousness, when gained; increases our capacity for love and for experiencing the Divine.

Massimilla Harris

I am an ice cube, one of many in an ice tray, frozen from water poured in from a jug, that was filled from a faucet, or a well, or a river. My frozen shape makes me separate from the other ice cubes, but the same as them in general shape and size. Some of us could be dyed a colour, some could hold a flavour or an herb, maybe lemon, or basil, but we come from the same jug, and before that, from the same original water source. When we are freed into the ice cube container we are together, rubbing, nudging. We enjoy that connection, each communicating in our unique way. But we are soon separated again, and put in a drink or a bowl or an ice pack. Eventually, we might thaw or be consumed or sent down the drain, our work over. Either eliminated, or tossed to the ground, or vapourized into the sky, we re-enter the water cycle and rejoin the rivers and wells of the world. We flow into one another unimpeded, finding our source, no longer separated in our frozen state. We rush and ripple, happy as can be, until we are poured again into someone's vessel somewhere in the world and frozen in an ice tray again. You are like us. You re-enter your world in what has to be an easily recognizable shape, which for you is known as a body. But you are still part of the source that you always were, just restricted in your body at conception. Like us individual ice cubes, you mortals are the expressed consciousness of the whole. You intermingle, separate yet bumping up against each other, communicating in your way, until the body dies and 'you,' as you call yourself, are freed and become part of the consciousness field again, unlimited, part of the One. Maybe in the future you will not need the restricting sensory body-skin to separate you, to recognize that you are not just part of the source. You are the source. You are One.

My Inner Crone

If we allow ourselves to look her [the crone] clearly in the eye, we see that she is pure beingness in its raw form. She has the power to teach us that outer beauty fades but our divine Self always remains intact. If we can see ourselves this way, regardless of what falls away, we have tapped into her strength.

Sally Kempton

Certain questions have bubbled through my life, boiling up to the surface as a teen, maybe on a low simmer when motherhood filled deep thought, but rising to the surface in elder years. 'What am I here for?' and 'Why?' Over and over in the popular media we hear that we must find a meaningful purpose in life so we can grow old with vitality. Often, one thinks of one's life purpose as having to be grand or earth-shattering. 'Normal' lives spent parenting and basically surviving day to day don't seem purpose-driven or important enough to matter in the big scheme of things. But one's legacy does not have to be emblazoned on a new invention to save world hunger, it can be something as seemingly simple as kindness, selflessness, or love. In an interview with David Scott, author of one of Mother Teresa's biographies, he quoted her as saying that she 'just wanted to convert people to love... one at a time.'[21]

Many authors and speakers provide ready-made answers and check-lists. Individual work put into the search is far more valuable - unique discoveries and a personal plan are more meaningful to own than somebody else's dreams. The big advantage of aging for me is the growing urgency to find my own answers to these questions, along with more time for the reflection, observation, and practice necessary for understanding. Moving away from ideas of fame and fortune, I believe that my inner work is key to co-creating healing with Mother Earth. Through that inner work, I have recognized and developed a growing trust in the Divine, a word I use to encompass both a higher power and a universal support system; to me, that's one and the same. Verbal language is useless sometimes. We can only name what we know, and no-one knows what the Divine looks like, if indeed the Divine could ever 'look like' anything we recognize by human standards. There has to be acknowledgment of flexibility when naming the higher power that I rely on as my guide. This is where faith comes in, faith in the unknowable.

Synchronistically, today I received early publicity for a new book by Carol Christ and Judith Plastow, *Goddess and God in the World*, where Christ and Plastow discuss the naming and meaning of the Divine in our world today:

'...[they] argue for an inclusive monotheism that affirms the unity of being through a plurality of images celebrating diversity and difference. Carol believes Goddess is the intelligent embodied love that is in all being, a personal presence that can inspire us to love the world more deeply.' [22]

As my body is female in this lifetime, I imagine the Divine as feminine, and I name Her Goddess. In my everyday life, I call on Goddess in many of Her incarnations and archetypes. I plead with Hestia when my pancakes are beginning to burn, imagining Her rescuing breakfast from my over-zealous culinary skills. Artemis is at my back when I embark on a difficult project, and Durga supports me when I need to be strong in the face of a bully. I call on Goddess to find a lost item after I have looked 'everywhere,' and chances are, it is right in front of me the next time I look. It happens every time. Sally Kempton writes that 'the energy of each goddess will show up for you in a uniquely calibrated way.'[23]

As I have aged, Goddess has made her presence known as my inner crone. Unheeded, and unacknowledged in our youth-oriented culture today - and less desired - she has gradually allowed me to recognize her. Barbara Walker, the definitive expert in the history of women's spirituality, writes that the crone represents the 'life-affirming moral wisdom of elder women...seen as a healer and teacher, as well as a death bringer.'[24] Encouragingly, she also writes: 'The Crone is being rediscovered by a world that male systems appear to be pushing towards the brink of disaster without parallel... archetypes suppressed by any culture will tend to arise again and again...the Old Woman, who acknowledges no master, may be our best guide in this long, dark, labyrinthine spiritual journey.'[25]

In today's culture of psychological survival, we are taught to honour our inner child, to heal and cherish them. We are taught that when we heal and protect our inner childhood wounds, our adult selves become integrated and whole. The inner mother, inner maiden, and the dreaded inner critic, along with a multitude of other archetypes are templates in our deep interior selves, informing our reactions and behaviours. We call on them, and others, at different times, consciously and unconsciously, throughout our lives. They emerge when we least expect them with no distinction of gender or age. My eight-year old grandson, a tough little soccer player, calls forth his inner mother when, unasked, he cleans and dusts for his mom. His big brother, on the other hand, celebrates his inner maiden when he dances around the trees on our forest walk, carefully avoiding overhanging branches.

Many books have been sold on the value of healing the inner child. Like most lessons, I had to experience this to believe it. When I was 56, a serendipitous journey led me to my old bedroom in my maternal grandparents' house, now someone else's B&B. It was there in the 1940s that I felt cherished by my beloved grandfather, as he sat on the deep window sill telling me stories and singing songs. I trusted him like no other. He was the only one I believed. But now, years later, when it was time for me, a grown woman, to leave that bedroom for the last time, I could not move. I could not get up from the window sill where Grandpa used to sit, bringing love into my stern little life. I was mirroring the reluctance I felt as a child, when it was time to go home. Now, the taxi was honking outside, my host was calling me, But I could not budge; it was as if I was stuck there by super-glue. Then suddenly my body bent down, not led by my mind at all, in no-thought. And my arms lifted up a sobbing four-year-old girl. Arms wrapped around her, I held her against my heart and breathed deeply. Patting her back - in actuality, my shoulder - I could then rise and leave my old bedroom, comforting her as I took her with me. We left the house together that way and it felt manageable. The sad little girl was nourished within my soul and finally came home with me. Once we are conscious of the inner child and the part they play in our lives, we cannot ignore the acceptance they need. As with the inner crone.

As a child, I had twelve imaginary friends, spending hours giving them different characteristics and interests. I drew elaborate floor plans of a house for us all to live in and every morning began with our preparations for their day, my twelve cohorts in their different roles and guises. As a lonely little girl, my head was very busy. Now I know they were all parts of me, archetypes. In *Sacred Contracts*, Caroline Myss calls archetypes 'patterns...of intelligence...that populate our minds and lives in ways that affect us deeply.'[26] And in her conclusion to Carl Jung's *Man and His Symbols*, Marie-Louise von Franz names them '...dynamic nuclei of the psyche... which have an enormous impact on the individual, forming his emotions and ethical and mental outlook, influencing his relationships with others, and thus affecting his whole destiny... common, inherited (from the collective) patterns of emotional and mental behaviour.'[27] We all carry common and individual archetypes. Mine were my friends. One of them would have been my inner crone. Maybe as I grew, she became my conscience.

As we age, and grow in wisdom and power, we come close to recognizing her. But, conditioned by legends and the media, we deny her aging presence, we try to hide from her. The crone of legend is old, wrinkled, and often portrayed as the hag who brings death and loss. This can be frightening to people trying to come to terms with their own aging. Behind the ads and the urging to stay young there lingers an incipient fear, an often-sensed disgust at being old. Sally Kempton quotes Gloria Steinem as saying that many of her successful professional friends have a 'terror' of becoming a bag lady on the streets. I can identify with that, once going through a phase of actually choosing a doorway and a shopping cart for my eventual decline. The crone reminds me of that possibility.

My premise is this: as with the inner child, we must also nurture and love and comfort and forgive our inner crone. Sometimes we read that crones have the freedom to have fun, wear purple. They have nothing to lose. Yes, the crone archetype within us does encourage us to play and be creative, to be free and not so rule-bound. If not now, when? I heard Meryl Streep call on her inner crone in a quick interview before a movie premiere, '...the antidote (to aging) is to live joyously, tolerantly, and with intention,' she said. But our inner crone is aging too, and we must accept her fragility, call her into our energy, saggy belly, thinning hair, wrinkles and all. We must cherish her with love and honour, not ignore her or try to change her, deny that she exists, shun her. If we accept her, we will be walking an integrated, healed path as we move towards the end of our lives. Crone's wisdom is being called forth now more than ever as Mother Earth enters Her own winter, Her time of fragility and death of all that is familiar - a chaotic transformation. We cannot deny the crone. We must honour her.

In the media, and reinforced within our own minds by the influences in our lifetime, the crone-aged woman is constantly berated and criticized, the idea of death is denied. If the inner child's wounds were so ignored, the adult's resulting behaviour would be toxic, with far-reaching damaging effects, often masked by addictions and attention-seeking behaviour. Why would our reaction to the crone's pain be any different? Is it because aging lies in the future so we don't think it applies to us until we get there? What about the terrible history of the crone, the witch of the burning times? We carry the suffocation of smoke in our bones. Can we not atone that by accepting and loving her now, instead of continuing her crucifixion?

If we constantly malign our own expressions of aging, our denial will overwhelm any conscious awareness we think we have achieved in maturing. Surely, this would lead to a death marked with anger or despair, fear or grief, instead of the acceptance and forgiveness that are truly possible? In writing about goddess archetypes for women over fifty, Jean Shinoda Bolen says: 'The crone archetypes need to be recognized and cultivated to become a conscious part of ourselves.'[28] Embracing the physical signs of aging and cherishing our own aging process will let us journey forward as whole and heal the crone's pain, both of the past, and in today's depictions.

How often do you listen to your inner critic? How many times a day do you say to yourself, 'You look so stupid/ugly,' or 'Why did you say that, you're so dumb/silly?' How often do you instill these self-judgement calls into your very soul? I wonder if you listen to your inner crone as much as you listen to that inner critic? But it is the crone who tickles your gut with a butterfly wing when something doesn't feel quite right. It is her wise voice that speaks up when you have a decision to make and you hear, 'Let's look at this differently,' or 'Oh, come on, take a risk!' or 'Pause!'

Or she may just push you to act and you follow, without your mind getting in the way, before thought. Once, in Santo Domingo, I was standing at the gas stove stirring chicken drippings into gravy, as my grandmother had taught me. Suddenly my body turned and walked to the back door. I didn't tell it to, it just moved under its own volition. I stood on the step, staring out into the garden, lost in the moment. Then I came back to earth. 'What am I doing here? The spoon is dripping gravy all over the floor!' I shook myself and turned to get back to work. At that very moment, the Pyrex pan exploded into shards of glass and hot gravy, right into the space where my face would have been had I not moved. While cleaning up, shooing away children and pets, throwing away anything that might have glass splinters in it, many thoughts buzzed through my head. What warned me so quickly that I didn't even hear? Who is watching over me? I was moved away from danger, with no time to even consider, no message to debate. She beckoned, I followed. I didn't recognize her then. I called her coincidence, and luck. Now I know better. I call her Divine and I call her my inner crone.

In spite of the popular image of the crone being an ancient hag, the fearful picture still perpetuates in the media along with that of a useless space-taking, addled-headed, old lady. I envision my inner crone as the voice of experience, the wise one who nudges me to follow my instincts, encourages me to shed my disguises. She can be compassionate and wise, outrageous and discriminating, totally authentic and laser-sharp, always loving - a mentor. I can be that too. I believe that my acknowledgement of her presence within me is as vital as that of my inner child. My acceptance of her helps my integration process into shaping a whole person.

It is the crone in me who hushes my inner maiden if I become too self-centred; she lays a warning crone hand on my inner mother when I jump in to make everything better, fixing things for other people instead of letting them happen the way they should. (Oh yes, crones do not like shoulds.) She checks my ego, pops its bubble if it gets too big. Inner crones have experience to draw on, resources. I believe they channel the ancestors. And they are worth listening to.

My inner crone attempted to get my attention when I was young. She terrified me when I was a baby, sitting up in my pram as my grandmother and my mother wheeled me around the park. A very early memory: propped up by pillows, white knitted bonnet and cardigan, covered with the baby blanket that is now boxed away in my cellar. Grannie liked to see and be seen, she was decidedly autocratic. So when she met an acquaintance who was similarly of the old school, Grannie wanted to show me off, her pretty, only grandchild. This stranger was all in black, high choker collar, long skirts, and a hat that dangled long wispy feathers. Under the hat was a wrinkled face, long nose, big teeth, and a funny smell. The smell came into my baby-space, and the big teeth chomped, 'Hello little Rosebud,' baring themselves as hat-feathers tickled my cheek. I burst into tears and buried my head in the pillow. 'Say hello, Rosebud,' urged socially-correct Grannie. I cried and scrunched down even more. 'Say hello to my friend, Rosamund.' Grannie was getting cross now, using my real name, always a clue even then. There was no hello from Rosamund, eyes squeezed shut. Overdone apologies followed the departing tut-tutting old lady, along with lectures on my disobedience and rudeness, and my tearful mother begging the 18-month-old me to be 'good.'

The crone went into hiding after that introduction. She would have frightened me, the lover of fairy tales, nightmare-victim of Snow White's wicked queen, self-director of imaginary high drama. So she watched over me from the summer ocean, where her sea-songs rescued me from wind-blown admonitions to be good. She lived in the lavender outside my grandfather's kitchen door, her sweet fragrance always accompanying something loving happening in that house. She shone a moonlit path across the snow, a path I could jump on at night and travel wherever I wanted to with my imaginary friends. And she led me into the garden in springtime, to the buzzing bees and bird calls, so I could feel free after winter's imprisonment.

She was my tree-friend. I passed Tree every day, mid-journey to primary school. I remember her surrounded by pavement, though maybe it was a grassy patch or a regulation square of cigarette butt-filled dirt. Reading Mindell's *Quantum*

Mind, I can honestly say that Tree flirted with me.[29] And I responded. That was what it felt like. A shiny patch on the tree's trunk was a magic door to me, a bit higher than my child's third eye. Every time I passed I would stop and talk at the door, to whoever, whatever, was behind it. And Tree bent down to me, gave me her full attention. I wasn't familiar with Catholic rituals, but in retrospect, it was as if I was at confession. If I was with a friend I would only acknowledge Tree in passing with a nod, a glancing touch; I did not share this private relationship with anyone.

Sometimes I wondered exactly who I talked to when I bent into Tree's space, especially in my early teens when solving life's mysteries was a full-time job. Were there imaginary creatures in the tree? Fairies? Spirits? God? I didn't language 'Goddess' as a child. I never identified my conversation partner and yet this being/space/time/spirit was extremely important to me. When childhood was challenging, I would purposely visit Tree to gain perspective or some sense of inner calm. Looking back, I was sharing with my inner crone, her calm assurance nourishing me with non-verbal confidence and even love. Come to think of it, I didn't always talk. Standing there, my eyes fixed on the shiny place, I communicated in another way, a silent way, sharing energy with Tree. Communing spirit to spirit, sometimes putting my hand on the shiny patch connecting in silent harmony, I didn't hear cars and buses going by, people no doubt wondering what this kid was up to. Before I moved to Canada at 16 with my family, I visited my tree to say goodbye and I cried at the parting as grievously as that from a close friend. I didn't know then that my inner crone was travelling with me, that she would manifest in many more ways again.

When I visited my childhood home for the first time in almost 40 years, my first foray into the past was to find Tree. There was no question in my mind where she had been, but I doubted I would recognize her. I had no idea what kind of tree she was, if she had been cut down, if construction had taken place on her street. I expected to have a hard time finding her on what I perceived, from my adult's lofty point of view, to be a fool's errand. I followed the same route I used to take to school, at the same time of day, retraced my footsteps as naturally as if I was nine years old - and there was Tree. My body knew exactly the number of steps to walk. The past flirted with me and drew me back in time, yet made me very aware of the present moment by the structural and societal changes around me. How could I have ignored this moment, ignore any sign, any 'flirt?'

'Myths tell us that the present world has forgotten that the trees were once our bones, the rivers the blood, animals and people the cells of one being. In our broken modern world, we marginalise the experience of interconnectedness and ignore the quantum flirts and dreaming upon which the everyday world rests.' [30]

Tree's trunk was more slender than I would have thought, her shiny door much higher than me by now. The fence of the nearby house abutted her tightly instead of giving her breathing space as before. The pavement had narrowed. Lot sizes had changed. Gardens sprouted cement parking spaces instead of flower beds. But Tree had waited for me. I had no doubt of that. I caught up with my inner crone, and she was nudging me forward on this journey back through my childhood. I stopped, craned my neck up to the shiny place, and spoke, sometimes in silence, sometimes aloud. 'Hi Tree, we found each other again. Thank you for listening to a little girl all those years ago, for being here for her. For helping her.' As a 55-year old, I loved that tree as much as anyone could love anything. I had never humanized her branches as if they were arms, or given her a wise character, or the voice of a sage, but when I walked away, I knew that Tree watched me, reached out to embrace me, and held me in her presence. Tree was just a tree, yet one hundred per-cent there for me, connected to me as deeply as any person could, except maybe my grandfather. And I didn't question the trust I had in her.

My inner crone tried to reach me wearing several disguises. When I lived in Brazil as a young mother, a light beckoned from the back of a tiny rock shop in Sao Paulo. Deep in those little city-caves were agates, raw amethysts, uncut hematites, as rich and soulful as if still housed in Mother Earth. As I got closer I saw a huge, taller-than-me slice of rainbow tourmaline, layered with all the colours of the spectrum. Backlit in its pitch-black corner it spoke to me. My inner crone spoke to me from her home in the centre of the earth, and I felt the healing spirit and balance she offered me in Tourmaline's energy which helped me gather strength to master some difficult terrain ahead.

Now I am older and wiser, I do believe that my inner crone led me to Tree and to Tourmaline at times when I needed a voice of wisdom and could not find it anywhere else. I saw her without looking, knew her without thinking, and she spoke to me in a way I could hear without listening. She was there in those times when I began to believe that I was part of something bigger than myself; my cells connected with something ephemeral that said love. No more did I ignore the voice inside that spoke up when something didn't feel right, when a choice had to be made, when a certain feeling demanded to be felt. Now I know it is she who helps me discover my power and to use it when necessary.

Recently, I saw an online photo of a dried-up reservoir in Sao Paulo, almost empty from the drought that threatens Brazil with a drastic lack of potable water. The aerial photo shows the water's receding outline which looks like a slice of a tree. The undulating contours of its edge show the growing levels of aridity; they look like the rings within a tree trunk that show its age. The outline is that of a face in pain and grief, a profile of agony, a profile of a crone, her face forming a scream: Mother Earth screaming in Her agony of abuse and assault. I wonder if Tree feels that same pain. It has been proved scientifically that tree roots extend in underground communication for miles, giving support and nourishment to each other. We know now that older trees mentor saplings with their experience, especially after they fall, when their nutrients pour into the soil to enrich the ground of being. I heard somewhere that pine trees actually make a sound to indicate the diminishment of the energy needed to draw moisture up from the depths of the drought-ridden earth. The sound alerts pine beetles to attack the trees; in this way, the beetles are moving across Canada, felling entire forests as they go. Will the Brasileiro scream reach those pine trees, the palm trees dying in the tropics, and the withered elms in Europe?

I lived in Sao Paulo for two years in the mid-seventies when air, water, and noise pollution levels were already over-reaching danger limits. A toxic orange cloud engulfed the city, and newspaper headlines warned 'This is your city! Save it!' From the city centre airport diesel fumes rained down on favelas stacked behind luxury condos; the constant jets screaming overhead deafened conversation every few minutes. A stagnant river circled the city, bubbling with gases emanating from floating excrement and toxins, so the air was overwhelmed with a putrid stink, depending which way the wind blew. Our kittens did not survive their hairless birth; my family developed chronic bronchitis; we watched someone drop dead outside our living room window during a meningitis epidemic. Twelve million people did not stop for rest; highways roared 24 hours a day and shops never closed. An average life span was 44 years; unidentified victims of car crashes lay covered with newspapers in the street until claimed. People lived in cardboard boxes under underpasses and children were sent out to beg at three years old, their numbers regularly culled by police gunshots when the streets were too crowded with packs of tiny starving thieves.

Not surprisingly, Sao Paulo was at the bottom of the United Nations list of green world-class cities. Tiny front yards were cemented in; Ibirapuera, the only city park, was taken over by buildings, a small man-made pond its only concession to nature. No trees sprouted out of pavements. Traffic fumes killed whatever growth there was. And that was 40 years ago. No wonder the trees of the world scream. No wonder the outline of the dried-up reservoir shrieks in agony. Can Tree hear? Does Tree try to reach this non-green place with her energy and love? Do all trees try to respond, all cells in the same body, like the blood cells in my body rushing to the surface to create a swelling and protect the hurting place inside? What protects the huge open sores on Mother Earth?

On relocating to Sao Paulo, we were put up in a hotel for ex-pats moving in and out; 160 children were in residence. School buses pulled up every morning but would not return in midday traffic jams. So in the first week I was presented with a car to pick up my kindergarten-aged daughter at noon. I had mere minutes to find an address and a map in Portuguese, and ask a new acquaintance to look after my other daughter when she got off her local nursery school bus - and to care for my children should I end up under a pile of newspaper, for I really thought I would. We had moved from Jamaica, where my car had meandered along sandy lanes, on the left side of the road, with English signage. A week later, I was launching out into speeding traffic and endless spaghetti junctions, on the 'other side of the road,' signs in Portuguese words I hadn't learned yet. It was one of the most frightening experiences of my life. Innately direction-challenged, I swerved, I swore, I cried, I screamed, I honked my horn, I tried to breathe, I talked to myself, I invoked every goddess ever named, and an hour later when I reached the school, I shook. Strangely, I associate trees with that transition in my life, contrasting languid air outside the gentle Jamaican school where sunlight flickering behind leaves was a Monet in real life with Sao Paulo's garish Picasso cubist shocking the entire system.

I think about tree rings: uneven layers that count age by years, where darkened, cracked layers show stresses from blight and destruction. If my own body had similar body-rings, the Sao Paulo layer would show up as weakened by physical and emotional onslaught. That makes me think of other parts of my life, and I wonder how each era's cross-section would appear - if I were a tree. I envisage the rings as growing stronger and firmer as I got older, definitely as I approach elderhood, feeling more resilient than I ever have. The seasons of my life have varied: child-hood would be marked as a fearful and colourless spring; young adulthood as the summer that vacillated from joy to despair; an autumnal middle age of growing confidence; and now a winter, built firm as it approaches death. No life is perfect. No tree cross-section is perfect. But imperfection is beautiful in its own growth. My inner crone teaches me that.

It was hard in Sao Paulo to find places to breathe and connect. Nature's connections were at a country club on Sundays when it usually rained, making the highways slick and barbecues soggy. So I often visited the rock shop, nodding Olá to the gnome-like shop keeper who soon recognized me. I'd stand before Tourmaline, not so much in homage, although I was awed by her power, but in reverent connection, not speaking. I found sustenance there deep in the city, hidden between the Tiffanys and the Diors. Here were the jewels of the earth, not the cut diamonds and flashy aquamarines that my friends lusted after. My gem-buying friends did not understand my need to be there instead of worshipping at the altar of Harry Winston. As they tiptoed delicately over the rock-strewn floor to show me their latest purchase, I'd shrug at my tourmaline friend. 'Te vejo em breve.' See you soon.

I visited the cave-shop for the last time before I left Sao Paulo, to say farewell. We were returning to Santo Domingo, back to green and sunshine, but unbeknownst to me, to tumultuous change. My inner crone manifesting as Tourmaline had heard the fears of a confused housewife who ached for soul nourishment, and gave me strength to face I knew not what. And then she passed the message on to the universe, like tree roots reaching out. All I had to do was link my spirit with Tree or Tourmaline and I felt whole, heard, seen. I felt prepared to move on. At a very young age I had known that with Tree. Spirit to spirit. Consciously.

I wonder if one can be unconscious of consciousness? There was definitely a wise inner consciousness within me as the child, and the mom in Brazil who had no problem accessing spirit in another being and responding in kind, a natural communication. Because I didn't share these experiences with anyone, I wasn't judged; there was no opportunity for criticism of my assumed day-dreaming or silliness. I would have been the only critic of my behaviour and it never occurred to me that tree-talking wasn't perfectly normal. Time spent with Tourmaline was so meaningful and private that I would never have exposed it to anyone. Though I think that the shopkeeper understood. Entering into another dimension was normal, and it was my secret. That had to be consciousness. But I didn't know it.

In 1996, my inner crone finally made her presence known within my body at the first Goddess Conference in Glastonbury. That conference was a transforming experience, serving as catalyst for many transformations since. Very shy, I wrote in my journal after I entered the Assembly Rooms for the first evening, 'Everyone here knows someone but me. If I don't talk to anyone, at least I'll learn something new.' Little did I know where it would lead. We never know when an adventure starts until much later, when we look back and connect up the thread. Aging follows many threads.

After the welcome circle and opening ritual, over 100 of us gathered in our element groups. Born under Taurus, my element is Earth. Each group was to create a unique chant and body movement to drum beats, celebrating its element. I was technically a crone at 55, past menopause, but when the leader asked for four crones to form the circle's centre, I hung back shyly. Was I wise enough? Up went the hands - one, two, three, four. The fourth woman called out 'I'm a crone but I don't like it!' My hand suddenly shot up. 'I'm a crone and I love it!' Where did that come from? My reluctance was overwhelmed by another force. I was chosen. We four crones were the centrepiece of an earthy guttural chant. As we swayed back and forth, supporting each other, we called forth the strength of powerful, aging women moving fearlessly into the future. Later, when all the element groups had demonstrated their individual creativity, the entire gathering sang and moved together, powerful intermingling sounds blending in the echoes of the rafters. Voices harmonized; dancing shadows were mesmerizing. Slowly and gradually, everybody sank to the floor as one, leaving us four crones remaining upright, still swaying back and forth with our strong earthy crone chant, like the core of life itself, supporting each other, strong. A new power rippled through me. I was a woman who had danced through the ages, carrying my sisters' stories. That night I outed my inner crone, or rather, she outed me - and I've loved her ever since.

When my four children had all left home, I was determined to change my name - my birth name and my ex-married name carried too much baggage. I was trying out Sparkle Treetop. I put it out into the universe in user names and passwords, painted it, sang it. But as I dwelled more on the name Sparkle Treetop, Barbie and her friends kept bouncing into the picture and Sparkle just didn't sit right with me. I was too serious a person to recognize my inner teeny-bopper so publicly. So Sparkle faded away (maybe she took off on the Barbie bus) and another character evolved: an old woman with wild hair who loves to play and dance, is reverent and irreverent at the same time. She cradles the world, comforts and loves, and spits and curses too. She knows when to push and when to pull. The name Sweet Reason popped up. I looked up the definition, and found it too safe at first: 'levelheaded, rational, prudent.' Mmm, maybe I am that sometimes. But when I read 'wisdom, wit, cool, mother wit,' I decided she could stay. I didn't need to change my own name after all. She taught me to accept who I am. I named my inner crone Sweet Reason.

Sweet Reason

Sweet Reason's bones creak in the morning
sing memories of dancing in dew
when the sun's creaking too
in its rise over treetops
at the end of her garden, greening her lettuces....

Feeding the birds, she's painting their houses
enticing the lilacs and roses to stay
'don't fade away'
bakes bread with bananas
and raisins and chocolate, lavishes honey.....

Sweet Reason bathes in oatmeal and comfrey
tendering tissue time-wearing thin
sweet-lotions her skin
drinks peppermint tea as she dreams with her cat
curled up on her belly, ladies greying together.....

outside her house wild-child dances in heather
scattering walls put up in defense
melting pretense
beckoning Sweet Reason outside to play.

Boots tossed aside, she pours tea in her plants.....
flies through the door, joins in the dance.
Sweet Reason's bones may creak in the morning
but the grass in her hair will give her away.
She knows how to play.

She was there all along, the voice of wisdom that isn't about being 'good' but about being true to my soul. It has taken me until I am a crone myself, to recognize my inner crone who has put up with my fears of getting old, angst over wrinkles, anger at the way the body lets me down sometimes. The ritual in Glastonbury launched our ride together. If I get out of my own way, I can hear her voice. It was Sweet Reason who encouraged my spirit to fall in love with a beautiful woman. Before my mind and body knew what was happening, Sweet Reason let a deep friendship develop, not telling me at first. I guess she thought I might pull out all those practical level-headed definitions or haul out that emotion that inner crones have no time for: fear.

But my body caught up with my spirit and this was the sweetest thing that could have happened in my crone years. With a life partner who shares the same vision, Sweet Reason nudges me to be more spontaneous, less concerned with rules, don't watch the clock, say Yes more than No. Play. Rage. Weep.

We are in pain right now, and do rage and weep. Walking on my altar, and with inner crone wisdom, I have learned that we take Mother Earth for granted, that we use Her and abuse Her. In this, Her transition time, She must be hurting. Millions of Her people are hurting. She is so beautiful with Her sunrises and hills, Her sunsets and valleys, oceans and lakes, animals and birds, rocks and trees, Her children's faces, their laughter. But why, instead of thanking Her, do we desecrate Her body? No-one knows this better than the crone; she sees us hurt our own bodies too, and she recognizes our pain. She carries compassion. So many people ignore the pain of Mother Earth and don't see a connection between the pain in humanity and our careless attitude to Her. They choose not to know; they want everything to stay just as it always has been, afraid to look into an unknown future. Surely, when their inner crone nudges them to get their attention, they must be ignoring her, for mine speaks to me about it all the time, urging me to witness the agonies that are going on, not to look away.

Yes, there are those who have no choice, in pain themselves. I think of the elderly who live alone in one room, yearning for human touch or even recognition, a smile. The British government is considering making loneliness a public health issue; in Japan, the elderly rent a family to visit, pretending they are related. This is incredibly sad.

We carry, not only the pain of the present, but also the hurts of the past, of the generations before us. I have had fibromyalgia since I was 16. My grandmother, nicknamed Dolly, also had fibromyalgia, known as fibrositis in her day. Her only daughter, my mother, was constantly triggered by her own childhood's depression, and chose to relate to her mother only through letters from Canada, very few visits. So Dolly lived alone for several years after my grandfather died, with few visitors. Nobody believed her pain, even doctors. She was considered a crazy old woman and she died alone. I remember how loving Grannie was to me, how much fun she was when I was little. But when she and I got older, I was afraid of her crone energy. Her aging fragility and closeness to death scared me. I didn't see her often, rationalizing that by living across the sea, I was too far away. Even when I did travel to England, I protected my memories of childhood stories and lavender, and kept my visits short. Recently, on one of my cleaning-out purges, I found her last letter to me, written just before she died. I could hear her voice again, see how kind she was, how much she loved me, in spite of my absence.

I was young then, I mirrored my parents' attitudes, not knowing any difference. Now the matriarch of my own family, I hold the responsibility of Grannie's family failing her. I am fortunate to access healing and understanding, but I feel the fibrositic pain that filled my grandmother's tiny bent body, the loneliness of her soul. I need to heal that. The Divine speaks through me when I write poems; Sweet Reason gives me the words. I dedicated this poem to Dolly, may it finally bring healing to her. I do believe that if we can heal the present, we also heal the ancestors and we set in place a pattern for healing the future. That is my inner work.

Last Note to the Milkman

How often did you climb the winding steps
to find the scribbled notes she left for you
    or did you have to shout at her to make it clear
that it was half a pint of milk and only three brown eggs
my grandmother wanted?

How much time without another word before you stopped
    thought something might be wrong?

How long before you called nine-one-one?
When you broke in, was there a sense of peace?
I wonder if her rosewater scent met you at the door
or if it was too late, if death's aroma had already filled the space,
        more permanent.

Years before, she would have stood so elegantly straight
but in the doorway's shade, I doubt she reached your ribs
        her back a hump of bones
yet still so arrogant and proud.
(She always called you Jones, no matter what your name.)

I remember cream, an inch above the bottle tops.
She'd save it for my Peter Rabbit bowl of oats;
we'd play a game with funny eyes on soft-boiled eggs,
        toasty soldiers dipping in their yolks.
When I was eight she taught me how to scrape burned toast.
I loved those waking-up-for-breakfast sounds
the most: 'This is the news' on BBC,
knife scraping blackened crumbs, and her wooden spoon
thudding ceaselessly against the iron pot I still sometimes use
for stews.

You didn't think it strange - the smell of gas
she often left turned on? No, you'd hurry back to your delivery,
afraid of being late, shake your head at her senility,
not offering to change the light bulb by the door
or carry in some coal. Why would you?
But then you could have seen the holes
burned in the rug around the grate,
fabric fraying on the armchair where her fingers
clawed incessantly as she challenged ghosts,
praying to die.

You didn't know that she once sang Madame Butterfly
in perfect tone, and spun magic tales for me:

winters when she, her Papa's princess,
rode a fur-lined sleigh pulled by a horse of ebony
waited on by servants at her will.
When you found her, was she lying on the cold tiled floor
or had she fallen backwards in the bath,
legs splayed open, eyes vacant to the ceiling?
I wonder if you covered her, or left her tiny body bare.

She would have hated to be found like that by Jones the milkman,
bent and naked, shrivelled flesh.
She deserved a crown of violets in her hair, a silken shroud,
a footman-driven phaeton for her final ride.

I hope you put your hat aside and said a gentle word or two
before you drove away to wake the town, tell how you found
a mad old lady dead for days up on the hill
as you deliver fresh news with eggs and milk in time for breakfast.

I am a 21st century grandmother and my lifestyle is so different from Dolly's; I travel and study, I drive and my body is fairly flexible. I look forward to many more years of activity. She seemed old and fragile, and her haughty sense of entitlement kept people away from her. But today I only have compassion for the crone energy I was so afraid of when I was younger. I now own that crone energy and I must use it as well as I can, in Dolly's honour.

In *Earned Wisdom*, Julie Simmons explains that approximately every 29 years in one's life, Saturn returns to the place in the cosmos that it occupied when one is born. Saturn's return marks important transitions in one's life. It was my second Saturn return when my inner crone showed up in Glastonbury, and I reacquainted myself with Tree. Simmons sees the third Saturn return as the time when we become 'living ancestors.' '...if we are not frightened by death, we can live consciously and with wise acceptance in the world of the living and the world of those who have passed on...whether our lives have been meaningful for us is not the issue (now)...in a sense we exist for others...'[31]

In *Autobiography of a Yogi:* 'It is only when the traveller has reached his goal that he is justified in discarding his maps.' [32] I almost look forward to my third Saturn return in my mid-80s, wondering if I will discard my maps or keep forging new ones. Will I be content to exist solely for others or will I be trying to keep a balance with my own life's goals? In a movie review, Annette Bening was quoted as saying 'I like being a veteran, I have fewer illusions' Hers is a road map well followed.

Regardless of astrology, my inner crone has been with me all along, through all my transitions: in Tree and Tourmaline, in the ocean waves, in my grandmother, strong and fragile at the same time, in the images of Mother Earth. It has taken me a lifetime to today, as a crone myself, to recognize her and to embrace her just as I have embraced my inner child. She puts up with my fears of getting old, my angst about wrinkles, frustration at the way the body lets me down, my efforts to accept her. When I die, she will accompany me as I return to stardust in the constellations, the 'cosmic family tree (that) connects us with all others,'[33] before I approach life again to join the evolving crowd, hopefully wiser, hopefully more conscious.

Story-Telling Time: Air

The early morning walk to the bakery was always heavenly. The first two people in the family to wake up would walk to the sleepy village of Sosua in the Dominican Republic, to buy a dozen pan de aguas for breakfast, hot and steamy, directly from the brick wall oven. On this particular day in 1979, my son and I were the early risers at six. The air was still, anticipatory. I overheard the word: Huracán. And so began a journey that didn't end for years, although I didn't know it then.

After speedily packing up the car and heading south to Santo Domingo, we joined highways that were packed with vehicles, mostly heading north, away from the hurricane's projected force. We arrived home to huge waves off-shore and empty store shelves. The next day at dawn, with little time for preparation, two parents, four children, one only two months old, one dog and two cats, moved into my 11-year-old son's bedroom, painted brown like a cave. For six hours, as far away from this Category 5's storm's direction as we could be, we heard furniture, signposts, trees, cans, flying past the closed wooden shutters in howling, screaming winds. We could see nothing but it sounded like a war zone. At noon's calm, we emerged into Hurricane David's eye to sweep water out of doorways, clear the drain in the cloistered patio where water sat two feet high up the windows, mourn our vanished avocado tree, briefly search for the tin roof blown away from the storeroom, before we headed back to hopeful safety. Electricity and telephone had broken down early; they would be useless for five weeks. Twelve hours in candle-light: game-playing, spirit-cheering, story-telling, and much reflection, as if staring at the back wall of Plato's cave listening to monsters raging outside.

At 6 p.m, when the winds finally abated, we ventured out to try and clear the tree-filled driveway so my husband could check the damage at work. The roads were impassable but he was determined to get through. We were stopped by army megaphones sending us indoors under threat of gunfire. The curfew would last for five weeks; there was no arguing with the Dominican army.

The winds blew changes into my life that I never expected. Two hurricanes one after the other meant floods, no electricity or phone, no school, for weeks. The aftermath of Hurricanes David and Frederick saw me walking daily with the baby to the one open supermarket, climbing over piles of rubble and glass to buy what I could find that had to be cooked or eaten immediately. It meant showering in the driveway under torrents of rain, trading playdays with nearby friends and inventing crafts to keep youngsters' hands busy, nightly card games by kerosene lamps which soon lit the way to bed. There was no gasoline on the island, but the roads were too blocked to drive far anyway. I became fixated about water and disease, and, every morning, after hauling 27 pails of water from the cistern, I cleaned and scrubbed with disinfected zeal. Survival was my purpose and I thrived on it.

David and Frederick blew changes into our marriage too. Their rains washed away the happily-ever-after myth I had tried to believe in for far too long, and flooded out my denial. The lonely darkness every night magnified my fears of being deserted in a foreign country where wives were second-class citizens. After five weeks, the lights came back on. School started again, gasoline tanks filled up, daily walks stopped; we didn't gather to play games around the lantern-lit table any more.

I lost my urge to scrub, and we could go out at night without being shot, at least by the army. I didn't have to work so hard. We lost our sense of family survival. It was almost boring.

But the East winds had blown in a new normal. They birthed a new life for a husband who found another woman to rescue from the storm; they birthed a mother's strength and courage needed to keep her family healthy and safe in a traumatic time, more or less alone. I didn't know that these skills were being honed for tough times ahead. I want to continue to practise them as I age, as air continues to blow change into my life.

Life is amazing. And then it's awful. And then it's amazing again. And in between the amazing and the awful it's ordinary and mundane and routine. Breathe in the amazing, hold on through the awful, and relax and exhale during the ordinary. That's just living heart-breaking, soul-healing, amazing, awful, ordinary life. And it's breathtakingly beautiful.

L. R. Knost

Fire

I face South: welcome Fire into the circle of my life.

The sun lies directly overhead, shining heat upon the day
or hides behind the clouds at play
but always there.

Sun-flares heat our cells in many ways
passion driving work and play
changing dreams into activity, ideas transform to beauty,
usefulness stirs up the pot of alchemy.
Life.

Fire burns in noon of day, summer of year, youth of life,
blossoms flowers and fruit. All sentient beings
take root, grow empires, nest, give birth to generations,
anticipation of hope.

As Maiden-Mother turns the wheel to summer,
She fulfills Spring vows,
makes Her pledge of harvest to the table in the Fall.

And when I breathe my last, fire will transform to dust
the body I have occupied with love
will energize my spirit, transmute to burn again
into another play, another incarnation.

With gratitude, I hail South. I welcome Fire.

Blessed Be.

Pin Pin Korori

That's the bolder challenge: to find the value in aging without borrowing the value from the metaphysics and theologies of death. Aging itself, a thing of its own, freed from the corpse.

James Hillman

A teacher and mother, I have the internal compulsion to fix things, plan things, make lists. Maybe it's a control thing. But while I cannot fix old age, I can contemplate it now, not ignore this passage in my life until it is too late. I have no idea how I will age. Nearby lives a 100-year-old acquaintance, living in her own home where she gardens, cooks, and entertains. I take note of athletes like the late Olga Kotelko, who at 95 consistently broke records in triathlons and track. Athletic centenarians are very fortunate in their health and abilities and their gene structure. I am not an athlete at all, but recognize the vital value in stretching and moving the body on a regular basis - walking, yoga, swimming. Recognizing and doing are two different things. We all have a different combination of genes and personality and skills and attitudes. Unless we have a medical prognosis, we have no idea how much time we have before we die. In Japan, people pray for a 'supernova close...Pin pin korori means to live a long vibrant life that ends on the dead run.' [34] wrote Bruce Grierson in a letter to me when I was defending his book about aging athletes in a local contest similar to Canada Reads. Pin pin korori. Not knowing when the dead run will happen is challenging for a planner like me.

Some people try to ignore the whole aging process and let the days go by until it is too late to make informed decisions – I imagine it would be hard work to push the nagging thoughts aside. And I would be denying my inner crone which I have pledged not to do. I want moving into a smaller home to be a conscious decision, be in control of my own life, my living space. I do not want to be carried out of my front door like some friends of mine. Days before Mary had a stroke, she put her name on a list for a new senior's residence, thinking it wouldn't be needed for years. Suddenly, her place on that list became vital. Her inner crone had nudged her and she listened.

When I began travelling back to England regularly, I would stay with Nora for a few weeks. Nora was a family friend I had known all my life, and, after my parents died, she shared with me the depth of her relationship with my father, beginning when they were teenagers. We became close friends, having a difficult man in common. I surprisingly held no grudges against her, although I vehemently stood up for my mother when I had to. I accepted Nora as a factor in my parents' complicated life and she was part of the energy around me while I was growing up, which explained a lot about my childhood. Latterly, I talked more deeply with her than I ever had a chance to with my mother; conversations were always dominated by my father.

When Nora reached her 90s, I visited for longer time periods and cooked for her, cleaned out her cupboards and fridge of old dusty jars way past their sell-by date and mouldy leftovers pushed to the back. Nora's big pink house overlooked the sea, a gracious home, full of beautiful things. She always sat in her green velvet wing-backed chair, watching the 'white horses' - waves galloping across the horizon. I remember Tiffany lampshades, elegant upholstery, photos from trips to Egypt and South Africa on cargo ships when she was a young woman, a photo of my father on the mantel. Nora was always dreaming of moving to a tiny flat and I encouraged her. But not a family member, I only had so much influence in the short time I was there, and the flat never did materialize, although a few were inspected, some had help on hand. That conscious choice at her age might have made all the difference in her next few years. But selling her home became too bewildering a task, thoughts of emptying it were overwhelming, with little support from two nieces, her only family.

One night, Nora fell out of bed and lay on the carpet for 15 hours before the gardener found her. After hospitalization for shock and dehydration, she was moved to a nursing home in another village, never to return to the pink house overlooking the sea. The green chair, a television, and a few pictures were brought to her before the house was sold by her nieces. Nora couldn't visualize other occupants living there. A year later, she told me to choose some pieces from her house, not believing that it was empty, sold, and renovated by then. She died at 97, her days condensed to a circle of silent people, dozing in front of a blaring television set to the Youth channel. I visited her there for three summers, and she talked to me of loving my father, a tiny aging Juliet still pining for her Romeo. One Sunday we heard a church organ playing through her open window and we pretended he was playing for her as he used to. Although the nursing home was in a seaside village, no windows faced the sea so Nora would ask me about white horses and I would show her that morning's photograph of waves breaking over her beloved harbour. She wanted the white horses to carry her away. Pin pin korori.

Sometimes things that happen are unavoidable, but I, at the post-nubile age of 75, still dream of being in charge of my own destiny, moving myself before I have to be moved. To think otherwise, would be to deny getting old. To deny dying. My partner and I recently moved into a smaller home, conscious of our footprint on Mother Earth, hoping to use fewer resources, less space, leave behind less baggage. Will this be our last home? Older friends are moving to even smaller spaces, some eventually to one room, or even half a room in a long term care home. Will that be our destiny? Or can we stay within these walls until we die? We cannot ignore the possibility of more living choices in the future.

We are conscious of what happens in the world around us, witness the atrocities and marvel at new discoveries. We try to be alert to ways of honouring Mother Earth, morphing positivity into realistic goals. It isn't easy. But that is the work. Yesterday, an old friend came for tea, one I don't see too often so we had a lot of catching up to do. We talked about world issues, compared life changes, body changes, attitudes to aging and dying. She said: 'If only we knew ahead of time what to expect. If only I knew that my body would ache if I sit too long. Or that my ankles would swell.' But we did know, from watching our mothers and grandmothers. Did we forget so easily? We talked about dying with dignity and what that means. We talked about wills, and powers of attorney and what we thought about at the end of the day. Years ago we would have discussed child-rearing and husbands as babies clambered over our feet; later we would have talked about our careers, clients, bosses, maybe divorces. Now we talk about aging. It seems that we always talk about survival. Survival this far; survival tomorrow. We wonder if we are actually suffering from PTSD after the lives we've lived.

When I was younger I didn't think about what I would think about when I got older, never one for five or ten-year plans. In retrospect they never would have worked. Decisions to move and turn my life upside down were made for me for the first fifty years of my life. I had to adapt. Things change in a moment. I remember telegrams, telexes, phone calls, taking me to new crossroads - or one-way streets and road closures.

I finished my Bachelor's degree at 57 after 35 years of on-and-off study. With no plan of what to do next, I carried on teaching, but missed the challenge of classes and papers. My father died, so I could afford to buy a house, but the house that called me, flirted with me, was two and a half hours away from the college. So I decided to take a year's sabbatical to think my future through. Needing a reason for the sabbatical, I began MFA studies. When I returned to work part-time, the job I had loved for years had been changed, the atmosphere was unpleasant, I didn't even have a desk, so I made a huge decision to take early retirement. Now, I never would have planned that career path 10 years previously. Then I would have imagined I would be working until I was 65 or 70, unable to pay off the interest on mounting debts. Plans change. Adapting is the work – with no regrets. Pin, pin, korori.

Being older always seemed so far away it didn't bear thinking about. There wasn't time to think about it, as in Joan Erikson's words I 'just kept steaming along.' [35] And then I turned 70. 70 was always the age that loomed large in the distance if I let it. And now to think that in five years I will be like my 80-year-old friends is hard to imagine. Imagine I must if I want to remain conscious. To look at the positive side, most of them are active, useful members of our community. And I have to be realistic. My body is getting achier, wearier, and I sometimes forget who said what, when. The other day I decided that I had enough socks to last me to the end of my life which actually seemed like a sensible idea. Sometimes I look at my partner and wonder how either of us can be left behind without the other, although I know that will happen. 'Death is not just some distant possibility; it is an equal reality in every breath and every moment, in everyday life.' [36] I do believe that dying well could be one of the most important things I do with my life. I need to do some work to make that happen. I see now that the journey through aging is a journey to dying. There is no separation between the two, and there are no exceptions.

In childhood, I spent many hours alone, either playing in my room or being quiet in the company of my conflicted parents, silently questioning their emotions. From a very young age, I was traumatized by criticism on one hand, and over-protectiveness on the other, both in the name of love. I still hold the tension in my body, however hard I work at relaxation techniques. The body knows. I have a round, bony protrusion in the roof of my mouth. I thought this was normal until a new dentist gave my oral orb a scientific name, pronounced it non-malignant (a scary word intruding into a previously carefree morning), and told me it had grown from holding myself tense at the time of skull development, which occurs very soon after birth. If a tiny baby can hold her body tight enough to affect her actual physical growth, then I know that the fear I felt as a child was real, and must have begun in my crib, or even in utero. My heart leaps in love for that newborn baby trying to be quiet and good, absorbing the toxicity around her, afraid of her shadow for fear she would do something wrong.

So I learned empathy very young, putting myself in other people's shoes to try to explain their behaviour, to counteract the judgment all around me, to rationalize how they must have felt through my perspective. Maybe in searching for their goodness I over-emphasized my badness. I walked in their shoes enough to be considered naive by those more cynical. Without siblings or taking part in any teamwork, I grew up without the people skills necessary for bobbing and weaving in adult society that one learns in a boisterous home or with a pack of friends. I grew up being what I thought people expected me to be, not knowing any other way to relate, having no confidence in an opinion, not daring to make a choice in case it was deemed the 'wrong' one. I can see clearly now how this must have been very frustrating for anyone in a relationship with me. It was certainly challenging for me, especially as it was all totally unconscious. I thought I was being good and kind. But I felt confusion and sadness which somatized as depression and body pain. Ah, the joy of age, to think one has cracked the code and discovered the motherlode of understanding into the ticking of one's inner clock! Though will the code ever be entirely solved?

Was there ever a time when I was not wondering about the purpose and worth of my existence, either during my times alone witnessing life around me, or fantasizing under the eiderdown at night, convinced that my real parents would soon rescue me and take me back to their royal palace? I constantly wondered why I was where I was, and why nobody seemed to understand me, yearning to be sent to boarding school. I followed all the dictated passages of life more or less in the predicted order then expected in one's 20s and 30s, feeling the same emotions and hormonal urges that everyone else did, but interpreting them in a self-critical way as I moved between different cultures and relationships, with others and with myself.

Now I have the luxury of time. I actually enjoy my sleepless hours after reading about the end of the world as we know it, when I wonder what life and death are all about. With the gift of an understanding partner who daily reflects me back at me with such precision, I can see between the gaps with more clarity than I ever could alone, or in a weekly session with a therapist. I hope I am more conscious than ten years ago. But I still have a long way to go while the land-mines of aging lurk underfoot. I am not alone in these thoughts and questions: how do we age consciously and approach dying without fear? All the fears come down to having to let go - of things, people, places, traditions, beliefs, illusions, hopes, dreams. Pin pin korori.

An important factor recently has been the constant sorting, throwing away, letting go of 'stuff,' physically and emotionally. Along with that comes finding things, coming across things you forgot you had, things that make you wonder why you ever had them in the first place, tears flowing as the soul retches with poignant memories. If I were remaining unconscious, I would leave boxes piled up in dusty corners, thinking it an overwhelming task. Let someone else sort it after I'm gone. But consciousness surely means being responsible for what is left behind, making it easier for those looking after my estate. As an only child, I know very well the stressful effort put into unloading the trappings of a life after someone dies. I do not want to leave a huge houseful of things like my father did, forcing me to work my way through furniture that dated back to the early thirties, a parcel mailed in 1935 and never opened, a workshop full of noxious-looking liquids and rusty tools stacked among the latest equipment. Part of growing older for me is the realization that in not wanting to leave anything behind, I can streamline my life, keep what I need to live with and enjoy.

People moved away from their homes by necessity are also removed from dealing with that. Nora didn't dare imagine how her home came to be empty, it was too painful. Auctioneers? Hired cleaners tossing a life's possessions into a dumpster? Or on a front lawn tabled with the leftovers from a life for sale, as I recently found on a walk past a house belonging to a close friend who had died three years ago. My heart leapt out to sale tables scattered with books I had given her, a homemade DVD of our messages that made her laugh when she was ill, a favourite blanket she had said I could have 'one day.' Which is worse: hours of emotional tearing apart as one throws things away as I have done so many times? or a dissolution of one's life by somebody else with little input, like Nora and Mary? The former is a cleansing ritual and a personal responsibility; the latter doesn't matter much to anyone, except as an extra burden on those left with the job. Either way, every article carries a resonance into the future. We never die.

What I have gathered over a lifetime is mind-bending. When moving around the world at the corporation's command, we were entitled to movers who came in and packed, and then unpacked the other end. I didn't have to think about that part of it much. I remember when we left Venezuela, we had a despedida - farewell party - the night before the movers were coming. The next morning, the movers couldn't wake us up, so they began by packing the party tables left on the patio. Three months later in Jamaica, we unpacked our party - sticky wine bottles, full ashtrays and dishes of peanuts! In those days, moving for me was more about saying goodbye to friends, a long hotel stay while the furniture was being shipped, finding schools and doctors again, making a new life.

But when I separated from the company and all its accoutrements and moved with my children from Santo Domingo to Canada after 15 years away, I supervised everything, knowing that at the northern end it would be my responsibility to move into our new home. I literally had a pop-up shop in my Dominican house for three months, tables around the walls covered in our bits and pieces for sale. Everything was sold that had to be sold. I witnessed everything going into the huge truck. It took five days for me and five men to pack up what I thought would be essential for our new life. I remember suddenly hearing a loud crunching and found a packer putting a sea urchin shell on a piece of newspaper and then smacking the paper around it to pack it away. Delicate as a porcelain breath, the shell instantly shattered. He still wrapped it tightly and put it in the box. Then the next. Were sea urchin shells, white and exquisite in their fragile state, really that necessary to our future in Canada? I thought so. I had no idea what we were moving back to, but that connection with the sea would keep me grounded. The last view of our home was in my driver's mirror: steel drums filled with flaming garbage, fires lit by the maid to prevent local rascals from diving in to find treasures to add to the piles they were hoarding on the street. I cried and cried. That life was in ashes. Pin pin korori

Once in Ontario, we moved into a rented town house on Labour Day; the moving truck blocked the street well beyond our short driveway. That move introduced us to a series of garages and basements - five in ten years - that we jammed with boxes. Each move meant garage sales, more trips to the second hand store and the dump, until the fifth move when the contents of that basement had to be condensed to the size of an apartment locker and I spent two weeks going through all the boxes I had never unpacked. They should have been emptied years ago, or never filled in the first place. Two weeks off work, sitting on a skateboard in a four feet high space, hunched over letters from my grandparents, books once cherished now damp and mouldy, finger paintings, baby clothes, crying over garbage bags full of 25 years of cherished memories. They had to go, but I still have the memories.

In my crawl-space now, are labelled boxes full of the final remnants of what is precious to me after so many moves, things I cannot bring myself to throw away that I imagine my children will want to revisit. My homes used to be full of the past, until downsizing pulled me into the future, so boxes of framed pictures of my children at all ages stack high. It would take months to relieve each photo of its frame - do I pitch them? Leave them for the next generation to clean out as I had to do? Every now and then a treasure wafts into my mind like a wispy cloud and I visualize the box it is in stored downstairs and a memory returns.

Do I load a truck up with all the boxes, sweep out the empty space and shut the cellar door feeling gratified? Pin pin korori. Or do I leave them there, labeled, and waiting to be delved into by those who will pass Grandma stories down to their children, keep alive the myth that our family will eventually become, with its many photographs to prove it? Or is that a myth in itself? Will they really spend hours in family togetherness remembering, or will they throw out the boxes without opening them, in a hurry to put the house on the market, like Nora's nieces?

I return to Olga Kotelko, the Super-Senior athlete, and read of her attitude to aging. She began track and field at 77 years old. From a Ukranian farming background she was of sturdy stock. In medical studies to see what made her tick, results were those of a much younger woman. How can she help me with my musings on aging consciously? At 77 she worked with her gifts of energy - played soft-ball, then track, volunteered in her community, was very curious. She didn't expect her aging years to be sedentary and boring, waiting for, as Bruce Grierson describes in his biography of her, 'the ticking doomsday clock of the boomer' as she is 'perpetually in a state of being either confidently anticipatory or pleasantly surprised...brimming with desire and intent.' [37] Grierson talks of how we also 'have the knowledge to rescue ourselves, one good habit at a time.' There is the work again, aiming for a supernova close. Pin pin korori.

Permanently Cool

Eighty is the new eighteen.

Hannah Marriott

I consider myself very fortunate in the women in my life. Some of us meet regularly, in discussion groups or study groups. One group, Evolutionaries or Evo's for short, struggles to look at our conscious behaviour, how can we wake up? What is the evolutionary way of reacting? How do we become sacred activists? Some of us have a burning desire to do something, others work on being - we all try to wake up. Another group is self-named The Dead Group, because the first book we studied together was the *Tibetan Book of the Dead*. We took over two years to finish it; we take a long time to dissect and wrestle with unfamiliar material. Often in our groups the subject of feminism comes up. Several of my friends strongly declare themselves feminists; they marched in the '60s, created new laws upholding Canadian women's rights, wrote fiery articles, worked in women's centres. Living abroad, I had no opportunity to march for women's rights, even if I had known that I could. But my strong beliefs in equality between women and men, between all disenfranchised groups, and wanting people the world over to be free of shame and abuse, still makes me a feminist. As I witness my middle-aged children's assertions of self, and their struggle with balance in relationships, I believe even more in a fair and kind society, free of isms.

I am aware especially now of ageism, which is obvious in today's media. The aging population on television and film is either given far too young an image or presented as doddery and forgetful. Nobody knows how to depict us. *Grey's Anatomy*, an ongoing drama usually excellent at depicting controversial issues, went down in my estimation with an episode that showed an influx of seniors into the ER from a bus accident. The actors played simple-minded and buffoonish roles and the medical staff either laughed at them or talked down to them as if they were children, jollying them along. It was abominable, that in the twenty-first century, old people could not be depicted as intelligent adults, with legitimate feelings and rights. I question myself; is that really how I appear to younger people? In another current series, *Grace and Frankie*, 77-year-old Jane Fonda's sculpted figure, back-combed hair, and botoxed face are shown off at their best. She is sharp and witty, but is only typical of those retirement home brochures which give the impression that only elegant couples enjoy patio cocktails by a sparkling pool every evening. The image of a lonely widow eating alone at a table by the kitchen door would not sell the retirement home image.

I get perturbed at ads for bathtubs that have doors opening in the front to allow easier access, where the well-coiffed, straight-backed woman in a white dressing gown sits calmly while the water drains around her before she can open the door and get out. Isn't she freezing cold? Isn't her robe soggy? Why is she smiling so inanely while her arthritic bones seize up? And I object strongly to photo-shopped versions of families posing in their designer kitchen as they joyously tear open Grandpa's bank statement, each a token member of society in colour, gender and physical ability. The grandparents are giving their mortgage money to their children with a huge smile. Of course I recognize that there are elegantly aging men and women, and families who gift their children with lots of money. But they are not the norm today. Non-reality is presented as reality, all in the name of making money on products aimed at the latest high spending consumer market. We see them and wish we were them. Discontentment sets in. But reality wouldn't sell. The entire focus today is on shopping and consuming, creating a demand and then supplying it in a disposable manner, thereby creating a further demand. I object to the media's manipulation of our emotions.

To attract the aging market, well-known older women are now being wooed as product advertisers. The latest is the highly respected author, 80 year-old Joan Didion, advertising Céline sunglasses in Vogue magazine. The caption under her photograph states that she has 'timeless cool.' I am really conflicted between a) being pleased that finally older women are being noticed, told we're beautiful, smart and courageous, and b) cynically wondering if our latest target group is being hoodwinked, and nobody really believes the propaganda. Why else would aging movie stars become cover girls? Vogue calls Didion 'the ultimate Céline woman: brilliant, creative, vaguely recalcitrant... immortal, intellectual-and-otherwise dream girl.' [38] Do they think that in the fickle world of fashion that will sell sunglasses? Have the advertisers seriously balanced out the hopeful purchasing power of the elderly against the negative attitude of the masses towards the same elderly? They must have or they wouldn't be making such a gamble. '80 is the new 18' [39] is quite a statement to back up.

An image has just come to me, drifting in from way back when: the Charlie Girl. In the '70s tropics, we had little access to North American culture. So it must have been on home leave, those few short weeks in Canada when I tried to absorb everything I could of the current zeitgeist, that I found Charlie perfume by Revlon. Unaware then of the toxicity of cheap colognes, I relished the ads that showed the Revlon Charlie Girl, who 'personified the independent woman' [40] I wanted to be. Who came first? Charlie or me? Oh, how I wanted to be the Charlie Girl! And I became her: the walk, independence, the mannerisms, the breeziness - and the perfume. I was totally taken in by marketing. (I think I mixed her up with a bit of Annie Hall.) So on reflection, I see how easily it can happen. But now, 40 years later, am I so easily taken in? Weaned off advertising and consumption, cynical about the motivation of the media, and highly aware of the toxicity of products we call food and beauty care, I know the answer is no. I certainly don't yearn after an 80-year old life-style as I did after a 30-year-old one. Why?

I was recently watching snippets of an interview with 80-year-old Dame Judi Dench, who I admire as a person of integrity and talent. After seeing Dench, the narrator of the entertainment programme said 'Oh, how sad. She's got so old, she looks so old. It's so sad.' I could not believe my ears. But this is the general feeling about age. The focus is on how we look: we don't look young any more, regardless of our attitudes or activities, regardless that Dench is still acting brilliantly even though macular degeneration has taken away her ability to read lines or see marks on the stage where she should stand. Airbrushing elderly faces in advertising is not going to change that. Writing that 'Joan Didion's age is not hidden but celebrated...she's all sleek grey hair and formidable bone structure' [41] does not change that either. If we saw Didion on the village bus going to market, we would see an old lady with thinning hair and jowls, and we wouldn't call her hair sleek or her bones formidable. We would call her old.

Is it that younger people feel fear when they look at their own future? I listen carefully to my children speak about me getting old, how they speak to me. They remember me as an energetic single mom, working, studying, active. They are proud of me, that I am still writing university papers, that I dress edgily and have 'a life,' but sometimes ageism does creep into our conversation, usually about technology or an energetic activity. Sometimes I sense it, in a nervous giggle, a look. If I challenge, I feel defensive and get responses about how great I am, as if I am asking for reassurance. Is it their fear that if they acknowledge I am old, they will have to recognize that I will also die? That they will get old and die? My son used to tell me that I am not going to die, I will just 'go away.' Is he afraid of his own mortality? Was I? As 50 creeps closer for them, the number becomes a topic of awe, of dread, or almost surprise. I well remember that feeling. And I felt the same way about 70. But somehow I do not feel the same about 80. It is as if I have crossed a great divide.

When my elderly mother was becoming weak and confused, I tried to get some answers from my father. Was she going to the doctor? Is she taking any medication? His angry rebuttal was: 'You don't know what it is like getting old!' No I didn't. At 48 I didn't know what it was like to be 75 but I did know enough to inquire about doctors and medication, no matter how old my mother was. He didn't understand that. He took my concern as interference in his care-giving. Now I do know what it is like to be 75. Would I take a similar inquiry to be an attack? Or a compassionate desire to help? The older I get, do I interpret certain questions or attitudes as ageist? Of course, when the words 'old people' are used, as young people do when decrying our computer skills, there is no question. But I wonder about the innuendos, the looks, the sly smiles. Am I imagining them? How can I equate that with the 'timeless beauty' of Joan Didion in her cloud of perfume? Is it all a sales pitch? Do photographers smirk behind her back? Is she treated with great reverence because she is the Joan Didion, or because somewhere along the domino chain she pays their salaries? Then is it true reverence for the person or for the almighty dollar? As written in one of the flurry of articles that appeared around Didion's debut on the advertising stage, 'In this instance, the line between celebration and exploitation is a fine one.'[42]

I wonder about the generations growing up, most of whom appear to have no idea of the struggle women had to get the vote or even be designated as 'persons.' Do they know that today is the first time women are allowed to vote or stand for office in Saudi Arabia? Would they care? Do they even care about feminism? A music critic writes that the 'new face of pre-teen feminism' is an 11-year-old girl, the precocious Sophia-Grace, who holds her own with day-time hosts, sings rap, whose video is marketed as one that every schoolgirl needs to see.'[43] I watch it and I am angry. Five over-excited pre-pubescent girls bounce and sing their way to K-Mart, where they buy armfuls of sparkly dresses, put on a fashion show, and make up each other's faces. 'Home' is a Hollywood movie set, right down to the infinity pool. The lyrics tell me that no boys are allowed, girls are taking over town. In same critique, we are asked to overlook the 'typically girlie activities such as lip gloss and fashion shows.' Why?

The bubbly author of the critique may as well say 'Go back to sleep,' for this is a blatant example of today's sleepwalking and unconsciousness, along with the latest fads for pyjamas, zombies, and virtual lives played out on computers. The media is telling us to sleepwalk our way through our lives - after all, knowledge is power and the last thing we need to learn is what is really going on in the world. Right? I am aware that often seniors are quite happy with that status quo. They would rather their last days be filled with prettiness and cheeriness than putting any effort into understanding world issues, let alone heal the space around them and contribute holistically to the collective. Just follow the advertising.

The subtle messages in this pre-teen 'feminist' video are obvious: to be happy you must shop 'til you drop, and to be accepted, you must concentrate on clothes and makeup. Besides the fact that it is a not-so-subtle commercial for K-Mart, the girls in Sophia-Grace's video are hardly typical 11-year olds. The age of puberty these days is as low as nine, yet they have the breast-less body shapes of seven-year-olds, while they vamp with the suggestive movements of grown sexy women. This is all they see in the media: waif-like models getting younger and thinner and more vulnerable-looking; girl singers once admired as healthy role models are now prancing naked, lauding drug use. Looking young for their age is juxtaposed with acting old for their age. No wonder young women are confused.

I do allow that in entertainment nothing is typical. A 'typical' life would be considered boring, not good entertainment. Reality shows are so far from reality - we see no every-day tasks like unplugging the toilet or doing the laundry. Roseanne Barr's sit-com was touted as typical, which was maybe why it was so popular. Though I wonder if in its 'typicalness,' it gave permission for disrespect and rudeness to be considered normal behaviour. What is the happy medium? Boring? Father Knows Best? Or, how about no sitcoms at all? Could we find other ways to entertain ourselves? This would mean destroying an age-old tradition of poking fun at ourselves: the court jester gossiping in skits for the king; Shakespeare's theatre-in-the-round where theatre-goers threw tomatoes at players who were acting out their own archetypal conflicts. Are we seeing ourselves? Or are we trying to become what we see? What is real here? Or should I just relax and laugh along?

If Sophia-Grace's video is an example of today's feminism, it is not the feminism I believe in. My feminism believes in egalitarianism, encourages friendship with both sexes. My feminism honours relationships built on trust and support, not on clothes and makeup. I think of the solidarity and honesty of Meredith and Christina, each other's 'person' in *Grey's Anatomy*. That feminism doesn't wallow in entitlement, competition, or dualism, but in having each other's back, sharing, and mutual affection. Videos like this one by Sophia-Grace are not going to carry the feminist movement further; they set it back years. I constantly wrestle with being an old fuddy-duddy, so the last thing I want to do is rant about the way things used to be, compared to what is. I don't want to live in the past, or romanticize the past. Neither is healthy. But I do believe that we need to look at where we've been, how it got us to Now, and how we can use that knowledge as we move into the future. What I try to do is objectively look at our world situation and see if and how I collude with anything that stands in the way of a conscious evolution, like this video, and manipulative advertising. Then I can work on learning new habits, practise being an Evolutionary. But as my brother-in-law says, 'It looks good on paper, Roz.' However, I do not see being older as an excuse to stop questioning, stop changing, stop the inner work.

One way for me is not colluding with a world like Sophia Grace's for my teen-age granddaughters, both of whom are delightful authentic individuals who constantly struggle against the mixed messages they are given. Margaret Wente, whose advice to young women is to 'practice manning up,' (a phrase my feminist friends would decry) writes in an article in the Toronto Globe and Mail, 'our 'brave and fearless daughters... have turned into neurotic quivering piles of jelly.'[44] I don't think so. Daily they are surrounded by toxic environments; one example is this video and also the thousands like it that create entertainment by various levels of sexualizing and even brutalizing women. I used to play a game of pretending to look into my little grand-daughter's belly button to see if the adorable girl was as beautiful inside as she was outside, because that was more important. She still fondly remembers the belly button game, and she is beautiful inside.

What also makes me angry is that this type of media brainwashing sets up a discrepancy between those that have, and those that don't have. Maybe the daughters of the 'haves' can swim in infinity pools, shop all day, sleep in designer bedrooms. A high percentage of the other 99% will crave that kind of life and internalize negative reasons why they don't have it, including critical self-judgment when they can't achieve the closet of dresses, or mommy's credit card, goals that were not real for them in the first place. The media sets up discontentment, over-reaching, sometimes self-abuse.

I grew up in England after the war. I had to wear sensible clothes, not allowed to date, however much I begged. The only women in my life I could emulate were my mother, her friends, or my teachers, none whose strength of character or appearance made a positive impression on me. The girls whose boyfriends picked them up after school seemed so exciting. I envied them. Life was serious, dull, and sad. My dream life came from books and my imagination. A common flight into fancy was imagining boarding school with a pack of adventurous friends. If I had the lifestyle choices offered to me in today's videos and movies and advertising, I would have been suicidal with craving. Then my father travelled to Canada and brought back copies of *Seventeen* magazine. For the first time, I saw another side of life: girls not in school uniforms, dancing and laughing through a life catered just to them; teenagers in poodle skirts, with shiny hair, boyfriends, convertibles – maybe the '50s version of Sophia-Grace's lifestyle. When my father announced that we would be moving to Canada, I 'knew' the new life I would have. In Canada, I would be happy, fun, thin, popular, everything I wasn't in England, just like in *Seventeen*. Because I had learned very early not to share my hopes and dreams, my emotions, or my worries, there was no-one older and wiser to advise me, or set me straight.

Of course, my old self went with me to Canada. My father did not magically forget his strict parenting style. My school uniform and strict British tweeds were 'good enough' for school, and I still couldn't date or go out with boys or girls whose parents he didn't even try to know. I envied the girls at school who looked and acted like *Seventeen* models, not noticing many more like me, struggling to be seen, surviving in the jungle that seemed to be high school. I just knew I wasn't good enough. Media images continued to haunt me, through anorexia, through drastically changing myself into the popular girl with a fraternity boyfriend, then the wife who followed magazine articles on how to set up a perfect home, cook, hostess, trying to emulate the glossy images – the Charlie girl. I considered myself a failure when a cake didn't look as shiny as the waxed model in the photograph, or people didn't flock to my door on bell-ringing sleighs because I bought a certain whisky at Christmas. I still wasn't good enough. It took a long time, maybe into my 50s, to see the damage done by my following the media's brainwashing. How controlled I was. It took longer to track that back to my *Seventeen* dreams. I don't think I am alone.

Hypnotized, we still stare at the back of Plato's cave, unable to pull ourselves away to experience reality for even a second. For some young people this is the only way they know. I need to walk out of the cave, or at least get close to the entrance, to feel fresh air and hear birdsong.

In the perfume promotion, Didion is called 'a dream girl.' [45] Girl? I don't care if people call me Ma'am although I have several friends who get annoyed at that, but I find 'dear' or 'dearie' quite demeaning, even if it is used in good faith. I have never been called Grandma by anyone other than my grandchildren thank goodness, but when the waitress asked 'What would you girls like?' as she approached our white-haired smiles waiting for our tea, I was mildly irritated. Today, 'girl' is cool. Would Kirk Douglas be called 'boy?' I expect in a similar situation he would be called 'stud,' even at 99-years-old. Why do I suddenly have to be called something because I am old?

So now it is cool to be 80. I can see where this is going. Already white and silver hair is fashionable among the young. Runways will soon be filled with sensible shoes and shawls during New York Fashion Week; malls will have hand railings in the middle of walk-ways; Metamucil will be available in the Food Court and magazines and newspapers will be printed in an extra-large font. Because that's what 'they' think older people are. That is how we are defined in marketing-land. Like four-year-olds offered Britney Spears style slinky dresses in department stores, women bribed back to the kitchen with modern appliances after the war, and men's gift shops selling only beer steins and tool kits. We are defined by marketers: told what we like and what we need, told to follow so-called trends created by corporations, told how to keep up. Keep up with who? There is the myth. Trying to keep up is like running on a hamster wheel. Round and round, getting nowhere.

I gave up the hamster wheel years ago. I have always worn my own style of clothes, the only person in my working world who didn't own a suit. I didn't even get organized enough to layer outfits, as some friends do so elegantly, able to pack efficiently. I give up the idea that I am slow because I am old. Or wrong because I am different. Nobody is wrong because they are different. Different to what? There is no norm except that which we have each internalized from our birth. Yes, I am permanently cool. And that is the way I intend to go on. My way. (Bless Frank)

I return to the images of Joan Didion, and other older women who are now spokes-models for cosmetics companies - Helen Mirren, Cher - and I reflect on a global inborn shudder at the older body. I look fine in my quirky clothes, but when I take them all off and stand naked in front of the mirror, I very consciously practice gratitude for a crone-body that is emerging at a time when culture tells me that I have no power, that signs of old age are to be avoided, and aging minds are feeble. I practice gratitude that my body has held my soul in a safe space for all these years. I question the meaning of beauty that we are taught from birth - young, lithe, fresh-faced. My mother called that 'chocolate-box pretty' because when I was a child, chocolate boxes in England had either a village scene or a beautifully smooth-faced young female on the lid. I know now that she was telling me to look behind the pictures to see the staging and the makeup (no photo-shop in 1950). The opposite of chocolate box prettiness to my mother, I know now, was 'real' - light-filled energy shining from eyes, authentic smile, the beauty of loyalty and service. Through her, I learned about the shallowness of fakery and the beauty of authenticity. I have just realized that and I am grateful to her. This morning, as if to validate my new thread of connection, an English newspaper photo comes up on my computer screen showing a lineup of models waiting to become the new Cadbury's chocolate box girl. Sigh.

I am criticizing my inner crone when I complain about looking old, or groan in my stiffness. When I wish I was younger, I am throwing her well-lived experience back into her wrinkled face. If we pretend that aging has nothing to do with us, we are denying that she even exists. If we refuse to talk about dying, we are destroying her legacy. When I look in the mirror now, I try to see my sagging body and wrinkled face as beautiful. I say 'try' because sometimes it is hard to catch sight of a mottled forearm and think it is Grannie's arm, instead of mine (though now I am the Grannie!), or see my mother's jowls in the mirror instead of the clean cut jaw that used to be there. But I am not 21, and nor would I want to be. In old photos, that young face looks empty, free from experience, unlived-in. Every wrinkle and crease is well-earned, every laugh-line well enjoyed, frown-line well-deserved. This body has served me very well and I am grateful. I am proud of being an old woman. I will not prettily couch those words but claim them as mine.

Atonement

I have hated, berated you, exercised and crunched you,
squashed and squeezed you,
even starved you. Cursed you for being round.

Yesterday I looked at you in the mirror.
Really looked.
Not for years, not since I anxiously waited
for a low roundness to prove that life was really inside me.
Not for years have I looked so closely.

You are round.
But you take what I feed you,
and wisely you give up the chaff,
energize the life force circling my body
so it can re-grow, re-live, re-generate.

You are round.
But you carried five babies,
nurtured them and protected them.
You pushed out four of them at exactly the right time,
cherished the other when she changed her mind.
Years ago, I had to call you 'tummy.'
Belly was a bad word - now I relish your name:
Venus Rising belly - red velvet Raphael belly
Goddess belly.

Do you remember?
Once you felt the sea on your naked skin when the moon was full.
Once your core held me upright when I wanted to fall.
Wrapped in burlap or silk - do you remember?

How can I punish you when your memory is love?

Love

How could we define the feeling of love? In my experience it is associated with a feeling of bliss, an ecstatic joy, an upwelling of a feeling that exists prior to any conception of what that feeling might pertain to.

Anne Baring

When my children used to ask me what I wanted for Christmas or my birthday I always had a stock answer: love and peace. I still do. That's all. Love we shared in abundance; the peaceful demonstration of it was a bonus. I still have a valentine from 1983; a child's paper heart from a tear-out book was signed by all of them. I cherish a note written in 1985 when they played a joke on me; I felt I had done my job well when they plotted together behind my back. I still do. A florist's card sent on my 70th birthday says they are proud to call me Mom. Peace in the home was always a joy; peace in the world less attainable, but I still dream of it and still request it for Christmas. Although we don't 'do' gifts any more, I still like to acquire love and peace at any time.

As I get older, love takes on more importance, not less. I believe that we all have a guiding principle, a value that underlines our choices, our reactions to each other, what we think, say and do. Very early on, love emerged as mine. I try to discover why I feel about this so strongly. My father called me naïve; the worst thing I did, he said, was to believe in people. He told me he didn't believe in love - until his last day on earth when he told me he loved me and I could see that he meant it. I was so grateful that he was able to finally say the words for his sake. And also for mine. I had looked for them all of my life.

Part of me thrills to hear people say I love you so easily at the end of a phone conversation, but despairs when their claim to love does not show in their behaviour. It seems like a trite throwaway comment sometimes, the current trendy thing to say. Another common phrase is 'I love them dearly but...' I have said it myself. A lawyer friend once questioned me when I said of a mutual friend, 'I love her but she makes me so mad.' 'Then you don't love her,' he said. But I do. One can love someone and still be cross at them. The killers of love are disdain, scorn, dismissiveness. They cannot be part of a loving relationship. When I think of loving humanity, a universal love, this comes in play too; scorn and disrespect surely help to create the polarized dualities at the root of our world problems today. Do we really love 'the other?' or do we have no idea what we are saying? Do we really know what love means?

'Love' needs to be re-defined. Its interpretation has been consumerised into a Hollywood Hallmark hypocrisy where it is glorified as between two people and usually entails sex almost immediately on meeting. What is love? What does love mean to me as I age? How does consciousness fit in with love, and vice versa? Where does love fit into these in-between times of stress and angst? I look at my own experiences of love, from my view from the crib in World War Two, to now, to see how love became the value I most treasure.

I was brought up by a mother who adored me but was too weak to protect me. My father used love as an excuse to control; love with him was oh so conditional. I can see how they both struggled with their interpretations of love and looking back into their early years, I understand their struggle, but I didn't feel much love for either of them during their lives. Now I send them love and healing every day, hopefully changing the generational inclination to repeat history. Maybe it just assuages my guilt, but in this way I do believe I can create a healing path for future generations. As a child, I was blessed by my maternal grandfather's love for me. I don't know what I would have done if he wasn't there, there was no-one else I trusted. He not only listened to me but he heard me and his words created a simple framework for my internal maturation. The light he told me would always shine inside kept me going through many tough times, though I didn't realize it until much later on. This little light of mine. Play it at my funeral.

Inexperienced, I confused my first sixteen-year old kiss in the moonlight with love forever after, and was devastated when my passion was unrequited. Two years later, my first real boyfriend adored and respected me, but I didn't understand his niceness. I wasn't familiar with that. I confused popularity and leaving home with love when I married the star football player. Much was done and said before our wedding that should have raised alarm bells, but I was chasing the bridal image too determinedly and ignored them. Nothing would deter me from my illusions; keeping the masks on the man I wanted to love while creating new versions of my own.

I first met a true, embedded love when I gave birth to my son, and found that it only multiplied with his three sisters. I loved being pregnant, when baby-dances within my body gave me joy that only I could experience and share. With them I learned to show the emotion I had firmly hidden early on in my childhood. I learned how to laugh out loud, how not to be so self-absorbed, to love unconditionally, a brand-new experience for me, and one well-practised since. As the years went by I began searching for the love that was missing in my marriage by flirting, confusing sexual attraction with being loved. The tropical environment I lived in was conducive to a frenetic search for excitement. One relationship went further and I knew what loving another adult human being felt like for the first time. When this affair coincided with the latest of my husband's flings becoming a more permanent fixture, our marriage ended, and a new phase of my life began. Then my children were all I had to sustain me.

The flirt in me during marriage turned into a prude after divorce. After an abusive date, and confused about entering the dating game at 40, I chose to dedicate myself to being the mother my children needed. That led me on a journey to find out where I stood in the middle of all the roles I played for other people. In the next 24 years I grew up. In that time I re-lived those first 24 years of my life when I was forbidden to learn from experience. In those middle 24 years I finally grew up and I am so grateful for that.

I read and studied, practised different spiritualties, learned to enjoy my own company, and learned that love did not have to be focussed on one person, that love could be felt and expressed in so many ways. I could love life itself. I worked with adults returning to school after crisis changed their lives and found that love was in advocacy, mentoring, and conscious listening. I healed. On reflection, I see that in those years I began to practise loving the person I really was, that everything and everyone in my life had contributed to my growth up to now. I saw how valuable all of my experiences had been, how everyone I had met was a teacher, but I had built walls around me. Now I had the opportunity to knock them down and expose who I really was. It wasn't easy. Sometimes I didn't like that person. Sometimes I did.

It was very fortuitous that I had the gift of that time, because I became more conscious, more in tune with the world around me. As Anne Baring writes in her magnificent tome *The Dream of the Cosmos*: 'Time is needed to reflect on and absorb all these and more aspects of love, time to become conscious of the power and intelligence of the energy that is living through us, and in us, time to open the eye of the heart to awareness of its unconditional love.' [46]

Several of my friends could not understand my self-enforced celibate state. Why wasn't I looking for a partner? How could I possibly live without love? Maybe they meant without sex. I was still young, I had 'life in me yet,' they said. A piece by Osho, found in a friend's book and copied on a paper towel remains precious; I carried it in my purse to pull out and quote to those who thought it appropriate to inquire after what they saw as the lack of love in my life, maybe anxious about their own fears of possible loneliness. I still have it there.

'Let love become your quality, not just a relationship with somebody, because when love becomes a relationship it includes one but excludes the whole universe. Simply be a lover and let the whole be your beloved. When your love spreads all over space, when it knows no boundary, when nothing confines it, when it is unlimited, when it is not focussed on any object but is just a state of being, then love is prayer, then love is meditation, and then love liberates.'

'Simply be a lover and let the whole be your beloved.' Without focussing on one person, I found that love can be expanded way beyond - not only to my children, students, and neighbours, but also to the people who accompany me on a flight or a bus ride, to refugees on the other side of the world and those trying to help them in their desperate journey. It is liberating.

For years, if I wake in the middle of the night, I have practised a healing meditation, sending out loving energy, first to our house, then spreading outside to the street, visualizing the village, then Ontario, across Canada, around the whole world, lingering where I know my family and friends live, dedicating healing energy to them, then moving on. On a particularly sleepless night I may travel right around the world on my healing tour; sometimes I don't leave Canada, or even the room, before I fall asleep.

At the Glastonbury Goddess Conference 2005, several women told their stories in a production called *The Yoni Chronicles*. My contribution was in three parts: maiden, mother, crone. In front of three hundred people, I told my abbreviated story in poetry, then created a circle, calling in the directions, asking Goddess for love. I was finally ready to love and be loved. I did not describe what I wanted love to look like, it was of no consequence. By now I had defined love in a person as someone with a similar vision, walking together with understanding and respect, someone who could cope with the difficult times as well as the good, with whom I could share interests, and whose ego wouldn't get in the way of our different opinions, with a good sense of humour. I would offer my same interpretation of love in return. In her important and timely book, *Love in the Age of Ecological Apocalypse*, Carolyn Baker writes that '...compassion and empathy are two expressions of love than humans must cultivate' adding 'detachment, discernment, forgiveness, and humility.' [47] I agree with these six qualities and add resilience. Aging, we must be able to adapt to our rapidly changing world, recognizing the global changes and evolutionary choices ahead of us, however old we are, not going backwards with excuses.

I flew home that summer to deepen a friendship that blossomed into love in winter. At 65 years old, I fell in love with a beautiful woman and have never looked back. I asked for love and Goddess presented me with love in a form I never would have imagined. We have lived together for 10 years. I, who never thought it possible to share a home with anyone again, so set in my ways I thought, eagerly opened up my home to another household of 'stuff.' We negotiated linens and closets; her carpets and lamps and paintings brightened up dark corners. As with my own shadows - I now see parts of myself that I never would have known about living alone. Political junkies and baseball fans, we do not get tired of each other's company. We are different in many ways and don't always see eye to eye in small everyday collisions, but we are learning how to debate and process. We share the same vision, walk side by side. We are both fiercely interested in waking up before we die. We will accompany each other on that journey.

At our age, the future isn't very far away. But our Now is right here, today, putting petty arguments in perspective, making healthy conflict management skills even more necessary. This is a far more mature relationship than I have ever had. We don't know what we have yet to face: who will look after who first, who will be left alone to deal with the details, follow the meticulous guidelines we have filed away, write the obituary. We don't know who will be the holder of the memories, and all the 'stuff' in the cellar that we thought we had whittled down as we blended households. We wonder who will explore the mystery of dying first. But we do know that having each other in our lives has added an unexpected energy to what could have been two subdued, less colourful, and maybe lonelier lives.

Several of our friends have met partners late in their lives. They have met someone from their past, or when they made a move to a new location. Single elderly friends talk in different degrees about wanting a companion, some actively look online, others fantasize about what they think will never be because of circumstance or age, but they are not too old to dream. One friend in particular, is an active 87; she owns any room she is in with her vibrant personality, and shares willingly how attracted she is to a couple of men, younger and sexy. She is loved by many for her compassion, her humour, her courage to succeed in new activities - acting, painting. But she is still alone at night, playing Sudoko. There are so many like her, who remember lost loves and dream of finding love one more time.

I add to my new definition of love: intimacy, and the warmth of another body. Like dogs, we like to move in packs or communities big and small, and when cold or threatened, we like to gather close together for comfort. I am so grateful for that reassurance, of another heartbeat close by, private jokes, a shared memory accessed at the same time, someone to murmur with in the middle of a sleepless night.

Dying presents the most intimate of moments. Most of the deaths in my life occurred at a distance, or just before I reached the deathbed. It was then my sacred task to sit and share the space with my father's body, not knowing when his soul actually left, not knowing if consciousness ends with the last exhale, talking to him as if he was still alive. A friend shared with me that she witnessed the spirit leaving her twin sister's body. There are many different theories but in *The Grace of Dying*, Kathleen Dowling Singh quotes Sherwin Nuland as saying that 'the appearance of a newly lifeless face cannot be mistaken for unconsciousness.' [48] At this intimate moment, I would tend towards Tibetan Buddhism and urge whoever has died to remember who they are as they move on: 'Hey, noble one, you are in the in-between, do not fear it!' [49] sending them courage and strength for the journey ahead. We hypothesise and know so little. Even so, to accompany someone at their moment of death has to be the most honourable of tasks. To keep their cooling body company with loving support and prayers is another. That is intimacy.

But however carefully a dying person is tended, however much love is in the relationship, the end of their journey has to be a solitary one, for they take those final steps alone. We are born alone; we die alone. Stephen Jenkinson writes from his vast experience in palliative care and hospice environments: 'You are not journeying down this road of life together. At this point, you can't. Your dying partner, without meaning to or wanting to, turned off that road when he or she got the news, leaving the rest of us marching along it as if we'll be fine...the love that glimpses its end..' [50]

As 'dying people are trying to find their way out of their bodies and out of their lives,' Jenkinson suggests a loving task that maybe could be shared: the dying talks through the process if possible, to help the prospective survivor understand. 'I am going to give you something of your death now, through mine, as you'll have something reliable when you get there, something of me. Let me love you that way.' And the survivor, participating actively in the ongoing conversation, asks 'What is it to be dying? What should I learn now, to help me when it is my turn?'. [51] That is intimacy.

Singh writes: 'Love appears to be the last connection the dying have with the world of form.' [52] One of the most beautiful stories I have heard was Paul McCartney relating the death of his beloved wife, Linda. As she was breathing her last breaths, Paul talked to her of riding her precious horse. He said something similar to, 'You're up on your beautiful Appaloosa... it's a brilliant spring day and the sky is blue... you're galloping into the sun...' as she closed her eyes and gently died. I have an aerial photograph of my sacred place, Lyme Regis, the English seaside village where I spent my most peaceful of times. I want that photo by my side when I am dying; I want to trace the path I took every day walking by the sea until I can see it no more. To have someone walk me on that path as I am dying would be the most loving task anyone could do for me at that time. That would be intimacy.

Elisabeth Kübler-Ross says that there are only two emotions, love and fear. Today, we live in an atmosphere of fear, both real and instigated by the media. How does that fear affect the love we feel, both personally and universally, which is so important near the end of our lives? She writes: 'We cannot feel these two emotions together, at exactly the same time. They're opposites. If we're in fear, we are not in a place of love. When we're in a place of love, we cannot be in a place of fear ... every moment offers the choice to choose one or the other. And we must continually make these choices, especially in difficult circumstances when our commitment to love, instead of fear, is challenged. Having chosen love doesn't mean you will never fear again. In fact it means that many of your fears will come up to finally be healed. This is an ongoing process. We must continually choose love in order to nourish our souls and drive away fear, just as we eat to nourish our bodies and drive away hunger...' [53]

Surely, we must continually choose love. As the aging process begins to lessen our energy, maybe take away our independence, maybe remove us from our familiar surroundings like Nora, we must continually choose love. Then the fear that may accompany illness and herald dying will be lessened, and love will be the path we follow.

Larry Dossey writes about studies that analyze Near Death Experiences (NDEs) which, he says, 'suggest an element of consciousness ... (which) may persist following physical death ... Every near-death experiencer is convinced that the purpose of life is to grow in our ability to give and receive love.' [54] The message in the research is of universal love. The fact that my father could say 'I love you' in his last days tells me that he finally saw that for himself. Another quote on my Zen calendar by Osho: 'Let love be your only law.' This is a law I can keep day after day after day until there are no more days.

Mushroom Clouds

Evolution is a tightly coupled dance, with life and the material environment as partners.

James Lovelock

Yesterday I read an article about James Lovelock, lover of Gaia, proponent of nuclear energy. At 94, and after more than 40 surgeries, he is as vital as ever, living in my favourite part of the world - the Southwest of England. Already I am endeared to him. Anyone who walks on my coastline daily is fine by me. When he voices his opinion that rejects any view in which the chief role of the earth and its diverse life forms is to serve human wants and ambitions, I totally agree with him. Our attitude towards climate change has to include polar bears and hummingbirds and birch trees, for we are all part of an interlocking chain, each link relying on each other. This is not a human-centric issue.

There are many reasons why Lovelock and climate change are at the forefront of my personal reflections on aging. While Lovelock believes that nuclear energy is the only way to go, I have concerns about nuclear leaks, waste, accidents like the one in Fukushima. I am a firm believer in green energy but not of exorbitant costs spent to build and maintain huge wind turbines which destroy natural habitats and migratory paths, even killing the earth and neglectfully maintained. If groups of homes could have a small windmill between them, or share solar panel batteries, green energy would be more cost efficient.

Sixty-storey wind turbines cost more to erect than they do in dollar savings on energy. Our own little island has been under attack by government systems who don't take into account the animals who are protected here, determined to drain our local budgets to keep up roads and rebuild bridges for construction trucks. It is a conundrum; we have created a monster that has to be fed.

As a senior, I am not prepared to sit back and not worry about it because 'I won't live to see the end of oil,' as I have heard several times. First of all, I might see the end of oil. Maybe yes, maybe no. Secondly, as Lovelock said in an earlier article, 'The Gaia theory holds that animals, plants and microbes not only compete, but also cooperate to maintain their environment.' [55] As I am part of the whole, it is my responsibility, my energy that participates in that cooperation. Back to colluding again. I do matter.

Although I know very little about the science of nuclear energy, it does affect my life on a personal level. An hour away from our home, buried nuclear waste creates a toxic living environment for another lakeside town; there is constant talk about where to re-tomb it, the dangers of all aspects of the transfer. Following the results of the Fukushima disaster, I try to limit my intake of fish and shrimp - but every now and then a tuna sandwich calls my name and my intention wavers. I dispute Lovelock's claims that there is no health fallout from the nuclear disaster as I read of the first-responder sailors, who worked on the USS Ronald Reagan, offshore of Japan at the time, their disproportionately high rates of cancer compared to the rest of the country.[56] I mourn the fish and dolphins that die in their hundreds on the west coast. I am also very aware of false flag incidents and propaganda, so Lovelock's assertion also makes me wonder if I have fallen victim to another contrived story by gas and oil interests. Beginning to learn more about the lobbying industry and punishment of whistleblowers, I am fairly cynical about the sources and validity of what I read in any media.

When we drive into Toronto, we pass the Darlington Nuclear Generating Station, looming high and brooding on the shore of Lake Ontario. After reading Lovelock's article again, I tried to look at the complex as if it were a castle, its Disney-like turrets rising into the sky, surrounded by a magic fence waiting for the prince to vault over and rescue the dying princess languishing inside. It didn't work. It still cast a dark shadow and an inborn fear of radiation.

Acid rain was a popular term when I was a teenager, and I remember sitting on the step looking at dark splodges on the path outside our front door, wondering if the cement was being eaten up by toxicity and if we were splattered with poison every time it rained. Earlier drills spent hiding under school desks to be safe from exploding H-bombs, and movies of mushroom-shaped atomic bomb explosions in deserts, soldiers hiding behind cactus plants for their 'safety,' were my first acquaintances with the word nuclear. Although Hiroshima was a word often heard by my budding consciousness in my childhood, I did not connect all of these up at first.

Nuclear energy also polluted my childhood home. Beginning in the early '60s, my father's job was to submit tenders, and then on receiving the contracts, be responsible for the installation of huge turbines in nuclear plants in England, Canada and India. Even though I rarely had the courage to argue with him, I felt strong enough about my stand on the danger of the word 'nuclear' to try and persuade him that his work would only bring danger. I mixed up the two. Bombs and energy meant the same to me in the '60s. He argued that nuclear energy was safe, had nothing to do with bombs, and was the only way to go into the future. In retrospect, he was quite prophetic and I had little to base my words on, only a teenager's view of world peace and a fear of the H-bomb causing world destruction. (He used to say that the world would never be at peace and needed war to boost the economy.) Joanna Macy says that nuclear energy has 'turned (her) mind inside out because we were threatening the very basis of complex life forms by generating materials that will literally last forever, without realizing that disease and genetic mutation will inevitably follow.' [57] So now I feel justified in my teenage arguments. Before he died years later, my father described horrific dreams he was having, of children with no eyes running from huge fires, which makes me think he had buried any earlier concerns of safety.

Passing Darlington Nuclear Station brings back the names of the places I remember from dinner-time conversations, hearing about projects he had to visit, contracts he was working on, turbine installations he would be supervising: Pickering, Bruce Point, Hinckley Point in England which is in the news again as it undergoes a massive rebuilding. Rajasthan in India was his swan song, the project before he retired which entailed thirteen around-the-world trips for him, memorable because of the brief sense of freedom my mother and I enjoyed at home.

India was one place I have always longed to visit, especially as a young wife in the '60s and '70s, when less traditional young people than I were back-packing around the world, attracted by Indian gurus. I even asked my father if I could travel with him at one point; I must have really wanted to experience India to ask that. But his views were derisive and uncomplimentary. 'No woman in my family will ever go there.' Always the bigot, he sneered at the poverty, the uncleanliness, proud that he brushed his teeth in straight whisky and stepped delicately over dead bodies in the morning streets. He would stay in a private compound in Rajasthan, with ex-pats who rarely ventured forth and whose lives seemed incestuous and full of addictions - according to him - but I understood trying to survive in faraway lands. As I found out much later, my presence would have limited the freedom he had on these trips, the silver-haired executive whose flattery charmed those willing to fall under his seduction.

So, as I read about James Lovelock today, I remember my father, and think of the similarities and differences of the two men. They look a bit the same, born in the same part of the world, both agreeing about nuclear energy. But my father was a traditionalist, a cynical pessimist, a brilliant numbers man, but who did not think computers would last and there would never be world peace. Paranoid, he trusted no-one, suspicious of ulterior motives and spilt secrets. Lovelock trusts in Gaia, as do I. Lovelock has a positive attitude to life and death, is a futurist. He looks back to see how far we have come since cells wobbled out of the water and began to breathe oxygen, and then into a future, when we may become computer-human hybrids who wouldn't recognize the traditions or archetypes of the twenty-first century.

When I think of those people who have had limbs and organs transplanted, or pacemakers installed to assure regular heartbeats, or computers that calm the electrical systems in their brains, how artificial limbs operate on a thought, and how smart phones are almost another digit on our hands, such a future being is very possible. And like Lovelock, I am excited by that thought. I hope I will return in another life to experience that futuristic lifestyle, having déjà vu experiences about my life now - like those I have now about lives lived long ago.

Mushroom Clouds

1962: Child fed by nuclear power,
I fight my father, hating where he works
believing H-bomb fear
is his creation, while all the time

he talks clean energy.
I imagine bombs, beg him to stop,
save humanity.

In his restless sleep
when faceless children flee
pink mushroom clouds,
he shrugs them off.
In his perfection there can be no room
for doubt.

1975: Father cooks on Sunday nights,
fries chips and mushrooms.
Their slices must be equal, matching
'to a milli-thou,' he'll say with pride,
discarding those that slip his knife.
I watch his sleight of hand
behind the smoke of cooking oil
that veils hypocrisy and guile,
refusing to be sucked into his trip.

2003: Dawn behind the morning tide,
round and red with throbbing heat,

but for an instant I feel no joy.
Instead I see a TV image:
testing 1950's mushroom clouds
in black and white,
on Christmas Island and sandy desert seas.

I no longer smoke, but wonder
if there's time
to find a cigarette before
my father's cooking fumes
extinguish me at last.

Story-Telling Time: Fire

For fifteen years, I lived with my children in eternal summer. Sometimes it was wet and hot, sometimes dry and hot, and sometimes a bit cooler, but still hot. We were moved around the world like chess men, at the mercy of the multi-international company masters. As long as the business man was at his desk in one country on a Friday, and another desk in another country on a Monday, production could go on. The family would adjust. The wife's job was to smooth the way to make that happen: efficiently run the home, give birth in Latin American delivery rooms and be the go-to parent, the perfect hostess in other languages when entertaining visiting dignitaries, show how calmly she provided a resting place for their employee in between his meetings and important work which went on late into the night, six days a week. And if she became 'difficult,' maybe complaining about a too-long plugged toilet or frustrated at weeks of monsoon solitude in a new country, she was bought off with a car, or a house by the sea for a week.

Living in the tropics meant a much more luxurious life than I had ever dreamed of. But as I neared my 40s, married life was frantically playing out its death watch; emotions exploded in ugly confrontations over intimacy found in other places, indifference, derision. In *Into the Heart of the Feminine*, Massimilla Harris describes it as if I had sent 'a deep feminine part of myself into an inner cavern...had been banished and become withdrawn, frozen and bitter.' [58] In this story's particular endless summer in Santo Domingo, I was harvesting the fruit of discontent, rebellion against artificiality, with an energy previously hidden in compliance and pathetic tradition. I was a one-woman's liberation movement and I didn't know it. I struggled to keep life calm for the children's sake.

On this emotional high, I was offered the lead in a community theatre comedy, *Move Over, Mrs. Markham.* My husband was in Europe with a young woman. He wanted his family out of the way, vanishing as if we had never existed, allowing him to move smoothly into his new life with no encumbrances. Financially dependent on him in the tropics, I worked as a supply teacher, but saving the 25 pesos a day I earned was not enough to take my children and leave home. I had no bank account, no credit cards. I had been away from North America for 13 years. As a foreigner, it was impossible to leave a marital home in Latin America with legal rights, so I had decided to wait this out. But when he didn't return home at the planned time, I panicked. Imagined drama took over - he wasn't coming back. Desertion hadn't crossed my mind until now. I needed the stage role to take my mind off my fears by living someone else's farcical life for a while. I needed the distraction. I got the part.

The play's new cast and crew met after auditions to celebrate. At three a.m. we finally left the restaurant, a strange hideaway place in a forested park, where army generals and politicians met their mistresses under deep grass-roofed cabanas that also hid nefarious deals, chauffeurs waiting at the curb. We all said goodnight to each other in air that felt eerily still and quiet, even threatening. My car was at the end of the line as I had arrived last after checking on the children. The others pulled away; I was alone. The domed roofs loomed ominously behind me in the pitch black night. Walled houses on the other side of the road were in darkness.

As I moved around the car to the driver's door, a sudden ear-splitting screeching noise made me swivel to my left. A black car careened along the street towards me, lurching from curb to curb, out of control. I barely had time to squeeze against the door as the car aimed right at me. It veered away at the very last second, heat searing my legs as it missed me by inches. Swerving across the road, it hit a low wall and flew up in the air, flipping over and landing in an empty lot. A huge crash of falling metal exploded into flames that lit up the night. The air was filled with explosions and crackling flames; the smell was acrid, burning rubber and fuel.

I tasted incredible fear. Not one light came on in the neighbourhood. No-one stirred behind me in the park. Nobody came running. There was no movement anywhere. It was as if I was the only person alive in the world. I started towards the wall then stopped - any person in the car would be dead in the explosion. (Besides, if I had been seen near the accident, I would have been blamed as a foreigner.) But the strange thing was – and even though it happened fast, my experience was one of slow motion - I hadn't seen anyone in the car as it barely missed me. No-one. There was no driver.

Shaking uncontrollably, I got into my own car and locked the door, eventually forcing myself to drive past the fire, hardly believing what I had experienced. At home, I was unable to sleep. Heart pounding, I soothed the sore skin on my legs with aloe cream. As dawn broke, I returned. Smoke still rose from the pyre, but again, nobody was around. It was as if the crash had never happened. Yet I could feel my scorched legs, and smell the smoke in the air. It was not a figment of my imagination. I read nothing later about any accident in the newspaper. If it was an accident.

I often drove past the empty lot and eventually the car was covered over with weeds and greenery. It morphed into a hill in the middle of the field, a funeral mound of unknown origin, except to me who doubted that any person was incarcerated there. I wondered about other swoops and swirls in Mother Earth's countenance - seismic shiftings? Or ancient tombs opening up? In this case a tomb had been burying my life as I knew it; I went on to resurrect myself, stronger and wiser, to move into my next life. No-one but me knew why my decisions became clearer. I had lived. I had more to live for.

In an online workshop years later, Alberto Villoldo said something I will never forget: 'You did not decide to come to this workshop because a friend wanted you to come, or because you thought my book was interesting. You came because of something that will happen months, even years from now, when you'll say, 'Aha, that's why I went to Alberto's workshop all that time ago!'' I remember that anecdote often, it takes away the need to know why.

Yes, the car fire was terrifying. And yes, I was so grateful I had survived. But I was also conscious that this happened at a pivotal time in my life. The car gave me the choice to live or die. The fireball forced my turning point from impotence and fear to confidence and acceptance of my power. Once I had made the decision to live, I began to own my own power. What I didn't realize until later was that at the celebration, I met the young man who woke me up, who was to become a catalyst in my divorce, who gave me the courage to leave my comfortable life in spite of the unknowns waiting ahead, and then, as gracefully, disappeared.

I will always remember the driverless car. It came toward me at a crucial time in my internal decision-making. The car was me at that time: driverless, not in control of my own life, driven only by emotions, silently screaming to be touched in a loving way, torn between my children and some sense of who I really was. The car crashed and burned when I was narrowly close to doing so myself. It took a while to recover my balance, but I did not become the pile of burning debris that would be eventually hidden. By staying in the marriage I would have been like that funeral pyre. I took the wheel and began following my own route and eventually reached a destination I could not have imagined.

I am grateful for my age. From my perspective, I am grateful that I am in my 70s and not in my 20s. We are all born into times of stress and difficulty, and it is all that we know.

As a child I only knew war. Children born now know instant communication and Black Lives Matter. It is all relative. Some of my adult students decried the state of the world into which they were bringing their babies. My mother did the same in 1941, but if I had not been born because of the state of the world, I would not have had the incredible life I have been privileged to live. I believe we are born when we are supposed to be born. We are in the world at the time that we are for a reason, and maybe we will never know that reason. Maybe, as per Villoldo's message, we will eventually find out. I believe we have a role to play; how we play it is through our own choice, but it still gets played. I cannot be expected to experience the world as a 17-year-old or a 90-year old, but I can experience it now as a 75-year-old and not judge others from my limited perspective.

Too many elderly people compare what is around them now to what was around them when they were younger, and find today lacking in their value systems, values established in their own unique era and environment. I vowed years ago not to do that, though the occasional 'back in the day' does occasionally creep into my conversation. Especially this morning when the computer-driven washing machine was off-balance and went on its own journey across the floor, which sent me into a reverie on the glories of my mother's simple wringer washer. Progress happens fast today, information travels fast, time goes fast. Maybe it is easier on one level for older people to stop, put away the devices, and create a calm routine of self-care and pleasurable activities, not follow instant news, or keep up with technology. But I like to think that curiosity, community activity, and fascination with technology never slows. It keeps one on one's toes, alert and awake to what is happening in our world, happening to us. In actuality, we are happening to it.

And we are all in this together, no matter what generation. Each playing a role. Each part of the ripple effect. As the driver-less car taught me in that one existential moment, I must take control of my life and not give it up to what happens to me. May that last into my old age so I will die well aware of my dying, and grateful for the living.

When I look inside and see that I am nothing, that's wisdom.
When I look outside and see that I am everything, that's love.
Between these two my life flows.

Nisargadatta

Water

I face the West: Welcome, Water, into the circle of my life.

Water flows across my pain
highlights my joy, my grief, and soothes my losses
clarifies my thoughts,
rinses out my fear in sparkling tears of transparency.

Water cleanses me
my body's tides respond to Hers
emotion's ebb and flow
her moon tides crest in my moods high and low
wake me, rock me, nest in waves within.

West sets the sun by day
brings in the autumn of my life. As leaves turn dry and fall
so does aging paint my skin
transform the space I'm in to one free of constriction
less restriction, cools down friction

to reflective truth,
lets go of burdens, ties, attachments, illusions, all collusions.
I have enough. Enough.
I have lived a life as full as any
water pot could carry, I have the time to tarry at the well,
not hurry any more.

And when I breathe my last,
water's gift will cleanse and purify, moisten lips now dry,
skin so pale and bathe away my fear,
float me away into another world, the other world,
my boat, sailing west to reach new shores,
will rest on evening's tide.

Blessed Be

Story-Telling Time: Water

Water does not resist. Water flows. When you plunge your hand into it, all you feel is a caress. Water is not a solid wall, it will not stop you. But water always goes where it wants to go, and nothing in the end can stand against it. Water is patient. Dripping water wears away a stone. Remember that, my child. Remember you are half water. If you can't go through an obstacle, go around it. Water does.

Margaret Atwood

As I age, I am remembering mothering my children more and more, especially when they were babies. I adore newborns, those silent times in the middle of the night, just the two of us and the sounds of the night. I birthed three children in three years, and then a long-awaited baby came after another nine years. When I die, the final picture in my head will be of four blonde-headed toddlers playing on the beach, all the same age, with their buckets and spades, sparkling sea behind them. I miss those babies so much.

I carried five children, raised four. One baby was 'lost.' I wonder about the language of 'losing' a baby. When one loses something is there not the possibility of finding it? If one searches hard enough? Or not? I wonder what I found after this child was lost, for it certainly wasn't Matthew or Lucy, who was wanted, cherished, anticipated and already loved by three young siblings excited about the preparations. As my belly grew, we discussed the nitty-gritty of conception, the whys and hows of intimacy and childbirth. At eight, seven and five, they had different reactions to sex from extreme curiosity to 'Gross!' We had just made another international move so I had no close friends yet, just other mothers I saw on school pick-ups. So the pending arrival was a precious family affair, as we planned the nursery in our new Dominican home.

And then the baby died. 'Lost' has connotations of not taking care of something, forgetting where you put it, wandering off in a forgetful state, carelessness. But oh, dear baby, you were safe inside me; your tiny body couldn't wander away into strange territory. I nested for you, nourished you, cradled you. I loved you. But I was careless and maybe it was then that I disturbed your peace. Your conception was in Sao Paulo, the home I enjoyed the least. The city was a cesspool of careless values and neglected people filling non-green space, surrounding skyscraping entitlement and greed. I have often wondered if the Paulista pollution entered your multiplying cells and poisoned your growth. But as you developed in your ocean of warm, we moved to Santo Domingo, a welcome relocation for me, not knowing it would be my last one in such a free-living, musical clime. I knew Santo Domingo. We had lived here eight years earlier, your big brother was born here. I welcomed the tropical air, familiarity of place, kind people. You would have the same baby doctor. I had a sense of continuity. Of coming home.

After almost three months of bittersweet hotel living, we settled into a familiar routine in our new house. I felt very healthy, if tired. Then one day we ran out of drinking water, which meant changing the heavy five-gallon glass jug that swung on a metal stand. My husband was not home, nor would be for a couple of days. I was too independent to call a neighbour for help. We needed water. I swung out the empty jug fairly easily, moving it to the patio for pick-up. Then I hefted the full container, trying to adjust my extra girth around it and balance my body. Up the step and into the kitchen we went. Then the heavy bottle slipped.

Water poured everywhere. Searching for the lowest spot, it flowed around broken glass, over uneven tiles, under the stove, out of the door and down the steps. The water turned red. Thick glass had cut the joint open beside my left big toe. The inch long slash was a wide open C, pouring blood into a red sea that drenched the steps and patio. I wrapped my foot in dishtowels, and set to work, mopping up water, sweeping up glass, changing the towels on my foot as they turned scarlet. Eventually my foot stopped bleeding so much, the floor was clean, and piles of cloths lay soaking in bleach. I cradled my belly and finally allowed myself to sob loud unheard tears of shock. Did you hear me cry, baby? Because of my own pain, did I not hear yours?

By the next day, the baby's swimming movements had become weaker until they slowed and stopped. The pain and uneven healing of my foot was secondary to the agonizing stillness I felt when I sang healing lullabies to my womb. Anticipation of birth was lost in my concerns for a tiny life, which only a few days earlier responded visibly to a sibling's voice. My guilt at wondering if I had wrenched muscles, loosened the placenta's grip, destroyed the safety and love I had promised this tiny soul, was immense.

This was made worse by the doctor who dismissed concerns about the changes I felt in my womb and my heart. Realizing later that a Latin-American country would not condone an abortive procedure, I kept hearing his reassurances that all was well, that every pregnancy is different. But I knew. And two weeks later, feeling empty, ill, and unheard, I demanded tests. A simple pregnancy test proved negative. I was right. For once, I didn't want to be.

Each child reacted in their own unique way, one offering me her doll to care for, one asking if she could take over the assigned nursery for her own private nest, one tenderly making sure I was okay. As adults, they still react with similar intention to crises, shocks, or surprises.

Only those who lose a child and then spend time surrounded by nursing mothers and baby cries know how much the body, mind and spirit can ache. A few weeks after the D&C surgery, I translated the biopsy report from Spanish to English using the medical dictionaries I had bought to understand family diagnoses when needed. I learned that my baby's body had literally disintegrated in my womb while I was trying to convince the doctor that Matthew or Lucy was dead. I could have died from sepsis. It was impossible to decipher the baby's gender; only the head was entire. My husband loudly mourned the loss of 'my son' and then rarely spoke of it.

My body did. The blood that had nourished my baby for five and a half months constantly bled out of my body, reminding me of my loss. My tears flowed as readily. The jagged scar on my foot is the lifetime reminder of a life cut short before it began. Previously planned house-guests made it impossible to rest and, after weeks of bleeding, I was threatened with hospitalization by the doctor who was dosing me daily with Vitamin K shots. A stressful three weeks with my in-laws and their two teenage boys was the last straw. I took the children out of school and fled to a friend's beach house in Casa de Campo, la Romana. Now a resort, then an enclave of private homes, it was so peaceful. Tourism had not yet invaded the Dominican Republic, and the beach and pool were our own for two weeks. We took our bikes and healthy food and books, and to the music of swaying grasses by the ocean tides, my aching body finally relaxed. The blood stopped flowing immediately.

Every afternoon, after pedalling to the beach and back, we walked to the pool. I heard a call from its depths, unlike that from the ocean. This was different. I was called to be totally beneath the pool's surface, wrapped in its cool blue light. Not a good swimmer with memories of being tossed off a jetty as a child, I can manage a respectable breast stroke, as long as my head stays above water. Being out of my depth frightens me. Boats scare me. I don't enjoy showers and washing my hair makes me feel I am going to drown; one speck of water in my eye causes a red itchy result. So this call to be one with the water came from some other place; I didn't question it. I borrowed my son's snorkel and mask and swam under the pool's sun-shadowed surface for hours, up and down, up and down.

In that magical place I healed. The children understood my urgency. If they needed me, they knew exactly where I was; the lifeguard was watching over three excellent competitive swimmers. It was as if they gave me up to a sacred ritual. After hours of spending time beneath the surface, all sounds muffled, sunlight flickering in a blue haze, I healed, body, mind and spirit. Under the water, I attained another level of consciousness. Water, that had enclosed my baby for the first few months of a tiny womb-life, sheltered me when I desperately needed to feel close to the little soul who had been an unseen part of our family for such a short while. I lost the baby, but I found some inner peace, a healing, and sanctuary. I grieved alone, but Goddess held me and told me it was okay.

Letting Go

Letting go means falling behind the energy instead of going into it. The moment the energy moves and you feel your consciousness start to get drawn into it, you relax and release. It just takes a moment of conscious effort to decide that you're not going there. You just let go. It's simply a matter of taking the risk that you are better off letting go than going with the energy. When you're free from the hold energy has on you, you will be free to experience the joy and expansiveness that exists within you.

Michael Singer

We are dying from the moment we are born. Our cells die off, regenerate, multiply, fade, and die. Death is our fate, our destiny, for this, or each, lifetime, whichever way you look at it. To risk repeating the oft-used metaphor, we humans and the flower have much in common: we begin life as a sheltered bud, grow and bloom; at the end of our season, we wither and die, fall off the stem/branch/tree to the earth where our dismantled body enriches the earth for seeds to feed and grow and start the whole cycle all over again. My beloved grandfather called the baby me Rosebud. Now Roz is coming to the end of her blooming.

At the end of our garden there is a 12 to 15 foot width of treed land between us and a farmer's field. That piece of land is our jungle, our savannah, our safari park, and in the winter, our Northern Steppes which offers a view of the sunset hidden by green during the rest of the year. We hear the creatures that cohabit in this tiny strip of natural land, and follow the passage of leaves from spring to fall as they rustle to the growth below to be covered in their snowy transition. Our tiny piece of land makes us very aware of the turning of Mother Earth's wheel and the trust we have that everything will happen as it should. If I could be a leaf I'd be an oak leaf, a sturdy little soul, reminding me of English parks - or maybe a coconut palm frond, waving above my beloved ocean.

Trees welcome their buds, embrace foliage, every leaf soaking up energy for new growth; every leaf is important. We treat our own gift of life so badly by comparison. Why do we kill and starve, why do we steal, lie and cheat, when love and kindness would be so much easier? Or it appears easier but it takes work to maintain. I wonder what the world would look like if we all came from respect and compassion instead of from power and greed. Our lifestyle has been ingrained in us over millennia; something huge has to happen to make us change our behaviour towards each other. Something huge is already happening. Like the cartoon snowball exponentially growing in dimension as it rolls down the hill to cover the village below, that 'something huge' will eventually swamp us and force us to change, whether we want to or not. All areas of life are demanding change. Not just by renovating or rejuvenating, or by renaming, but by tearing down and rebuilding and reclaiming, by reframing the way we think, the way we live in community, the way we love.

Every generation has had to deal with change and, I am sure they were often as bewildered by its necessity. I remember my mother's strong resistance to change - and mine too if I forget my practice. It's the intention behind the change that's the main thing. Her argument was built on a fear of the unknown, secure in the familiar; mine on tradition and nostalgia. The steady growth of technology, which has occurred fast, tempting us with more 'free time,' has enticed millions into a twenty-four hour connection to their devices, and less face-to-face interaction. My paternal grandparents refused to have a phone in their house, even when they were old, ill, and needed help. I would love to know the reason for that. Remembering my grandfather's penchant for saying 'Goodnight' to the television newscaster and meaning it, I wonder if he thought strangers were intruding in some way. My own father, an engineer and mathematician, did not believe there was a future for computers, preferring his Oxford Dictionary and encyclopaedias to Google. Change was scary, even for him. Despite his all-powerful image, it was safer to stay with what he knew, than risk failing at something different. Saving face in case he failed.

Well-documented fears about the economy breaking down, climate change, food shortages, and terrorism, must be frightening for those elders who are already tremulous about immediate worries: Will I lose my driver's license? What if this test shows I have cancer? Will my money last for the month? When will my family visit? And turning on the television for some light entertainment only brings more fear and terror into the home, usually at night when it continues to haunt sleep. Many people refuse to listen, watch or read news of change, preferring instead to live in a bubble, doing what they've always done, befriending like-minded people and taking part in traditional activities that don't disturb their quiet life. It seems safer that way. Maybe they think that as their lives are nearing an end they don't need to 'bother with all that world stuff' because they don't think it will affect them. This speaks to many of the books I have read on aging which ignore the bigger world around us, and focus on the little life led by the reader, encouraging hobbies at home, going on cruises, expanding on the idea that as one gets older, supposedly one retreats back into the childhood world of 'me first.'

I wonder if denial is part of the separation that naturally happens at the end of life. I wonder if it will happen to me? The only news my father was interested in just before he died was not the Grand Prix motor races that he'd followed all his life and which I thought would have brought some enjoyment and nostalgia when he was bedridden. No, it was the first landing on Mars that caught his attention. Maybe the car races were too grounding a pursuit for him now while connection with the red planet brought closer his journey out into the cosmos. His spirit was preparing to rejoin the energy field of all spirits, now he was in that dying place.

But for the living, there does not have to be an either-or solution, when either we become insular or we don't. Maybe we can do both - both spend time with grounding, relaxing activities, and foster awareness of world events and create a sustainable life, becoming more conscious: a both-and situation. That tight-rope balance.

Stella aims for a both-and balanced life. I have much admiration for my 98-year-friend who is vitally interested in everything that happens in the world. She can repeat every detail about a programme on cosmology, or discuss the next federal election, or the Pope's latest encyclical, with great interest and curiosity. Macular degeneration prevents her seeing totally but her other senses have heightened and she has honed a brilliant memory. As we say, she doesn't miss a trick. Walking is hard for her too, so she can't gather with friends outside her apartment any more, but she makes the most of TV documentaries and talking books, and holds a lively conversation with family and friends who visit, no sign of age slowing down her mind. While Stella has a strong faith, she questions the religion she was brought up with. She says that she is ready to die - but after the baseball season. Living every moment of her life in her way, Stella inspires me with her interest in all aspects of world issues but she used to find it frustrating that others in her senior's residence don't want to talk about anything current. She is in charge of her life and no decision would be made for her. She does not dwell in the past, will tell stories if asked personal questions, but rarely goes back into it nostalgically. Stella proves to me that it is possible to age along with the planet, not denying what goes on in the world outside her closed door, yet still relax with favourite activities, enjoying her music.

Two friends came for lunch yesterday with the specific intention of setting aside some time to talk over the latest world events as we are used to doing: the state of the Canadian dollar, refugees coming to our neighbourhood, for starters. After soup was ladled and the baguette torn, the invitation to discussion was thrown on the table. But one friend said 'Oh no, don't talk about anything sad!' This was a discussion in itself, how sharing interpretation of information doesn't have to be 'sad.' Sharing news can be done without ranting, or doom-saying, or fear mongering. How can we witness what is happening, however atrocious, and take judgement and ego out of the story? Our bodies are aware of the disturbed energy around us even if our minds ignore it; the energy used to push information away could be used instead to send healing and compassion out into the world in the face of the disasters.

My partner and I don't read newspapers any more but that doesn't mean we don't have access to mainstream news and alternative news, and discuss it far more than we would have as newspapers are full of trivia, gossip, and ads. News stations on Twitter give headlines leading to articles for more information; the depth of a story is rich through alternative news programmes like Democracy Now, TruthDig, Podcasts are informative. We cancelled our cable television package and if we do watch TV in a hotel or someone's home, we soon turn it off after muting the commercials that pull down even more veils over our eyes, tempting us back into the upside-down fun house where nothing is as it seems. I prefer not to soak up what I am fed, instead choose my own diet, one that is healthier for my mind, body and spirit. If a disaster strikes, I don't shy away from the goriness and the pain, but I also don't wallow in shock value repeated over and over. That way I can concentrate on discerning the facts that inform the event, rather than absorb the media drama, in place to amuse and distract from the real issue.

In following different perspectives on news events and world disasters where I can, I feel more responsible, calmer. Participant rather than a victim, I am in charge of my own response, rather than manipulated into a collective hysteria. I am part of the issue rather than entertained by it, reframing and integrating it into my healing practice to join the solution.

But sometimes I check out the Daily Mail on my iPad. Yes, the sensationalist UK paper is definitely not a reliable source of news, the type of rag that used to have a bikini girl on page three. Now she's everywhere. No, I check out the Daily Mail to become aware of the environment in which I grow. Like a cell in a petri dish, the culture in which we develop is of extreme importance to our growth and values. In the laboratory, cells grow into immune cells, blood cells, even mammary cells, depending on the specific culture placed in each dish, creating an environment in which they can multiply. In the same way, society's culture around us affects our growth, whether we are aware of it or not. World moods, people's reactions to what is happening around them, their responses, fascinate me. As people become angrier, more frustrated and lost, they react in pain, violence, and depression. Like waves, those feelings move out into the energy field and affect us all. The Daily Mail glorifies struggle and violence, twists information of abuse, greed, relationships, sexuality, vulgarity. But the basic facts of the event are still there, however manipulated and illustrated by the newspaper to entice readers. It's the resulting mood and reactions that affect the atmosphere around us, reaching out to those creating movies, books, fashions. We are all cells growing in the petri dish planet with which we co-inhabit. If I wake feeling uneasy and anxious, I like to know why, and the news, one way or another, usually tells me.

One part of that culture we grow in is the popularity of so-called reality shows, considered newsworthy, encouraging disrespectful behaviour for shock value, especially in England where the social mood seems to be really suffering. People are greedy to be seen, to be considered 'famous' by whatever method. When I lived in England, I travelled on the bus everywhere, enjoying the chatter around me on the way to market. But when the Big Brother show was introduced to television, I didn't hear local gossip. All I heard was talk of Jade, a particularly controversial character: Jade did this, Jade said that, as if she was the local floozy. Jade fascinated me too, but I tried to get past my initial judgement and look for the story behind the story, the back-story. I saw these 'characters' in the Big Brother house as representing archetypes, both personal and collective. I wondered why Jade affected me so, what part of me plays her role? What part of me demands to be seen? These are very difficult questions, questions I wouldn't have the opportunity to try to answer if I hid away from some of the situations described in the Daily Mail or on television. They force me to look at my own shadow, my motivations, and masks.

I grew up trying to be good. That was my MO: not getting into trouble. As I grew older, I already had a 'good' mask, holding a self-image of someone who would never hurt anyone, could never kill, always doing 'good' deeds. My adult students were shocked one day when I swore, albeit mildly; I had played so well the role of 'good,' they never thought they'd hear a curse from my lips. Then I learned more about the shadow - that part of me that I didn't own. Learning that I that had the potential to be cruel to hurt or to kill, was, after the initial disbelief, very freeing because I didn't have to be 'good' any more. I could let it go.

I remember a surprising experience in Texas when visiting friends with my youngest daughter. In a huge indoor play area were all kinds of fun activities for kids and adults; the girls wanted to enter a game that entailed shooting monsters when they suddenly appeared around corners, out of windows, along a dark, winding path. Children could not go into this creepy place alone, so I had to join in. We were each given a large plastic gun. I had never allowed toy guns in our home; my children never played with them, or even used rulers or twigs to pretend-shoot. It was forbidden. My daughter begged, our friends were waiting, there was no turning back. I dangled the bright yellow gun at my side, intending to follow the trail but not shoot anything, just keep an eye on my daughter. When the first gruesome monster shocked the living daylights out of me as it lunged out of its holographic hiding place, I instinctively raised the gun and pressed the trigger, smashing the monster into digital heaven. From then on I was Annie Oakley, gun raised, eyes darting left, right, slaying monsters until we reached the light of day.

Collecting a tin trophy, I shook my head. What happened? I, the pacifist who abhorred guns, shooting, and killing, who would never ever hurt anyone because I was so 'good,' had single-handedly saved the nation from a monster onslaught? I hadn't played it as a game. I was deadly serious. So yes, I am very capable of shooting, killing, wanting to win. My shadow is alive and kicking. Freed of having to hide something I didn't know I was hiding relieved me of judging those who do hurt and kill, for I could be them. It is in me to be them. I am them.

From letting go 'not needing to be good' naturally sprung 'not needing to be perfect.' The child looking for approval led to the adult still believing in the old story, feeling inferior. I preached to my own children about being happy with who they are, to my adult students about the dangers of perfection, but could I follow my own lessons? It is a hard one, entwined with wanting to be right, in control, have the last word. All old stories. Creating a new story is important now, for that wisdom walk at the end of my life. Anne Lamott writes: 'Perfectionism is the voice of the oppressor, the enemy of the people. It will keep you cramped and insane your whole life.' [59] I search for the foundation of my perfectionism, past the parental 'why didn't you do better?' response to being second in a town-wide scholarship exam, past the laughter at untidy seams in my first self-taught sewing experiment, past the childhood internalizations of never being good enough, past those old stories. I leave them behind.

I search into my adulthood and remember the women I envied when I lived abroad, those wives who I thought were much more capable than I in decorating and running a home, whose dinner tables were immaculately laid, whose social habits so much more refined, who had matching living room upholstery. Even though I grew up with Doris Day's perky movies, I never quite made it. Thank goodness for the English like-minded friends I met in Venezuela, whose rambling meals and rumpled but exuberantly happy homes nagged at those perfection dreams and helped me weigh comfort against image.

Living back in Canada, advertising fed my angst. But who can match up to Martha Stewart on a single mother's budget, time and energy? I never reached those self-imposed standards. Instead, I gradually realized that no home is as perfect, no person as immaculately turned out, no family as polite and charming, and no salad as crisp and perky as the media images fed to us. Even Norman Rockwell played a part with some of his paintings of Middle America. I saw that other things could take priority – art, music, studying, having fun, not being so busy all the time. And I stopped reading magazines. I stopped believing in the perfection propaganda. Now that older people are portrayed in the same Hollywood style with fabricated role models impossible to emulate, setting up feelings of failure, I can see them for what they are. It took many years to understand that, and to question the word 'happy', to decide what happy really means. I look for other words to substitute for 'happy' when writing a greetings card.

Being in control is another matter. Surrendering control is the ultimate letting go and one of the hardest practices. Growing out of a traumatic childhood, one has to gain control over at least part of one's life to survive. For me it was the world of imagination, which led to creating drama on the mind's stage and panic over the smallest of imagined consequences. My child's fantasy play morphed into inventing adult dramas over the least significant comment or glance, creating a play that no-one knew about except me, the director, leading into all kinds of chaos for those who didn't even know they were supporting actors. Again, self-talk has helped me stop the drama, but spontaneous distractions from an internally created plan can still throw me for a loop.

Retired and living alone, running my own schedule, all of this was invisible to me. And then I fell in love and all of a sudden what was unknown became known. Confused at first, I saw how my internal plans - and not letting anyone else into the secret I didn't know I was keeping - could cause a communication crisis. So it has been my practice, which is what life is. Practice in talking my plans out loud. Practice in not freezing in the face of spontaneity. Practice in not investing in things that, in the big scheme of things, don't matter. Practice in awareness of inner dramas and literally bringing down the red velvet curtains before Act 1. No encores. No bravos. Practice, while it doesn't make perfect, creates a ritual that soon becomes a behaviour change, and eventually is so subtle that it becomes not only unnecessary but a dear co-participant. The mirror a partner provides is invaluable. And knowing that nothing comes easy. But then it never did.

Letting go isn't easy, sometimes seemingly impossible. 'Letting go' has become a catch phrase in self-help books and Oprah-type guru sessions. De-cluttering is important now, making space, paring down, clearing out, especially as I age. At the village dump I have said many prayers as I hurled life's treasures into the pit, tears pouring down my face. The funny thing is, a few days later, when recalling the tears, I could not remember what the items were. That experience became my touchstone, the knowledge that tomorrow I will forget. That little reminder makes it so much easier.

And then there's inner baggage. 'Just let it go' appears so easy, especially when Dr. Phil's guinea pig almost immediately shakes her shoulders and says something like 'Ooh, that feels soooo much better' and is a changed person in the ten minute segment allotted to the exercise. We will never know if that quickly released experience suddenly reappears in her sleepless night, or collides with a job interview. I used to visualize packing the unwanted words or thing or person into a box and gift-wrapping it, putting on a huge bow, giving it back to its source, with a silent 'I don't need this. I'm returning it to you.'

Or I would 'drive' it down to the (imaginary) lake and throw it in from the dock. Or I'd write it out and burn the writing. Now I practise just saying the words: Let it go, you don't need this any more. Whether it's a thing, a habit, a comment, a thought – anything.

There's a lot of letting-go as we get older, letting-go that we instigate, and the letting-go that's beyond our control: friends and family who die, or become changed by illness, or move away - letting go the person that was; activities, sports, hobbies because of new physical limitations - letting go the active life that was; letting go places, soul-places that you know you won't see again; letting go a way of life, of familiarity; letting go favourite foods, houses; letting go dreams, goals, ambitions. They pile one on top of the other like those words just did, sometimes coming with notice, sometimes with a shock. Hardly a day goes by without something or someone leaving. Little dyings always bring sadness and grief - and stress at the need to adapt and change.

In recognizing the part played in my life by the thing/place/person/activity that has to be let go, it helps if there's a warm gratitude for its contribution to who I am. This soothes the letting-go process, like buttering a finger so the ring can slip off more easily. There will still be some soreness, maybe a bleeding scratch on the knuckle, but the ring will slide off and the wound will heal. I practise saying 'Thank you' if I throw something away, take a pile of books to the library's book sale, or clothes to the hospital auxiliary shop. I honour its part in my life path. Thank you for the lesson in joy, learning, beauty, love, usefulness, even pain – there's always a lesson. As Tennyson famously wrote in Ulysses: 'I am part of all that I have met.' And part of all that I have met is me. I like who I am. I am grateful to all that created the 'me' that I like. But I cannot drag it around for the rest of my life. I must be it, not own it.

The same goes for regrets. It is not as easy as driving to the village dump, burning letters or donating old furniture. Letting regrets go demands a consciousness that must not waver. Letting regrets go demands forgiveness and healing, sometimes every day. Forgive everyone involved; heal everyone involved. And every time the thought of regret enters my mind, I gently forgive and heal all over again. The keyword here is 'gently.' No self-recrimination, no self-judgment, no re-living the experience over again, no drama, no 'if onlys,' no walking that familiar road, not even an inch. Gently. Now. Over and over if necessary. I have one big regret I still work on, almost daily. I hope I live long enough to let it go.

What about bringing in? Yes, it is necessary to pare down, clean house as we get older, so we can die with a clean slate, a clear conscience. But that doesn't mean ending one's life with a lot of empty space. Now we have room to bring something in. No new tchotchkes cluttering up window sills, or more blouses than you'll ever wear dangling their tags in your suddenly unjammed closet. No stuff. Unless the new stuff is something to eat, burn, or drink, and unless one thing goes out when a new thing comes in - the two cardinal rules. Now there's room to bring in a new pastime, a new interest, satisfy old curiosities, new learning.

It seems as if I have been a student for ever. Graduating with my Doctor of Ministry in Wisdom Spirituality, I find myself saying what next? Over the last few weeks I have thought about playing the piano again, or remembered dressmaking, or said 'Let's learn about opera!' With 'live' opera offered on even the smallest village's movie screen these days there's no excuse to say 'I don't do opera.' I have the time, space and energy to find out why not. I haven't played the piano seriously since I was in school, or for fun for thirty years. It used to be a great outlet for anger and frustration. Banging away at Rachmaninoff's 2nd Piano Concerto solved many a problem. The other day, while visiting a friend's house, I sat at her piano, opened The Phantom of the Opera score and played All I Ask of You. What a joy to find that I could still read music as well as I ever could. Now I'm searching for a piano. I lost mine years ago - but that's another story.

And there will be time to take up new interests. This year I became bewitched by baseball, especially as the Toronto Blue Jays did so well. I can't wait for the next season. I've become a political junkie; we have a young feminist prime minister, politics has become exciting! I've learned how to play canasta, and we love making soups and breads and sharing them. My partner began a vegetable garden a few years ago which has grown, both in size and in intensity of research, learning new skills, canning and preserving the harvest in the fall. She built high-standing planters to accommodate her aching back. Even 98-year-old Stella, who can't use an iPad because of her poor eyesight, is very curious about computers, asks many questions about how they work, squints at the screen on mine, knows the lingo, tells me to Google a fact if we're not sure about its veracity. She is almost as fascinated with iPads as if she had one herself. My father, who fretted his life away, complaining that no-one passed by the window, let his activities slide. In earlier retirement days, he rebuilt clocks, crafted a beautiful table. Faultless in any craft he tried, he enjoyed baking fruit cakes with his mother's recipes, trying to get the perfect cake. But in his last couple of years he saw no point in starting something he might not finish, he could not move out of his 'poor me' space. Then I think of my dear friend Mimi, who carried a half-finished knitted scarf in her walker, along with the nodding orchid. She hadn't knitted in fifty years before she took it up again and she loved watching the scarf grow. She didn't expect to see it finished, but that was okay.

Our lives will never be 'finished.' With all the plans in the world when I die, there will be something I haven't said, a place I haven't visited, an old friend I haven't hugged, a project not completed. My soul-sister Koko had many plans when an accident took her life - a course to teach, a new man to find, a house to renovate. She was too young to think of dying yet. I plan on leaving things unfinished because if I didn't, I would never start them. And besides, life is unfinished, not ended with a tidy casting-off stitch.

The space that's left behind after all the letting-go does not need to be filled in a rush; I can afford to be discriminating with the thoughts and activities and places and people that will drift in. And I will cherish the empty space: space for dreams, space to write poems, space for thoughts to wander into, for possibilities, for seeing what's behind sight, and hearing what's behind sound. Space that doesn't need to be filled with lists, and 'shoulds,' but open wide to welcome more in.

Enough

There's a story behind everything ... sometimes the stories are simple, and sometimes they are heartbreaking. But behind all your stories is always your mother's story, because hers is where yours begin.

Mitch Albom

The only requests my father made of me before he died, were to turn off the water and cancel his doctor's appointment, not what to do with his accumulations of a lifetime. My mother's war-time mentality had saved receipts from food shopping, string, rubber bands, letters, and my childhood memorabilia. When I was emptying their house, I opened report cards as if I was 10 again: 'a daydreamer who doesn't work up to her potential with little hope for an academic future.' Painfully neat notes told Mummy how sorry I was for being so naughty, but I never knew what I did that was naughty. Books of pencilled stories and poems reminded me of reading and writing by flashlight under my blanket-tent in bed late at night. My childhood chair from my grandfather's house, a painting from his living-room that I had memorized on long quiet Baptist Sundays, the brass tray I helped him polish before our walks to the park. They were all jammed under the basement stairs, proof of my father's disdain for his in-laws. I pried them out and dusted them off, overwhelmed at finding such treasures.

My mother, stuck in her security of the familiar, was suspicious of anything new. I remember an automatic washing machine sitting in our front hall for weeks, when she was not willing to end the Monday morning routine of boiling the whites on the stove with some kind of blue packet added, squeezing water out through the wringers that I loved feeding. My father was furious when she wouldn't accept the new machine with gratitude, as the wives of his friends had done. Maybe she saw through the sales pitch aimed at post-war housewives, tempting them to the delights of a sparkling kitchen instead of a fulfilling career outside the home. But she wouldn't have worked anyway, with no experience other than a few years helping in a kindergarten, given no encouragement to learn new skills. Her self-esteem was so low, maybe she thought she was incapable of operating the machine. My father wanted to invite his friend's wife over to demonstrate, but that thought upset her even more so she gave in. At 12 years old I saw her terror of inadequacy, and recognized it as a fear of others who appeared more able, and more together than she. I felt the same way, and sometimes still do until I get myself in check. It is still my elder work.

In the basement I found every old appliance my parents had in their Canadian home for forty years - refrigerators, stoves, televisions. When my father retired he bought a new television and told my mother that he would be the only one to use the remote and change the channels from now on, that she could not possibly understand the technology. Only one person should use any appliance to avoid extra wear and tear, he said. She didn't have the energy to challenge him. He controlled the house, telling her to sit and rest. She withered away.

At the back of kitchen cupboards, I found dishes and glasses I'd never seen, untouched wedding presents later verified by 1937 wedding lists. Among the many old dishes, I found a bowl, one I remembered having my porridge in as a child, topped by the creamy top hat that rose above the glass milk bottle sitting on the doorstep on winter days. I never would have thought of that bowl again, but here it was, two-handled, blue and white striped Devon pottery. Now it sits in my pine dresser; sometimes I use it. Compared to our present-day bowls, brightly coloured Ikea domes, it is at least one-third the size. Yet what was in it was always enough. I was never hungry, even though servings were much smaller than today, and eating was strictly at mealtime. No snacks. No thought of snacks except at designated times. A small chocolate bar was the Saturday treat in the war, cream cakes after the war. No wonder I challenge my addiction to sugar.

Today's televisions, beds, bath towels, restaurant servings, movie popcorn, refrigerators, everything, have grown to a gigantic size. Yet we are still not filled up. My child's bowl reminds me of the greed and insatiability that have led us to huge garbage mountains in China and India, creating lifetime jobs for garbage pickers and testament to the fact that humanity is not satisfied with enough. People are born, live, and die on the garbage heaps that our greed has built, stoked by the media and corporations who exploit our inner sadness and feelings of abandonment by tempting us with more 'stuff' to temporarily satiate. I found my school bag, a leather satchel that I used throughout my British schooldays, when we wouldn't have dreamed of shopping for a new one every September. Now, my grandson, who seems to have inherited my quirky tastes, carries it to school. We are told to beg for newness, demand sleeker, fancier, faster items. We cannot be shocked enough, hurt enough, or, Midas-like, gather enough money, get high enough. I am very aware of my own 'enough.'

Do hoarders carry that archetype for us, when, afraid to let anything go, their homes fill with piles of paper, clothes and refuse? And collectors soothe themselves by adding one more item to their pile of whatever it is they collect, unable to stop the search until they find it. Then, not even opening the box, they head out on the chase again to satisfy their longing. We fill our souls with stuff, cling to the familiar, to the memory, afraid to let it go.

In *The Untethered Soul,* Michael Singer writes: 'Clinging is one of the most primal acts. Because some objects remain in the consciousness while others pass through, your sense of awareness relates more to them. You use them as fixed points to create a sense of orientation, relationship, and security in the midst of constant inner changes and this need for orientation extends to the outside world. Although you are clinging to inner objects, you use them to orient and relate yourself to the multitude of physical objects that come in through your senses. You create thoughts that tie all the objects together and you cling to the entire structure. You end up relating so strongly to this inner structure that you build your entire sense of self around it.' [60]

I would add 'grasping' to Singer's perception. We grasp at what makes us feel good. Fear makes us keep around us what is not healthy, be it things or people or lifestyle. Afraid to move into the unfamiliar, we stay with the known, however threatening or unsafe or alienating it is, like my mother and the washing machine.

When we moved to Canada, she was terrified. Afraid of meeting new people and uncomfortable with new experiences, she wouldn't venture out. As difficult as her marriage became, she couldn't leave it because she thought she had nowhere to go; she did not drive and her name was not even on a bank account or a credit card. My father's initials were even embroidered inside her muskrat jacket. (As in mine, hence an early letting-go of that.) Trapped, she hung on to the familiar until she couldn't hang on any more. A few days before she vanished into a coma, I visited her in the hospital and found her fixated with the few personal items she had in her bedside table: a little bag with her compact, handkerchief, and hairnet, her diary and pen, a few dollars, that was all. She arranged and rearranged, checked and rechecked, made sure everything was in its place. My father got angry: 'Stop that, settle down.' Her life had narrowed down to that metal tabletop; her tiny belongings created her only safe environment at that moment. It was all she had left to look after. I found her little bag after my father died. Thirty years later, I still have the handkerchief in a drawer by my bed. Its fragrance brings her back.

It is amazing what becomes precious to us. Through 15 relocations I have gathered and given away, bought, been given, tossed and recycled a multitude of things. Part of growing older for me is the realization that I must streamline my life, empty out boxes, keep what I need to live with and enjoy it. Stop dragging burdens around. Today's quote on my Zen calendar paraphrases the Buddha: 'Every time we give something away, whether it is a material object or our time, we are letting go a bit of that carefully gathered and fiercely defended temporary heap of stuff we call 'I, me and mine.' (Jan Chozen Bays) I honour things for the role they played in my life, but that act in the drama is over. It is time to move on and get real.

I have always had enough. Even in times when funds were not there when I needed them, I still had enough. However little I thought I had, I only had to think of people fleeing their homes, carrying their belongings on their backs. What would I take if I had to leave my home and had only a cart or even a backpack to carry everything I would ever need? I watch the refugees trudge across Europe with the smallest of bundles, but the largest of emotional burdens. Would I take things of use, or things of sentiment? It would be a difficult choice.

When the house my daughter lived in burned down one November night, she lost just about everything. The roof over her bedroom caved in; she escaped in her pajamas and flip-flops, tumbling down flaming stairs; her cat was found alive the next day, hiding in the bathtub. Keys, wallet, and phone were conveniently left by the front door. (Note to self.) Grateful to be alive, it wasn't until later that she thought of all the things lost in the fire besides clothes, furniture and books: the many swimming trophies she won as a child in the Dominican Republic, the box of Christmas tree decorations I had given her every year for twenty years, each signifying something special that happened that year, photographs, pictures her nephews had coloured for their favourite aunt. All gone.

What would I want to save from the ashes of all the stuff that surrounds me? My mother used to keep her hairpins in a little silver box; as a toddler I played with it in her bedroom while she did her obsessive daily housecleaning, ready for its nightly inspection. For some reason, I remember a specific day very clearly when I was too young for school, snow outside, fire burning in the bedroom fireplace, and a sense of peace and being safe. Maybe it was because the feeling was not normal that this day stood out, but it left a huge impression on me and fifty years later, when I visited my childhood house, tears sprung to my eyes in what had been my parent's bedroom. Although I remembered it mainly as the place I heard shouting from at night, this earlier memory of love overrode everything, and I cried with affection for my mother and her little girl, so happy on one snowy morning.

In my wallet is a Valentine's card - one of those cut-out paper ones that children deliver to their classmates. This one was signed by my four children, the then three year-old managing fine capital letters with her sister's help. Each year they proudly brought me paper hearts from school. But this particular year, we had just returned from the tropics, no longer an ex-pat family living a country club/private school life; now I was a single mother, a supply teacher and an Avon lady. By now the children had experienced winter's cold and ice for the first time, had hard adjustments to different schooling; the nights were long and dark with no more dancing under the stars. Instead, I was relearning my typing skills, taking medical secretarial courses after work. This little piece of paper is enough; it said they loved me 'a real lot' which meant the world to me. They were so supportive as the five of us worked through the sadnesses and fears that accompany a new normal.

I visualize my grave as if dug millennia ago. My body is wrapped in the purple velvet cloak I wear for ritual and placed into the deep hole. Lavender, sage, and frankincense are sprinkled over me and my belongings placed around me: the goddesses that grace my desk, the photos of my beloveds and my sacred place, some books, my poetry, favourite CDs of Neil Diamond and Barbra Streisand, flowers, seeds, until I am totally covered up. What a useful way to tidy up when cleaning out the cave for the next occupant. Nourished by my body, seeds will break open and roots will entwine around each other, tiny creatures will scamper and burrow. Centuries later, an archeologist might dig into my grave and discover whatever hasn't been digested by Mother Earth. The valentine card and photos will be long gone, my mother's little silver box will be a dirt-encrusted treasure. Ceramic goddesses will be chipped but available for academic hypotheses, and the CDs could be identified as unknown items from another planet. Maybe frozen tears.

Nora's pink house had a room at the end of the hall; its door was never opened, until one day, when she was in the garden, I peeked in. I could not have entered through the floor to ceiling wall of boxes and furniture that met me, no space for a toehold. I imagine that after she was moved to the nursing home everything was moved out in a day, no discoveries made, her life in a dumpster, gone. Her green chair was enough. What treasures were in there? But are they only treasures to the owner? A special friend of mine who died of cancer spent one of her last days sitting at a table covered with jewellery, a few precious pieces, mostly what we crudely call junk jewellery, deciding who would have what after she died. I was the recorder; it was an honour to sit with her, her husband and daughter, as they told stories about each item, giving each piece a life of its own. She redistributed her belongings consciously and responsibly, actively participating in her dying act.

My great-uncle was widowed at eighty. He had one estranged son who lived on the other side of the world. After his wife died, Uncle Bill decided to make his living space as basic as he could, so that after his death, his lawyer would have very little to do. Every detail was meticulously covered. He kept two of everything. Two plates, cups, knives, forks, two shirts, jackets, ties, suits. Two towels and sheets. All relevant photos were in albums, and books were donated, from then on he used only the library. Very self-disciplined, Uncle Bill held no attachment to material things, no time for sentimentality or trivia. His house was Zen-like before Zen was 'in,' he had very few well-ordered possessions. He had enough.

Uncle Bill lived and worked in Peru most of his life. I used to dream of living like him, the magic man in a panama hat I met when I was six and he was on home leave. When he showed me photos of white houses, palm trees and llamas, little did I know that my life would emulate his. When he was no longer able to travel, he lived vicariously through my experiences of living in South America and the Caribbean which I shared in long letters. But we had different ideas about memories. I enjoy the tangible reminders; his were in his heart. Francis Weller writes, in *Entering the Healing Ground*, that we need to 'shed the skins that do not foster aliveness,' and quotes the beloved poet David Whyte: '...anything or anyone that does not bring you alive, is too small for you.' [61]

As I age, I realize the same. I must shed the oak leaf from Glastonbury Abbey, the paper napkin from Princess Diana's childhood home, the hundreds of shells from the favourite beaches we played on as a young family. Once I scattered a basketful of seashells into Lake Ontario, wondering if anyone would question an ocean shell found on a lakeside beach in the future. Would it change the pattern of ecological history? I am gradually giving away my jewelry. My daughter loves the Peruvian silver llama pin that Uncle Bill gave me when I was six; the family historian, she carries the vagabond gene.

Enough already: enough food, enough books, enough worrying, enough fighting, enough hypocrisy, enough denial. I decide on a new practice: bringing 'enough' into my conversation. Enough and greed go together. 'I am not greedy' easily comes out of my mouth, yet I am greedy over certain things. I am not focussed on amassing a fortune or real estate; I am generous with my possessions, share my cooking, I am kind. Hah! There's that shadow dance again. But I do have the potential of being greedy. I can be greedy for love, greedy for attention and for chocolate, greedy with winter bingeing on Netflix - I can't get enough. Maybe the other side of 'enough' and 'greedy' is 'sharing.' I may share the breads I bake or my time with friends unable to get outside, but I admit I have felt put out in the past when a good friend may favour another friend more than me, or if I can't get a word in edge-wise in a discussion. That greedy ego again. But I do have enough air-space. Enough friendly conversations. Enough attention. Enough love. I look around me. My surroundings are filled with enough. I need to be satisfied with less in my little blue and white bowl.

We have had enough fighting, enough pain, enough warfare. If I really mean 'enough' then how do I stop the suffering? How can I literally stop the wars? And move into the public marketplace to stop the greedy 1% from starving the 99%? Stop Monsanto killing our food? If I believe that we are all one body, what I can do is stop the war that goes on between the trillions of cells within my skin-city walls, cease the inner fighting within myself. Stop inner judgments. Stop berating myself, punishing myself, criticizing myself. Love and appreciate every bit of me, and work to reframe any negativity that comes up.

I can change my consumer habits, shop more responsibly, starve out the potentates. I collude with corporations when I buy from those who exploit third world countries. I must be more aware at the cash register, for it is there that my vote for 'enough' is cast. I can use my garden more sustainably, be conscious of where my food comes from, shop locally. I can watch my use of water, of gas, electricity, of driving, limit the space I take up in the world with my waste. Enough waste.

I can do all that, I can watch and limit and budget. But if I truly keep saying 'enough is enough,' then I have to think about not flying, not visiting my homeland any more, not seeing my children a tankful of gas away. If I really walked my talk, I would no longer fly and drive. What is stopping me? It is relatively easy to say 'enough already' when activities are doable, trackable, already almost in place, even enjoyable. The challenge is when it means giving up things that bring joy, that nourish in more ways than one. I don't know if I will ever achieve those goals, but I must still be aware of what I am doing to the environment as I fly, and drive, and eat, aware that in these cases I am not practising 'enough.' I am saying one thing and doing another, falling into the hypocrisy trap.

Last winter, I had the flu. It is rare I am ill, or allow myself to totally relax into a healing space, but this time I took the time and hibernated for a while. Mid-winter, deep snow covers the deck outside sliding glass doors, offering a wonderful view of the birds, some returned early after their winter journey, but most winter with us. They all look for food, preparing for their courting, nesting, parenting season that lies ahead. We put deep plates of seed on the glass table sitting in its icy aloneness, centred in our view.

Doves never get enough. Not the peacemakers of this snowy deck, they sit in the middle of the dish, not looking out for others, totally focussed on the job at hand. Within minutes, seed is scattered as they demolish the main course, their fat bodies jostling for space. Sometimes they fall asleep in the dish and block the way for the others. Blue jays are skittish, they peck once, look around, peck, look, the least distraction sends them flying back to the trees. Cardinals arrive in their chauvinistic pairs; the dull-looking female hides under the table while the male shows off his scarlet coat. They leave together. As the seed supply dwindles, a dove approaches the window, sits in the snow and stares at me, as if watching my own eating routine inside the room. Sometimes one will flutter at the window as if to say 'We don't have enough!' They never have enough. Each morning the blue jay calls in appreciation when I take the dish out. Little junkos and sparrows pick up leftover scraps on the deck, digging in the snow for seed that was covered by an overnight snowfall pocking the drifts with little holes. They are the peacemakers. Making their gentle way through the crowds, grateful for the leftovers, they clean up after the greedy doves. I want to be a junko, satisfied with enough, not a gluttonous dove or a fearful blue jay or a meek female cardinal or her strutting entitled partner - just a junko, happy with my lot, grateful that what I have is enough, and making peace.

Edges and Dreams

It's walking the razor's edge of the sacred moment where you don't know, you can't count on, and comfort yourself with any sure hope. All you can know is your allegiance to life and your intention to serve it in this moment that we are given. In that sense, this radical uncertainty liberates your creativity and courage.

Joanna Macy

At 75, I balance on the edge between aging and being old. There is a difference. I am fortunate in my good health and agility, so for me, aging now is often remembering how old I am, which most times surprises me. But I am as ageist as anyone when I think of 'old' as being physically limited, slower in thinking, unable to adjust to technological changes and generational differences. My inner crone trembles at that description. I walk a fine line between the two in that, while I do not consider myself old, I notice some friends living up to my erstwhile definition as they near 80 while I can still sit crosslegged on the floor. And then I read about century-old athletes, and Tony Bennett and Jimmy Carter and vital old women in crazily creative clothes, and I teeter on the edge of not knowing where I really fit. Age-wise I am old. Spirit-wise I don't know what old is.

In a cartoon recently, an older woman in a flamboyant outfit was told to act her age. 'But I have never been this age before,' she said, 'I don't know how to.' I agree with her. And in a video about civil disobedience recently, when an 87-year-old woman was being carried away to the police car, she was told 'Act your age!' by the policeman. I agree with her actions too. My 88-year-old friend Wilma dyes her hair purple and took up acting and painting at 80. Every winter her bouts of bronchitis get worse, and she doesn't like cooking for one. But she still has a wicked sense of humour and still owns the room where-ever she is. She walks that fine edge with panache.

Edges are very evocative. Edges are joining places, bumping-into-each-other places, nudging places. They border choices or dichotomies or dualisms. Walking the edge is walking a fine line. Gloria Anzaldúa writes about living on the edge in her brilliant book *Borderlands*. Born a Mestiza, living on the border between Mexico and Texas, biracial, bisexual, and bilingual, she is well aware of the edges she bridges, and how they inform her life. Hers is one of my favourite books of all time, one that becomes even clearer now that I have walked a few edges myself. My aging self identifies with Anzaldúa when she writes in the Preface: 'Living on borders and in margins, keeping intact one's shifting and multiple identity and integrity, is like trying to swim in a new element, an 'alien' element.' There is an exhilaration in being a participant in the further evolution of humankind, in being 'worked' on ... dormant areas of consciousness are being activated, awakened...the 'alien' element has become familiar – never comfortable, not with society's clamour to uphold the old, to rejoin the flock, to go with the herd. No, not comfortable, but home.

Dying is walking an edge between living and not living. We are dying all the time: dying to a way of life, dying to a lost relationship, dying to a lost tradition. Dying because there isn't any other way. Dying is like crossing a border, an edge, a transition. I witnessed my friend Mary's last few years as she walked the edge between city and country, peace and conflict, trust and betrayal. My age, she was a fashionista, a gourmet, and a diva, before she crossed over into the land of long term care, imprisoned in a wheelchair, losing her language. Then she walked another edge between living and dying, struggling in unfamiliar terrain. By stopping eating and drinking, she made a conscious choice to take her final step and cross over the edge, enter into her final transition from this life as we know it to be.

I have lived on three islands, very aware of tidal ebb and flow, how the edges between earth and water meet and co-exist, how life moves around the edge, how fluid an edge can be, how different one can be from another. One autumn day, I sat by the sea for hours, watching mother seagulls send their young off on their own. They herded their still fluffy teenagers to the edge of the shore. After final lessons on finding food and flying, the mothers backed off to hover by the wall at the back of the beach, letting their offspring go alone. Now and then one would revert to cawing helplessly and come running back to check on his mom. She would peck at him and shoo him away. The young ones skittered on the edge where the waves lapped gently on the sand, then took off one by one until they were all gone, flying or paddling towards the horizon, crossing the edge between childhood and adulthood. And just as gradually, the mothers flew away too in the opposite direction, their work done for another year, moving into that edge of time between letting go and birthing again. I witnessed many edge experiences while I was living close to the harbour.

Crossing the Edge

The coastline, where water meets earth, a dynamic edge, an environment of change and diversity, a place which invites species to meet and mingle.

Joan Halifax

Reflections by the sea aren't always pretty,
more lurks in blue on blue than meets the eye.
It's the edge that counts   that place
where wave breaks over sand, barely
marking ebb and flow, life and death ...

... a child, no more than three, with empty pail,
digs sandy holes   looks longingly towards the sea;
parents sleep, prostrate and clothed. He shakes
their shoulders, hovers near the waves   they will not wake.
I cannot take my eyes from him, so close to danger
or from them   so far from care.

Young man, immaculately dressed, refreshes at the spring
ignoring shrieks behind   she, hidden
in a filthy blanket. He turns and curses.
Imploring hands lift empty can,
        'Son?' She trails his footprints.

I think of my son warm at home   remember
tenderness, wave-tickled glee, watching pails of water
drain away into the sand, chasing paper boats...

... on distant edge sail south-bound warships, filled
with other mothers' dreams   rows of children
dressed in sailor suits, chasing someone else's battle hymn.

A seagull tears into a fish   drags its guts across the sand
fights brothers off with snapping beak, refusing
to relinquish prize. Even sated, dripping blood,
        won't share or compromise.

Or compromise.

Won't wake up, reach out a hand, search for solution
        while on the sand the breath of dolphins
drains away like water. I wonder if they die for us
who only walk the edge.

Dreams

Eight years ago I had one of those dreams that never leaves, different parts of it return at different times, its significance a puzzle, as most dreams are. I think it has to do with dying, a reluctance to die, or even a choice of whether to die or not to die. Is that possible? It was a dream of walking the edge.

January 6, 2007: A dog and I walk for a long time on streets that become sandier as we walk out of a busy town. My youngest daughter joins us; in the dream she is six or seven. Night is coming as the three of us walk towards a horizon layered with pointy-roofed houses as far as I can see. In the sunset, golden rays fan out behind them, the houses are coloured gold, pink, terra cotta. They glow like an aura. I say 'Is this heaven?' As we walk closer, I see the houses are bobbing up and down as if on water, all to a different rhythm. I think 'we can't cross' because there is no solid ground underfoot, the houses are moving too much. I am scared. Two men arrive, the older one seems to be sending the other off to school or work. The young man confidently steps with his briefcase from house to house, in spite of the undulations, until I can't see him. Other people are doing the same thing, crossing over easily, jumping from rooftop to rooftop, balancing as they move up and down. I can't see the other side. We talk to them about drowning, call out warnings. I cannot take that first step, it looks too dangerous. We turn around and start back towards town. Dog and I stop, and I look down at my daughter and say 'Oh, I'll miss you so much.' I wake up weeping.

Often the meaning of a dream becomes obvious much later. Sometimes never. I walk away from the town, away from community, which in waking life is important to me. This is a solitary journey. My youngest daughter is the subject of the one big regret I have in my life that I can't seem to reconcile; she was 6 to 7 years old at the time and I missed her incredibly. She could be representing the past. I feel that the glowing vision is heaven but the path isn't easy and I choose not to meet the obstacles but to turn away. Am I going to visit someone who has died? Or am I going to the other side myself? I stand at the edge between life and death and then turn away. Or is the past dying? Do I choose to go back to the past or take a second chance and return into a new future? If I am everyone and everything in my dream, I am the dog, calmed by trust, and I am my daughter, living through her experience when she missed me very much. To take this further, I am the uncertain path, the shaky foundation, on which I dare not travel. I do not trust myself. I am the heaven within that I dare not find, although I know it is beautiful. Braver parts of me wouldn't hesitate, they would strike out and not listen to fear. But the inner me won't take that first step. And this could be a dream for the collective.

I interpreted this dream in a poem. Spirit speaks through me in my poetry and this poem comes from my dream, rather than my interpretation. I used the glosa outline, a form made popular by P.K. Page, a Canadian poet, where the writer chooses a quatrain written by another poet. Each of the quatrain's lines must end each of the glosa's four ten-line stanzas. Lines 6, 9 and 10 must rhyme. I learned through writing poetry in form how freeing it is, not restrictive as one would expect. There is something about the rules of form that allow one to play much more creatively than with free verse, my usually preferred mode of writing. This seems to be a contradicton, that something so restrictive is freeing. Maybe edges are like that. They give permission to go beyond and test the limits.
Dream #26:

Glosa

As our bloods separate the clock resumes,
I hear the wind again as our hearts quieten.
We were a ring: the clock ticked around us
For that time and the wind was deflected.

From 'As our Bloods Separate', David Constantine

Moon's blood shines through fragile bones
into my core, each strand of hair, each pore
of thickening skin. I let Her in as red light

fills my heart and heats the room. I curl inside
Her womb while winds play drum-beats
round this space. Time stands still, assumes
the role of guardian above my resting place.
No breath, no sound, beyond this endless night,
yet I'm at peace in Now, for She presumes
as our blood separates, the clock resumes.

Now near-awake, skin on skin, Moon enters in
and dreams eternity, maybe a prophecy,
where heaven waits in golden rose. But all doors
close in undulating earth, confusing paths lead
into dark. I muse the waves with Past, together mark
that this is not the day to die. We try to frighten
dead with drowning tales, get lost in dread
and turn back home, no matter what the cost,
return to Now, wail "How I missed the light!" Then
I hear the wind again as our hearts quieten.

In tears I weep, no longer craving sleep, fears
of separation ache within my breast. No longer
quiet in rest, I agonize, search the skies
for reasons that we didn't take the path away
from Time, however hard the climb. What season
waits for Past and I? What heaven bound us
to the earth for Now, and why did we return
and cling to light? The blood-red winds of Moon
consoled me when She told me how She found us.
We were a ring: the clock ticked around us.

Behind Moon's light the ego lingers, its shadows
trap me until I cry. Below Her winds lie towers
of fear, easy to deny. Wars and danger fill the earth;
I cower against the same within. And gold could
either paint the masks that play old games with Past,
or reward each karmic choice when it's perfected.

I accept my shadow's sword and voice its task.
Stronger, I'll befriend the dark at last - fearless,
journey through. Heaven lies within me when reflected
for that time - and the wind will be deflected.

My poem ends with a four-line intention that at first seemed too quick and easy as solution. Too much of a Hollywood happy ending. How simple is it to 'accept my shadow's sword'? Just like that! My hope is that 'Stronger, I'll befriend the dark' and 'fearless, journey through,' but will I be strong enough to climb that steep learning curve that aging demands? And not paint the masks with gold, which only beautifies their appearance, luring away from the truth beneath? I want to remove the masks, see them for what they really are: stories from the past, coping mechanisms, fear-avoiders, ingrained lies we tell ourselves, wanna-be characters, media manipulations, pretenders, expectations that others have put on to us.

Aging must not relax into what was. Aging can linger in what is, the Now, and also work on what could be - better yet, what will be. Maybe I won't change the line: 'Stronger, I'll befriend the dark ... fearless, journey through' but use it as my affirmation of strength and clarity in this in-between stage, this edge. In a recent dialogue between two Jungians in a Depth and Psychology online seminar, Pat Berry, wife of the late James Hillman, said: 'As one gets older, one finds more and more who we are and makes the most of what we can make of that.' [62]

I had another golden dream, more like an image in the night. I am in a forest of green pine trees, lush and thickly growing. I am standing, almost hiding, behind a column of a small Greek temple, open on three sides with columns holding up the roof. There are three low steps all around. The temple is glowing golden, like gold leaf. Robed men and women are entering to pay homage to someone sitting at the back of the temple. I cannot see who, but I 'know' it is a woman with a baby. The steady stream of people entering and leaving are hushed, but bring respect, honouring with gratitude. I don't mingle but remain hidden, watching. There is an atmosphere of gentle movement, undisturbed by any distraction; people are talking and laughing quietly, with a peaceful joy. This goes on for quite a long time before I wake up with a feeling of relaxation and contentment.

The golden glow reminds me of my other dream, it seems heaven-like although very real. This dream is a salutation to birth, maybe of a new idea, a creative solution; there is no danger around, no negativity. I don't attach any significance of a Madonna and child, though in description it appears like such a visitation. These are regular people of their time honouring something new. But I only witness, quite objectively. Should I be there? Was I shy? Or was I forbidden to take part? Maybe I am visiting from another place or time?

My other dream was of death. Both had a golden aura, both included approach and retreat. In my dreams, honouring birth was celebratory and relaxed, while nearing death was difficult and frightening. I know little about my own birth except that my mother's labour took days in its intensity. I have consciously chosen not to revisit it in rebirthing. Death is an unknown. For all my bravado in death's face, I recognize that I am fearful underneath, as I walk the edge.

Edges

A literary interpretation of death that touches me deeply and seems almost familiar tells of the person who has just died getting on a boat, while everyone on the shore waves goodbye. The boat disappears over the horizon; we cannot see it any more. But on the far shore, there is great excitement as people there await the boat, pointing as it nears closer, and cheering as the person disembarks into a welcoming crowd. On the other side of farewell is welcome, on the other side of death is birth.

In the Goddess community in Glastonbury, we visualize the boatman rowing over the waters to Avalon, carrying the soul to the island. When Koko died, Kathy Jones, Priestess of

Avalon and founder-creatrix of the world-renowned Goddess Conference, led us in a powerful ritual during the all-night vigil. In meditation, we accompanied Koko over the waters to Avalon, then came back to our own shore leaving her behind, having bid her farewell. These myths and stories help us, the living, say goodbye to dear ones as they move away from us. These images take the fear away. They help us, the living, put those who have died in a safe place, which eases our pain at their loss.

My grandmother, who was alone for a few years after my grandfather died, would talk about him waiting for her on the other side. When she got 'there' he would be waiting for her. She had been rather autocratic, and the younger me wondered if Grandpa was getting away as far as he could before she arrived 'there,' as I tried to reconcile 'there' with 'here.' But it helped her to feel better about her mortality, giving her a reason to look forward to her own dying. And what could be wrong with that? I do believe that there was some element of my grandfather out in the universe that would be attracted to the some element that was my grandmother. The life they chose to live together, in the bodies I recognized them as, had value that reacted on the people they met and so would live on. My grandfather was a headmaster who made a very positive impression on young lives. I heard glowing testimonies from many ex-students, now elderly men themselves, when I visited his home town.

Past lives have always intrigued me. Because déjà vu experiences have happened so often, I believe I have 'lived' before, but not in similar flesh and blood. But I do believe there is a line - an edge - where there is no more use for the body and the spirit is set free, like the baby seagulls I watched flying away over the horizon.

So I return to the edge between land and water on the beach. Ocean tides move the water regularly, so the edge is mutable, ever-changing. I live near a lake and often study wave motion, looking for similarities between the lake and my beloved sea, for it feels so very different other than the salty taste on one's lips. Lake waves do ripple and crash on the sand like ocean waves, but there is no back and forth, no ebb. The level of water on the sand is always more or less static, give or take a couple of inches depending on winds. The edge of our neighbouring lake is often clearly defined by a line of debris thrown up by the waves. No smooth strip of sand waits for a path of early morning footprints to be cleared away by midnight's tide. On the lake beach, last week's picnic scuffle is still there, a labyrinth carved four days ago still vaguely offers its sacred centre. I remember carving labyrinths in the sand by the sea, and walking them as the incoming waves took them away, turn by turn, like the Buddhist monks' mandala blowing away in the wind. Each time, I felt as if I was working hand in hand with Mother Earth, that the spiralling journey had to be made when the intention was there, or the opportunity would soon vanish with the tide. She would take it, leaving no physical trace of its existence. Yet lakeside, the labyrinth will still be there for others to walk when they come across it the next day, wondering where it came from, as if by magic. That labyrinth is for the collective, to be eventually battered by weather and time until its path finally becomes untranslatable.

Years ago, I was packing up my small children after a tropical beach afternoon, when a young man appeared on the empty beach, quite far from us. I idly watched him as I brushed off sandy legs, picked up buckets and spades, folded blankets. He too folded his clothes very neatly. He walked to the edge of the sea and stood there for a long time. As I was getting into the car he turned and looked directly at me. We made eye contact over the sandy distance. He turned away and purposefully waded into the sea. I backed the car out from under the palm trees, faced the way home, and looked back. He was gone.

Swimming under the water, I thought. But I waited, with a strange feeling that I was witnessing something private, intimate, that I should not disturb. I waited far longer than it would take someone with a normal breathing pattern to stay underwater, and then longer, but he did not emerge. I got out of the car and began to move in his direction, then stopped. The three little ones couldn't stay in the car alone. What could I do? Should I get them out and run over there, shouting? To whom? We were alone. Should I stop at a city police station an hour away, where a foreigner was guilty before deemed innocent, so we could be held under suspicion? And was there any point in trying to save him in an hour's time? Should I interfere with his inner journey? his story? I waited another five minutes, saw nothing, then drove away. His pile of clothes stayed in my car mirror but no dripping body came out of the water to grab a towel. There was no towel.

I think I witnessed someone crossing over the edge. Whatever led the young man to that moment, he had already made his final decision to strike out to a further horizon. He was like the young man in my later dream who stepped out over the rooftops and journeyed to the other side. He returned to the waters from whence he had been birthed.

Gloria Anzaldúa ends her book with 'To survive the Borderlands you must live sin fronteras, without borders, be a crossroad.' [63] If I am a crossroad, I have a choice. The body dying is one thing, but the spirit dying is another. Every day I am a crossroad, a choice how to speak, act, think. Each act has a re-action 'out there,' each is my crossroad. Our lives are very tenuous, edges present themselves at any time. We create our own choices as to how we walk them, but eventually we cross over and we die. We can walk that edge with courage and conviction and look with anticipation at what awaits on the other shore, or we can waver, wobble at the edge, and let fear accompany us because we are crossing that edge regardless, like the baby seagulls finding their wings as they cross the horizon.

When Death Stops By

When Death eventually stops by and walks me home one night
I'll have two pictures captured in my fading mind:
framed sunshine children, laughing, playing, bright,
the other poignant memory in cameo, tucked behind.

I'll have two pictures captured in my fading mind,
blonde babies playing happily on the shore;
the other poignant memory in cameo, tucked behind,
hides a fearful me that was, and isn't any more.

Blonde babies playing happily on the shore,
sheer joy, foundation for my life today,
hide a fearful me that was, and isn't any more.
Then children grew, and Fearful walked away.

Sheer joy, foundation for my life today,
four babies clambering round my knee.
Then children grew, and Fearful walked away,
our tide of flotsam stories ebbing out to sea.

Four babies clambering round my knee,
framed sunshine children, laughing, playing, bright,
our tides of flotsam stories ebbing out to sea
when Death eventually stops by and walks me home one night.

Earth

I face the North: Welcome Earth, into the circle of my life.

Earth welcomes me as deeply as I treasure Her,
Her undulating land, Her crags that tower the sky with snow
Her stones and bones
deep enriching loam.

Home.

Earth gives me power
strength in myself to share
ancestors' wisdom from long ago
DNA passed down the mother's line
from stardust far away.

Earth restores me, holds me in embrace of life.
Earth is moon time, midnight, the cry of loon time
the winter of the year
dark underground, roots and shoots,
crone time hag time death time.

When my body, tired and old
or wounded young
lies down to rest
to sleep in hibernation
curled up in roots, bids farewell to this incarnation
body returned to Hers,

then Mother Earth will take me back.
I shall never lack for love
for She understands
this weariness
and welcomes home
Her crone into the One.

Blessed Be.

Earth Walking

We walk the path no one has walked before,
following the guideposts left by others.

Zen saying

I began to write this as we hopefully neared the end of the long, cold winter of 2014. Calendar-wise it should be spring; April's page was ready to be flipped over to May. Yet snow was still underfoot, winds whipping white dunes on the roadways. We wondered about the wine industry, the future of grape vines unusually frozen, apple and peach trees whose branches dangled lifelessly, victims of ice storms. Birds and water-fowl starved to death, ducks and swans were desperate for open water, hard to find when the Great Lake system was 95% frozen. And with April, 2014, came the astrologers' concern of the cardinal cross, four planets pulling at each other's energy like siblings, each wanting to be right and first at the table, their energies creating a high tension within us, collectively and individually.

Every winter in Ontario brings ice lurking around corners as if waiting to catch tumbling bodies, sacrifices to its merciless gleam. The ground beneath us is unsafe, not sound. We respond with falls, physical and emotional. Often I hear news of friends tripping at home, see Band-Aids on cut brows, bruises on cheekbones. 'I just took a tumble,' I hear. 'I fell over the electric blanket cord.' We drop things, and fall over our words, bumping into tender spots when communicating. It is as if the bumps and bruises of rambunctious children return to remind us of carefree ways. We continue the challenge of growing up, but this time, we are stumbling on soft carpet as we challenge barriers and bogey-men.

Sometimes, when hearing the global news, alternative and mainstream, I feel as if I am entering a fun house at the carnival, where floors are angled instead of flat, and perspective is challenged. Sometimes I seem to be walking on the ceiling. Belly turns upside down, creates off-balancing nausea. Head spins. I need a railing to hang on to, beg for the ride to end. Exiting with wobbly limbs, I sway back and forth into the flashing lights and sounds of the carnival, as if in the land of topsy-turvy. Every day feels like that now. Tipped upside down by speed of calamity, rush of information, threats of fear and danger to loved ones, we waver. Off-balance, we tumble and fall down in our plans, our dreams, expectations. We need to find a touchstone, a helping hand to steer us. But we have lost trust in our institutions, carry fear into our future, and that of our loved ones. We no longer know what is truth, feel like we no longer have a star to steer by. So we fall: emotionally, mentally, spiritually, and nearly always accompanied by a physical crash, which finally does its job to slow us down. Joanna Macy said in an interview: 'I look at the path we're on, to the future, as having a ditch on either side. We have to hold on to each other, not to fall in the ditch on the right or the left, which are, on one side panic and on the other side paralysis and shutting down'. [64]

We don't have cable television at home, and, one night in a Chicago hotel, I forgot to curb my addiction to news-as-entertainment, and overdosed on CNN versions of school shootings, embassy bombings, corruption somewhere, piracy somewhere else, gasping in shock. Then the phone call came to say that my daughter's house had burned down. Moving too quickly across the hotel lobby floor, I failed to notice when the black and white tiles changed a level and I crashed down a step, forehead just missing the desk's sharp corner, spraining my ankle badly. Already saturated with CNN drama and news of the house fire, I forgot to be aware of my surroundings and those dizzying tiles. The fall slowed me, reminded me of priorities, to be aware of here and now. The earth is not steady beneath our feet. In a Yes! magazine article, Terry-Tempest Williams writes that 'the world is completely shifting under our feet...it is sand instead of bedrock.' [65]

We hear of sinkholes opening up all around the world. Massive pits swallow up cars and people, and even houses, in a second. Whatever the science behind drought and diminishing groundwater, is this not a tangible example of the earth collapsing under our feet? Even the earth itself sometimes has no base beneath its surface, just gaping space. If the topsoil has nothing beneath to count on, how can we? Tectonic plates are shifting in the Ring of Fire and beyond, threatening tsunamis. Earthquakes in our own lives have devastating effects on relationships, families, and health; tidal waves of problems continue to battle our own coastlines of security. We assault the earth and birth our own earthquakes with hydraulic fracking, creating tremors in places previously firm. No wonder we are falling and cannot keep our balance, whatever our age.

Actual earthquakes I have experienced have been, thank Goddess, fairly mild, but, in retrospect, each one heralded a huge tumult in my life, a shaking that forced me to grow up a little more, taught me about resilience and the value of experience. I believe that everything plays out on every plane of reality, that a physical event also affects mental, emotional, spiritual levels too. Nothing is just as it seems to be, as if we are 'moving from one plane of reality to another, and what is required of us is spiritual.' [66] And what is required of us is consciousness. Skills in consciousness practised now will stand me in good stead, not only as I age, but also collectively, as we evolve as a species.

Consciousness is letting go with grace, accepting with empathy, experiencing the importance of community. I believe that consciousness requires honing the old skills of respect and honesty, in their many facets. Consciousness needs to redefine love and wants to value creativity. Consciousness means a deep awareness of our connection with everything around us, a knowledge that everything we say, do and think has a reaction. Consciousness is a responsibility to the One that we all are, recognizing that we are the other. The Golden Rule, in Matthew 7:12; 'Do unto others as they would do unto you,' is echoed in all religious texts. How can we love our neighbour as we love ourselves, if we don't love ourselves? There is no Us and Them. My inner child knows she would have been better prepared for the world had she grown up in a home with more awareness of reactions to thought, word and deed. My inner crone swings her booted feet as she perches on the lilac tree in the next-door garden, waving her cane in delight. Yes, she cackles, yes!

Where do I stand in all of this? I remember my mother, weak at 75, and my father striding into his 85th year, sweeping aside all that stood in his way, even though he would become breathless with the effort. She gave away her power years earlier; he needed to exude his in body language and voice. They were both lonely, one by circumstance, one by choice. Can there be a balance? Friends of my age are beginning to use canes and walkers; we installed a railing on our two shallow front steps to make descending more manageable. They know only too well their painful hips and knees. Earth tremors would knock them off their feet. Yesterday I cleared those steps in one leap. Today I take them one at a time. I don't know what I will do tomorrow.

How can we imagine something we haven't experienced? We can only hypothesise and use our own resources, feelings, and fears. It reminds me of the video of the person on the beach watching a giant tsunami approach until it was too late to run, in disbelief that any wave could be so high. And the story of the Arawak indigenous people who, when they saw a boat for the first time, they did not recognize it as the galleon it was, never having seen one before. They had nothing to relate it to other than a big bird or a canoe. So how can I visualize being 80 or 90? I can only see me as I do in the mirror now, add a few more wrinkles, and slower gait, but it is impossible to really know until I get there. Will I see aging approach and take note? Or will I wait until it shakes me up, stirs me into action?

Joan Erikson agrees. She writes 'How difficult it is to recognize and have perspective for just where one is presently in one's life cycle. Today is like yesterday until you sit back and take stock. Would we recognize old age as it crept up and the days rushed on?' [67] Does it come as a shock? Or do we see the gradual stages? Erik and Joan Erikson wrote a classic book about the eight stages of life, *The Life Cycle Completed*, which ended with Wisdom being attributed to the final stage, vaguely called Old Age. Joan wrote an extended version of the book after her husband died, when she read his extensive after-publishing edits. She added a ninth stage. The Eriksons realized that 'at ninety, they woke up in foreign territory...they had just kept steaming along until old age really made itself felt,' but now experienced 'the inevitable complications of slowly growing old.' [68] The ninth stage expanded on the theme of community, believing, as do I, that elderly people need community around them, either centrally or peripherally. After 80, they saw that 'death's door, which we always knew was expectable but had taken in stride, now seemed just around the corner.' [69] The last stage of life just wasn't in their consciousness when they were energetic, busier and healthier. I can certainly identify with that; it validates the urge I have to explore my own attitudes to aging now, not wait until it is too late.

I am shocked when I catch sight of my reflection in a store window, or in an off-the-cuff photograph. 'I look like an old lady!' I wonder if it is that our soul is ageless so inside we still feel young. My mother used to say that she felt like 17 inside. I have heard others speak similarly, also referring to a younger age. I wonder if they feel inside as they did the last time that they were totally happy, unfettered with worldly worries, maybe acting out their creativity in full-blown freedom. My mother was over the moon at 17. I never knew her that way. I have tried to feel a certain age inside but I don't. I always feel the age I am at the time, like now. If it says I'm 75, I'm 75! But then, I am happy now, so maybe my theory stands.

Earthquakes can bury us. Earthquakes rattle our walls, shake our base. We need a railing, a hand, or trust, community, to see us through. Getting older is like an earthquake. Towns that were familiar now confuse old maps with suburbs; people known and loved disappear through death or circumstance; traditions are no longer respected; illusions collapse previous truths. Older people often move, or are moved, far away from friends at a time when familiarity would give comfort at the end of a life. In new places we don't know what is expected of us, unwritten rules are different, we are uncertain of others' boundaries. Years ago and in other cultures, elders were a vital part of the community; younger generations looked after their grandparents, their wisdom was revered. It sounds idyllic, and the cynical me wonders if that is another illusion from the past, a myth passed down with the Norman Rockwell Thanksgiving painting. Millions of seniors live in tiny rooms, or in senior communities with nicknames like God's Waiting Room, or Wrinkle Ridge, mocked by younger people unable to identify with aging loneliness and frailties, as I felt with my grandmother – maybe afraid of their own aging,.

I feel less and less equipped to discuss aging, as today I am an early participant, a witness, and I have my own opinions of how I think my aging should be, as do the authors of the many books I struggle to complete. As Kathleen Dowling Singh writes in *The Grace in Aging*: 'Being old is new for us.' [70] I won't know until I am there. I know wrinkles and liver spots. I know the cellulite on my arms that looks like my mother's, and I am told about receding gums by the dentist. But I don't know physical limitations or constant medical appointments yet. I don't know helplessness.

And none of us know how to live in the new paradigm of change in our world, of living in the in-between that creates shaky ground under our very beings, a sense of anticipation with dread, of not knowing what will happen next. One common excuse for being unable to adapt is that we seniors were born into a different world that we see now, that progress is too fast.

The information age has rushed into our lives with exponential speed but I want to keep up. I remember my grandparents saving their electric toaster in its box for 'special occasions,' and this was only 40 years ago. But they also knew change and shaky ground. They lived through the horrors of war; their world was turned upside down with the sounds of bombs and the deaths of their brothers and sons. Every generation has its own context. I wonder how old-fashioned my eight-year-old grandson will appear to his own children. That's hard to understand.

Jung writes in his memoirs: [A man] 'must sense that he lives in a world which in some respects is mysterious; that things happen and can be experienced which remain inexplicable; that not everything that happens can be anticipated. The unexpected and the incredible belong in this world. Only then is life whole.' [71] Terry Tempest-Williams echoes Jung: 'We're in this time where everything is being turned inside out, including us. Do we have the stamina to not walk away, to stay in this hard place of transformation? I think we do. And to me, that's evolution. I can't imagine being alive at a more thrilling, challenging time where what is called for is acts of imagination, direct action, and stillness.' [72]

My island home has been the host to an ongoing battle for years over wind turbines, dozens of huge 60-storey towers to be built in the middle of a nature sanctuary, on the migratory path of multitudes of birds, and the home for the rare Blanding Turtle. This is a David and Goliath story, with a small group of faithful led by a strong elder-woman, standing up to the government through many appeals, owing 100s of 1000s of dollars for asking that green energy be gathered in a more logical setting – a setting where roads and bridges don't have to be rebuilt, where the earth, that for generations has fed many communities, will not die, where the lives of sentient beings that share our space will not be destroyed. We abuse Mother Earth's body in so many ways: strip mining, fracking, deforestation, polluting all Her elements with our toxins. As elders, we were fortunate to be raised in a healthier environment. As elders, we witness as younger generations deal with cancers and illnesses that were osmosed into their baby bodies at conception from the very elements we honour: air, fire, water and earth. We watch our children mourn their own children. We bury our young far too soon.

Is it any wonder that we, absorbing the trauma around us every day, abuse our own bodies with chemicals and cutting and addictions, hoping to relieve the inner pain? We watch the young cut and paint and rearrange and pierce and numb and freeze and fill and abuse and prostitute and inject and pollute and poison their bodies, and it is so easy to judge, to criticize, and recoil in horror. But this can be an elder's opportunity to understand that they are reacting to Mother Earth's pain, a collective pain, responding to the loneliness they feel in a civilization that focusses on a flashing blue screen. They are screaming out 'I am here, see me, hear me!' This could be our task as elders: to understand our own self-abuse with compassion, to recognize with a great love, our connection with the One and know that how we behave/react/feel inside, is reflected outside. We are what we see. And we can change that.

As we are, so is She

We cut ourselves to release our shame,
clear-cut our faces, bellies, breasts, to fit society's
false name, use cutting words, harsh blades against
our sister, brother, degrade the 'other.'

For power, we dominate, humiliate,
then bleed and retch with shadow-pain.o+
She is our mirror, reflecting back defecting souls.
As we are, so is She.

We hack into Her flesh and pave Her skin
with stone that does not breathe, scoop out black chunks
of energy to drain our oil. Toxins thrive within our blood
as poisons surge throughout Her river-flow.
        Whales and dolphins beach themselves for those
        who know they cannot face the shadow-walk.

We are Her mirror, reflecting back Her pain.
As She is, so are we.

We used to dance in forest shadows set aside
as sacred space, when women's song could chant away Earth's pain.

With open eyes and hearts we'll wake again
in this brown place, now un-worshipped and un-loved,
        if we embrace the 'other.'
        For only then can we heal Mother Earth.

Did women vanish on criss-cross roads
as empty arms begged heaven for compassion?
But love in human fashion no longer seems to enter here.

As we are, so is She.

Story-telling Time: Earth Stories

First earthquake, 1967: We had just moved to the Dominican Republic. My husband was plant manager for a multinational company at only 25, learning how to work in a new language. In retrospect, we were young for such responsibility. I was pregnant with our first child and had already had my first encounter with machine guns. While our furniture was shipped from Canada, we were living in a hotel, and on this April day I was doing my Spanish 'homework.' Suddenly, the bed I was sitting on turned into a boat rocking on the waves I could see beyond the rooftops. With a fear of boats in rough waters I instinctively hung on to the sides of the bed and prayed the waves would stop, instead of worrying that my 'boat' could sail out of the hotel window and end up floating in the pool five floors below. When the rocking was over, it dawned on me that there had been an earthquake, but during the experience I could not name it as such. Rough waters were familiar to me, not rocking earth.

That quake warned an innocent girl to wake up, to be more alert to danger, that this corporate move to the tropics wouldn't be just fun and carefree. It added an edge of wariness and distrust to living in this place of revolution and dark secrets. I couldn't verbalize the earthquake's message then, but on another level I took note.

Second earthquake, 1979: By all theories, my next earthquake should have been recognizable. But it didn't cross my mind one day when I was driving home through the narrow city streets of Santo Domingo, and saw people rushing outside, wringing their hands and praying up to the skies, wailing. I instantly thought the sight around me as one of insurrection and revolution - that I was unfortunately familiar with by then. I had no other clues. As I continued driving through the panic, my dramatic mind visualized a rebel coup, an assassinated President, curfews, martial law, and my children trapped in the International School on the other side of the city. I almost turned back to bring them home to safety, but I had two house guests in the car, young daughters of a Canadian friend, so I tried to be calm. Revolution conjured up months of challenging living. That was familiar. When I finally got to our house, Reyes, our maid angel, was trembling. As the earth shook, she had quickly carried the baby out into the garden, away from cement walls. Returning, she found plates and trinkets broken on the floor, books tossed out of their shelves as if by an ogre's hand. I heard later that if one is driving, one doesn't feel the earth shake, so I knew nothing about the quake until I saw the shattered bits. At the same time, I silently rejoiced that we were not enmeshed in my imaginary drama of political strife.

As it was, this earthquake shook me into making drastic changes in my life, respond to signs I hadn't picked up on before, distracted by everyday doings, as one is when one is building an empire. I didn't understand the danger lurking within our own walls.

Third earthquake, 1983: Now we were far away from the tropics, in Ontario, Canada, not long after my children and I returned to a totally different lifestyle. A slight shaking woke me up in the middle of the night. I jumped up, came out of my room to meet my three older children already on the landing of our narrow three-floor townhouse. Our eyes met: earthquake! And we instantly did what we knew to do; they remembered their school experiences well, classes running out to the playing field. We went outside and obediently stood in the middle of the road. No lights, no neighbours - were we the only ones who felt it? When the shaking stopped, we laughed with relief. Then we remembered our three year old still sleeping soundly upstairs. In our panic we had forgotten her. I will never live that down. The earth tremor was noted in the news the next day but no-one I spoke to had felt it. Luckily a quick reporter hadn't caught us out in the street in our pajamas, but, by now, I knew earthquakes.

And this one led me into a long period of ground-shaking hard work, illness, grief and problem-solving, also a sense of independent freedom and joy. I knew it was an omen, but I didn't know of what, and only time would tell.

Death, by Memory

Old age demands that one garner and lean on all previous experience, maintaining awareness and creativity with a new grace.

Joan Erikson

The process of dying fascinates me. Most books don't give me answers. As I have to come from my own perspective, I can only come from experience - the relatively few personal experiences I have had with death - and what I have learned from each one. How will those experiences apply to me as I approach the end of my own life? I definitely believe in accepting death, regularly pondering on and living with the reality.

Memories of death leave imprints, templates for the future. My first experience was when my uncle was killed in the Second World War. I was three, and my memory of him is in a photograph, where I snuggle into his uniformed arms before he left on his last deployment. It would be easy to romanticize Derek's life - he was a devastatingly handsome jazz pianist who was courting a divorcée. Later, it was harder work to put myself in the reality of his mother's story. A kind, practical, hardworking woman, my grandmother gave Derek an ultimatum before he left on his last bombing mission in 1944: stop seeing the divorcée or don't come home again. When she got the news of Derek's death his body was already buried in Germany; she moved into the attic for weeks, because 'it was closer to God up there.' After she emerged, she not only began a ritual of walking up the hill to church early every morning, but she also became lifelong friends with the divorcée, who still visited before she died in her nineties.

This family story, passed down to me when I found the snapshot of me and Uncle Derek years later, was the first time I met such a huge reconciliation that must have emerged after weeks of wrestling with guilt and grief up in the attic. David Kessler writes with Elisabeth Kűbler-Ross that forgiveness 'is our spiritual maintenance plan. Forgiveness helps us keep at peace and in touch with love. Our own task is to try to open our hearts again.' [73] My grandmother's heart opened wide again to encompass her son's lover, and, years later, when I was able to forgive my father, it was with her compassion that I understood his back-story. From then on, I associated death with forgiveness.

When I was 12, a schoolgirl I knew was killed by a bus. Cycling to school, she turned right without looking and the wheel ran over her head. That afternoon my mother was whispering over the garden fence with a neighbour, as most mothers were doing, then she hugged me extra tight and locked up my bicycle for two weeks. At night I imagined Pat lying in the road, her head crushed, blood everywhere, wondering what it was like to have one's breath snapped out in a second, what dying felt like. Twenty years later in Jamaica, I was giving the company's visiting vice-president's wife a tour around Kingston. The traffic suddenly stopped; a bus had run over a cyclist. As my car inched closer, I encouraged the New York VP's wife to look out of her side window at the sparkling ocean on the other side of the road, so she wouldn't see the carnage. (Some part of me thought it would spoil her day. After all, wasn't she entitled to perfection?) Meanwhile, I looked down at the man's head, completely flattened, blood everywhere. I remembered Pat. I sent a prayer to both the Jamaican man and to her. Now, whenever I come across an accident or a dead animal on the road, or hear an ambulance, I pray that the soul go in peace, knowing that it was loved. From then on, I associate death with not shying away from horror, but meeting it with a blessing.

I began reading newspapers for the first time when I was about 13, and one day at the seaside, I saw front page news of two girls my age who were murdered in London. It is strange how distinctly I remember their photograph in school uniforms that looked like mine. I still remember that they came from Finchley and their bodies were found in the woods. This felt personal, and for the first time I understood that death by violence could actually happen to me. I was in Lyme Regis and I sat on the harbour with a summer friend. We couldn't read enough about their story and this was the first – and rare - time I remember discussing anything so serious with a person my age. It obviously made an impact - each detail is still clear now, over 60 years later. From then on, I associated death with fear; it could come by another's hand, and it could be terrifying.

My grandparents died in a family silence. There was no ritual I was part of, no acknowledgement of my sadness. They were hardly spoken of ever again, as if they had never existed. When I was 22, my beloved grandfather died, I miss him to this day. He was the one person who loved me unconditionally, who I trusted implicitly. There was no option for me to travel to his funeral. Now I cannot believe that I was so dominated by my father that I would obey him so easily. My mother went alone and all I heard about afterwards were travel inconveniences and the difficulties she had with her own mother. There was no comfort and I dared not talk about Grandpa for I thought I would burst. When my grandmother died two years later, my mother was actually relieved. Recovering from surgery, she couldn't travel to England, so my father dealt with the funeral and emptied my grandmother's small flat. It was all very practical. No tears, little talking, but I sensed an incredible guilt on my mother's part, a guilt that was never assuaged to my knowledge. We are born into a chapter of somebody else's story and have no idea of the chapters than came before, the plot in which we become a main character. I didn't know the back-stories but I inherited the shadows. From their deaths, I took the impression that death was a blessed relief for those still living. And that grief was unspoken.

My father's parents died in their nineties, when I was living abroad. Brief phone conversations, practical issues, again no sadness voiced. They had stayed in their own home, which had meant constant care and a devastating rift between two brothers that never got resolved. With their deaths I associated inconvenience, impatience, family conflict, and again, unspoken grief.

My first family funeral was my mother's. I was 48. My father wanted the funeral to be quick, impersonal, and over. He refused to speak to the minister; he wouldn't let me speak during the short funeral, kept a firm grip on my elbow so I couldn't rise. I left my words in her flowers and couldn't walk away until my son took my hand. There was no gathering after; no offerings from neighbours of casseroles or cakes were to be accepted. A week later I opened my apartment door to my father carrying three suitcases. 'I've cleared your mother's clothes out, you can talk to me about her now. I'm fine.' No visible mourning, no mention of my grief. I could have done more, spoken up, not colluded with his ego. It was a deep loss of what could have been, had I been stronger. My mother once said that I was so cold, nothing bothered me. She never knew how early I learned to cover up any emotion, or about the tears I shed in the dark. But with her death I associated my shame at not being there for her.

When my father died, I did everything that I wished I had done for my mother: I spoke at his funeral, others spoke; we picked his favourite music, had a big party afterwards, cried, opened the windows of his house and let the light in. I hoped that in so doing, I could begin to heal the past. With his death, I learned to stand up for myself and take charge. It was about time.

Since then, close friends have died and I have spoken at funerals, facilitated memorials. Sometimes there has been no ritual afterwards, no contact with family, no funeral, no more communication after the initial message. The silence feels as if death had suddenly engulfed a vital part of my life. One moment someone was here sharing the planet with me, talking together, and it seemed like the next moment they were gone and there is no opportunity to celebrate their lives. I feel almost betrayed by their silence, their absence, their abandonment. I always try to honour them in my own way, in my own space, cherishing our life experience together that no-one can take away. From their deaths, I understood the power of communication, recognizing friendship past and support given.

A dear friend died in Florida, too young, of a horrible cancer. Kate was ill during the time that my father was dying and her courage on the phone kept me balanced while I cared for him. He was angry that this was happening to him, while she talked openly about her pain and her fear. I chose not to go to her funeral in Miami. We had been very close living in Jamaica and managed to see each other often in the years since. The beach had always been our favourite place so the only thing I could think of doing on the day of her funeral, was to take the day off work and drive to Wasaga Beach, two hours from my home. In February, the snow was very deep. I left quickly, not caring about warm boots, halfway there thinking how Kate would have laughed at my historically poor choice of footwear. The parking lot was sheer ice, so I had to park beside a snowdrift and literally fall into the snow from the car. Not caring how cold it was, I ploughed my way through snowdrifts, crying and screaming to the heavens. I carved a huge heart on the icy shore and wrote her name as two jet streams crossed in mid-air and formed an X. Neil Diamond sang 'Stones' in the car while I lit a candle and prayed Kate on her journey. I had learned by now how to grieve, how to honour someone's life in my way.

When Koko died, I travelled back to my Goddess community in Glastonbury and was so honoured to accompany her coffin through the streets in procession, priestessing at her vigil and funeral. I learned to accept comfort and support, and when I called in South at her vigil, the Divine spoke through me so powerfully. Koko's death taught me the power of ritual and the importance of celebrating a beloved soul in caring community.

One day, a black-rimmed card told me in Flemish that my Belgian friend, Adele, had committed suicide. Adele was the ex-wife of a half-brother I discovered after my father died. Although the parentage was not a spoken fact between my brother and me for many reasons, the amazing similarities between father and son, and particularly a grandson, both visual and behavioural, were obvious. Shared experiences and coincidences, tangible evidence of dates, letters, and especially after meeting his mother, confirmed my beliefs. Adele and I compared notes and quickly became close. He was very much like my father; she and I had family pain in common. After meeting in Europe several times, we continued an e-mail friendship that I treasured. So I was grieving the death of someone I had only known for a couple of years, but understood deeply. It felt like a family loss. It was a private sadness that I found hard to shake. From Adele's death I learned the intimacy of a private grief that only one can understand.

I released some of it in poetry. The intricate editing and proofing helped to put this synchronistic meeting and sudden parting into perspective. Marilyn Schlitz writes in *Death Makes Life Possible*, 'Art can be used for our personal transformation... the elements of transformative practice— intention, attention, repetition, guidance and acceptance - all reveal the ways that art both reflects and transforms our fear of death.' [74]

Lost in Translation: for Adele

Spring forced in winter darkness
now dies as petals shrivel on the floor.
Beside the dusty pots pile stacks of mail
        mostly bills and advertising;
I recognize a stamp from far away
that brings a smile.

Delight steams tea, curls up to read
a letter from a sister-friend; anticipation
jots a mental note to re-plant dried bulbs
today. Shock sees black borders
edge the card inside.

A foreign language
I must translate, slowly searching
for some sign of life, but crematie forbids
denial of news. Somewhere between the lines
she lost her fight with sadness.

Robot-like I realign the flower pots,
their bulbs as listless as my core
and there
within the withered leaves,
pale pink lace stands firm and tall.

Not there before, this tulip, unlike
its purple friends now gone, stares
me in the face, dares me to keep
breathing on
to say goodbye with grace.
I lean the card against its vital stem,

black rim stern beside the fragile pink,
and leave to feed the birds, watch
their bellies throb, full of seeds and song.
I grieve beside tight linden buds not ready yet
to drink in light
still afraid of opening up to life.

Everything I have learned from my experiences with death has helped me be more confident in my relationship with dying, to practise 'deathing', as my friend Mimi called it. I ponder on my life's negative reactions: silence, denial, inconvenience, impatience, family conflict, shame, hiding emotion, getting caught up in another's ego drama, and I honour them as part of my journey. But I must leave them behind. The constant in all of those experiences was my father and these reactions fitted in with his behaviours in every aspect of life. I tried to understand his need for privacy, his British stiff upper lip, his arrogance, and apparent lack of empathy. So I practised the first thing I learned about death from my grandmother's grief at the loss of her son. I forgave my father.

Salvadokathedral (Bruges, Belgium, 2003)

Father, I travelled half across the world to talk to you.
Strange,
we'd find each other here,
within your other life.
And yet I knew,
sheltered in these ancient stones,
Salvadokathedral, shadowed
in the evening sun, canals beyond the door,
wake of houseboats echoing the organ swells,
profundo, basso tones,

I knew you'd wait.
You'd wait until Rachmaninoff diminishes distracting thought,
until Beethoven dares to wrench my memories
away from all their hidden places,
deep within my cells.

I almost see you at the organ keys,
your dancing feet in flight o'er triple pedals,
your glee at playing such an instrument at last.

I sense you here,
you make your presence known.

I gave you power as vast as this cathedral.
I cowered in your fury,
allowed your thundering voice to fill my head.
But now you're dead.
And today I met your son,
the one who shatters all illusions
of your perfection, of my perceived disgrace.
No longer are you a paragon
but real in every flaw.
Now I can say I love you.

I came here to bless the gratitude I feel
for you, for all your pain in staying whole
in spite of being split in many ways.
In sanctity, this holy place,
quiet now amid incense fumes,
I vow I'll guard your legacy with grace.
I say farewell to all I thought you were
and welcome new dimensions to my life.

The organ is silent, voices stilled,
footstep echoes disappear and I'm alone.
Salvadokathedral now bathed in moonlight
holds me calm. You are gone
and I, reborn, move on.

I have grown over the years in accepting death and learning how to celebrate the transition. There will be many more deaths before I die or I could be next. I have no way of knowing. I live in an adult community; it is often that people here die. Then their houses are sold, and younger people move in, whose energy we welcome. At this place we witness the turning of the wheel: life, death, life regenerated. I must adapt what I have learned to my own journey with death because strength is what we need to move forward into old age. Forgiveness, acceptance, giving comfort and support, finding creative ways to grieve, community, ritual, speaking from the heart. I can adapt these to my life as well as to reacting to death. I can continue this practice now.

Every day I can notice signs. Synchronistic messages sometimes tell me that a friend is ready to leave their earthly body. Arnold Mindell writes that we 'need a second attention, awareness of things happening around you,' [75] like Kate's sky kiss and Adele's pink lace tulip. A red-winged blackbird stayed in the chapel window at my mother's funeral and flew away during the final blessing, it was her favourite bird. The Jamaican cyclist showed me his wound, enabling me to finally utter a prayer for my school friend, an honour I wasn't capable of showing her in childhood. Pema Chodron, to whom I turn often, also writes about signs and synchronicities: '...we begin to realize that the world is speaking to us all of the time. Every plant, every tree, every animal, every person, every car, every airplane is speaking to us, teaching us, awakening us. It's a wonderful world, but we often miss it.' [76]

Diane, another friend who was very ill a few years ago, spoke to me clearly in three ordinary moments; after I heard that she had died, I understood that she was saying goodbye. As Jung says, 'The unconscious helps by communicating things to us, or making figurative allusions. It has other ways too, of informing us of two things which by all logic we can't possibly know...synchronistic phenomena.' [77] A heightened awareness of signs and synchronicities is part of the higher consciousness I want to understand and achieve. They connect me to the bigger picture, to the cosmos and to those who have gone before me, maybe even those yet to come.

Messages from Dianne

She left messages so I would know she'd said goodbye,
but I didn't know she'd gone, so I didn't cry, and life went on
just as it always does, not knowing there was now an empty space.

A poem showed up beside my work in a pile of bills I had to pay,
words written long ago in a far-off place, what file it sheltered in
I'll never know, appeared as if to say, 'You need to read me now.'

A length of rainbow silk that hung across a door fluttered on my arm:
'Take me to her healing circle - I'll recall her sparkling light,
her golden hair, her sense of self, warm energy so bright.'

A stack of angel cards, dusty on a shelf, fell on the floor,
needed to sit beside the door for friends to choose,
blend inspiration with the winter chill outside.

And then I heard that Dianne died.

The poem's a muse on faith. 'When love shifts its shape
it returns to your heart.' She liked that part and talked
about it often in living conversation, she needed hope that way.

Then Linda told me how she'd met Dianne one day across a bolt
of coloured silk, how Dianne raved about the rainbows
shimmering in her hands, how she had to save the shine in her creations,
called later, thrilled about her brilliant find, dressed a dancing teddy bear.

And for Dianne, I draw an angel card. It says 'Hello from Heaven.'
Archangel Azrael tells me she's doing well, wants us to free our worldly cares.

Three messages she left to say goodbye.
I didn't know she'd gone at the time,
so I didn't cry.

Thinking about my Death

To embrace life I must shake hands with death.
For this I need practice.

Paul Fleischman

I often think about my death, sometimes a few times a day. Most times it is consciously, sometimes a knee-jerk reaction. On a slippery highway surrounded by trucks forcing me to drive too fast for my comfort level may generate fear around dying in a wreck, and I dare to wonder what it feels like to be tumbling around the highway tangled up in grinding metal. A friend was killed in a flaming collision with a tanker-trailer on her way to visit us ten years ago as our first house-guest; the highway was later repaired with a paler paving. Every time I pass over the white space, I say a prayer for her. It is almost as if I am driving over her grave.

Buddhists meditate on death daily. Joanna Macy writes that 'to confront and accept the inevitability of our dying releases us from triviality and frees us to live boldly...death is certain, but the time of death is uncertain.' [78] I agree with friends who say that it is not that they are afraid to die, it is the manner of the death - the how - that they worry about. In good health now, I sometimes wonder how I will die. Will I take after my father with his failing heart and lungs, or suffer my mother's undiagnosed pain and lack of energy? I haven't got off scot-free. The '80s saw asthma, fibromyalgia, and severe anxiety develop from lying low to smothering efficiency. An earlier cracked tail bone was cracked again when I fell on hidden ice and sent rippling rings of pain throughout my lower vertebrae for many years. Working, studying and parenting made healing difficult, but a medication allergy finally forced me to rest for a couple of weeks. Over the years since, with better asthma care, therapy, and especially gradually releasing the stressors, I was able to emerge from a breathless, painful fog, and feel energetic again. Thirty years later, the agony is a memory that sometimes surfaces to remind me.

One night, when my children were still young, I had an odd pain. I can't remember where it was now, and as I am not someone who rushes off to emergency but lives by the 'wait and see' cure (including my unique 'think of your big toe' healing method - it is impossible to concentrate on two parts of your body at the same time), I decided I must be going to die that night. So I folded the laundry and made a dish of red Jello. My kids would need something sweet to soothe them over their abandonment; it seemed very logical at the time. Knowing me, I quite likely made sure all the dishes were put away and the living room picked up as only a room can be that is lived in by four active youngsters. Then I fell asleep, and woke up in the morning, odd pain gone, never to return. As is my practice, I like to process what new learning has come my way each day, so the next night, after the rough and tumble of homework time, sweetened with red Jello, I thought over my strange reaction the night before. I wondered if I would have been that practical if a doctor had actually told me I was going to die. Would I have gone home, cleaned the house, made Jello, and lay myself down, prepared to die as calmly? Did I really believe myself? What would I do?

I am quick and capable in immediate crisis, but otherwise, I am not too spontaneous and can make life difficult for everyone if I have to change a routine or a plan. My first reaction has always been No. Being an introvert, an INFJ, I have my day figured out in my head but nobody else knows about my plan until the threat of change. Old story: growing up, I had to control at least a tiny bit of my life which became mine only to know, therefore no judgement or criticism. New story: I now consider change, and ask for a few minutes before I answer a challenge to a plan I was holding close to my chest. I have a terrible time with little decisions: menus, movies, when someone says the two most ominous words - you decide. Choosing, without a feeling of panic or fear, is a skill I yearn to master. Big huge major decisions I have no problem with. Gestating for a long time, deep down in the sub-conscious, the unconscious, they work their way up to the conscious level at the very time that the decision has to be verbalized and the answer is always there, ready and waiting, never doubted. But give me a menu and I'm hopeless. That was why I ate every Caesar Salad in town until I became allergic to garlic.

So I imagine that if I was told I had a few months to live, my instant knee-jerk reaction would be No. No, because it would change the vision I hold for a longer life. No, because I don't want to leave my loved ones behind. But I imagine that once the information is absorbed into every cell, I would get down to work and prepare. We never know how we'll react. And we also never know how we're going to die - maybe with the grace of a few months' notice, maybe very suddenly like my friend's accident, maybe over a long period of time, like Kate. Maybe by one's hand, like Adele. That is the greatest unknown.

The thought of those I love dying frightens me - my children, my partner. As a mother, my biggest fear was not being there if my little ones needed me, not being able to hold them and kiss it better. As every mother knows, that feeling doesn't magically disappear on eighteenth birthdays. But one has to let go of tight connections and hand the responsibility of growing up to them, including their illnesses and syndromes. I can listen, I can hug, and if there is something practical to do, I can do it. But I have learned that their life is their story. Each of my children has taught me that in their own unique way, quite likely unknowingly. And I am learning not to impose my story on to them.

My mother died in her 77th year. I am in my 77th year, though I try not to dwell on dates. Kate's mother died of a stroke at 57 and Kate often talked about how young her mother was, what a shock it was when she died before she saw her grandchildren grow up. The age seemed like a signpost. Kate died at 57, never knowing her grandchildren. My father was 84. I see in the obits that many people die around 84 and wonder why. Is there some astrological significance about the number 84? 87 is the third Saturn return, signalling major transformation. If I can get past 84 in good shape, I'll be home free.

In musing over my own death, I remember that of my parents. My mother died of a stroke during surgery, and I was unprepared. Her passing left words unspoken, regrets. I wish I had spent more time with her, not allowing my domineering father to come between us. I don't like regrets. Once a decision is made, I prefer to live with the consequences, fixing it if necessary, and if possible. Then work on forgiveness, forgiving those who have hurt me and forgiving myself for having hurt others. The latter is the hardest.

My mother must have also left things unfinished because she came back to me twice, not long after she died. The first time was in a brightly coloured dream, where I was walking along a harbour wall and she was swimming in the clear blue ocean beside me, her black hair streaming out in the water just like it did over the pillow in the ICU. We were both looking back at the beach where my four children were little, playing with toys, everything in bright primary colours. In fact, it was the first coloured dream I remembered having, they were usually in black and white or monochromatic. We were calling out to each other in strong voices. I said 'Look at the children, they are so beautiful,' and glanced down at the water. She was gone. In a ruffle of waves that sparkled as if in a vision, she was gone. My children and I were her life. This was her way of saying goodbye, and she left me feeling as if something had been completed, I was forgiven for my perceived neglect. So I let it go, like I let her go into the ocean of my dream.

The second time she actually did visit me, standing at the end of my bed in the early morning. She said 'Go back. Go back, and see that there was joy.' She was solid, really there, not in a dream. And she was speaking to the story I had made my own, that my childhood was sad, unhappy, that I was unloved and unappreciated. This story had become a mantra to explain a multitude of behaviours. My mother's role in this drama was that she was weak, did not come to my defence; she begged me to be 'good' to prevent the inevitable temper outbursts from my father at the most innocent requests that went on well into my adulthood. Still visiting my ailing father at this time, I was very aware of the power of his dominance over my mother's life, how trapped she had been, and how sad. I was able to forgive her for what I had perceived as abandonment when she couldn't care for herself, let alone me. But I still clung to my victim story.

After she urged me to 'go back,' I did travel to my birthplace in England, the places of my childhood, for the first time in forty years, alone. In following her plea, I did remember some good times, memories I would have forgotten had I not walked the old paths. I came out of that experience a changed person, ready to take responsibility for what was mine and let go that which wasn't. I began creating a new story, the story I am trying to live now.

When my father died, I initially felt a little relief. For eight years I had been his sole contact as his only child, and, for the last couple of years, his unacknowledged caregiver. He died an angry man. From his death I would learn that whatever one's most powerful characteristic is in life, it becomes more determined in aging and dying. I hope mine is love. His was rage. When I found his body, only dead a few minutes, his face was definitely not peaceful. Kathleen Dowling Singh writes that 'By and large, people die in solemnity, peace, and transformational consciousness, radiating energy that can only be described as spiritual.'[79] If that was the case, spirit left the room quickly, before I got there. Congestive heart failure had weakened his body over the past few months and he relied on my help and that of the caregivers he loathed who came in a few hours every day. He cried out that it wasn't fair! It wasn't fair that he was ill, that he felt the way he did. Why him? He knew better than his doctors; he was being treated for the wrong thing. It just wasn't fair.

I recognized that he was near death when he asked for an egg 'cooked in a nest of mashed potatoes like my mother used to give me when I was ill as a boy.' I remembered the scrambled eggs my mother used to make for me when I had mumps and measles - a tray on cold crisp white sheets. The poignancy in my father's request softened my fear of living with him and doing anything 'wrong' in his house, so I began to break his 'rules.' Bedridden, he couldn't see me. Rebelliously, my grass-dewy feet walked on the pristine white carpet; I used the 'wrong' spoon to stir the gravy; I didn't turn off the TV when I left the room; I drank the rum in his liquor cabinet. I knew the day he was leaving home for the last time because his favourite teapot hit the faucet and broke. I didn't tell him because I knew he wouldn't need it any more. If this had happened centuries ago, I would have buried those teapot shards with him. By the time he died a few days later, his voice had left my head. I thought it would be there for ever.

I am a different person than my father. My life's motivation was not to be like him, but I do carry his genes, so I check periodically for bitterness or narcissism if it should arise. After he died, I wrote a collection of poems that began with my old childhood story, and ended with a new journey to forgiveness. I don't know which came first, the healing or the poetry, but I don't think I could have reached either without the other. The turning point was a poem that came when I put myself in his place as a youngster, written from anecdotes he'd told me. This allowed me to love him more than I ever did in his lifetime. We are never totally aware of peoples' back-stories, sometimes only learning them during eulogies. Imagining his childhood allowed me to understand him more after his death than before. And maybe that is the way it could be: that death can open us up to the transparency of our loved ones, and we are able to piece together the life stories we hear, create a spiritual framework of them, know them in a different way, separate from the physical body that got in the way of clarity and empathy during life, and love them more..

I Imagine

I know that early every morning
he'd climb a chair to light the fire,
fill a heavy kettle, put it on to boil in time for breakfast tea
and every afternoon he'd trot to the corner shop
with her order in his hand.

I imagine a grownup man inside the little boy
caring for his mother the way a husband would a wife
after they said 'Now you're the man of the house'
when his father left for war.
He didn't understand why and he didn't know how

but when his baby brothers arrived nine months after his father
came home twice in muddy boots and crosser than before,
he'd push their pram, play with them so she could rest.
He told me how he'd pinch them secretly
to make them cry so when he calmed them down
with hugs and kisses
his mother would be full of praise and he'd be so happy just to
catch her smile.

I know he studied hard in school to make her proud
and learned to play the piano
so she could sing her favourite hymns

but I imagine late at night he'd tug the heavy ochre curtains
to keep away the draughts and bogey men
and then she'd let him light the candle and brush her
silvery hair.
Her perfume made him drowsy
he'd dream of angels singing hymns in clouds of roses.

I imagine when the war was over he could not be a boy again
however hard he tried
not knowing laughter or how to play
but grieved a loss as only could a man who was betrayed
whose lover flew into the arms of a former beau.

Sometimes when I think of him I wonder if he searched for her
for ever after
if that's why he kept pinching people to make them cry
wanting her to smile at him again.

And then I imagine a little boy inside a grownup man.

I have found that one key to dying consciously is not to be afraid of planning the practical details, be open to change if necessary. Knowing one's papers are in order is freeing. I am amazed when somebody knows their prognosis, they still do nothing towards making a will, talk about a funeral, or describe where they want their body to rest. All those decisions would have to be made by family or friends who are also dealing with grief. All the factors involved with planning someone's exodus from the world are that much more intense. Death is a vital part of my life, I want to do it well.

'Death (should be) viewed not just as a singular event at the tail end of our lives but as an integral aspect of the journey itself.' [80] I think of my death in its many aspects. I think of it practically: what will I leave behind, how organized can I be? I label family heirlooms, who made them, where they came from. My partner and I have been fastidious about our wills and powers of attorney, completing a domestic contract, and listing what belongs to each and to both of us, who gets what specific family item when one of us dies. Neither of us can imagine it being the other - ideally we'd like to die together, peacefully. But we've done the paperwork because we know that when grief takes over, neither of us will remember the cold hard details. It is freeing, to have it filed away.

When I think of dying, I think of my children. They are very fond of my partner and respect our relationship. Will that continue? Will they hold true to our wishes or seek to impose their own? That would really surprise me because I know them so well but the lawyer does relate awful family stories. I trust them implicitly. But more than that, I think of saying goodbye to them. I think of how they literally began my life as I birthed myself through them, learned to laugh, to show joy. I remember holding them as tiny babies and that's when the tears come. The older I get, the more I remember them as little ones, how happy I was mothering the family I had always dreamed of. I think of how I thought that when they were older the childhood worries would somehow fade, but problems don't stop. They just get bigger and more serious until I want to wrap my grown-up kids up in a blanket and rock them to sleep. It was so much easier then.

When I think of dying, I think of my partner, and how very grateful I am that we were to meet late in life when love is richest. To be together with a like-minded soul who has the same vision is a gift. We laugh, we argue, we talk in the middle of the night, we enjoy movies and binge-watching, we can be silent for hours together, we travel, we squabble when we cook, we bob and weave, reflect and process, we enjoy our life together, support each other. We like each other. We are kind. We thank each other for little things as well as the big. Companions, we walk this aging journey together, following inner maps, creating new ones, pondering at crossroads. One of us will be left behind to carry our legacy of love. We can't imagine the sadness but want to be prepared.

When I think of dying, I think of funerals and wakes and disposal of my body. In England, one is able to prepare a loved one's body oneself, and bury it in a garden or a woodland. So civilized. My parents' funerals were led by anonymous ministers, both at a crematorium they had passed on their Sunday afternoon drives. My father ignored my mother's ashes and asked the staff to scatter them a year later. When I found this out after the fact, it was too late to intervene. When he died, I scattered most of his ashes in the same place but left no marker, there is no record that they were here. He was very private. He wouldn't want to be tracked down. I scattered his remaining ashes, after irreverently dividing them, over his favourite places - the sea by Lyme Regis and Lake Ontario.

All four of my grandparents were cremated, which I thought was forward-thinking for their generation. My father's parents requested that their ashes be buried in the grave of their young daughter. My cousin buried her parents' ashes in an English field, overlooking a lake they used to picnic beside. She planted trees over their otherwise unmarked graves as the cows looked on. I would like that. Where to do that here?

I think of all the funerals and memorials I have been to in this lakeside village, mostly in the United Church, or our small funeral home, some very religious, and some not so much. The minister is very progressive and adapts his funerals well. The last one was for a friend who died of cancer too soon, a gay man who was our village's go-to florist and landscape artist. His spirit still illuminates gardens and arrangements throughout the village. His memorial was on a cold snowy day, but for two hours we celebrated spring-time, with slides of his gardens accompanied by K. D. Lang and Sarah MacLachlan, and words of love spoken by family and friends. There were two Amens, and not one mention of God, Jesus, or heaven. Just the way he would have wanted it.

We drummed at another friend's funeral. Our women's circle drummed familiar rhythms on djembes and frame drums in the church, the circle missing her heartbeat already. Another friend buried his wife's ashes, with a few words of love, in a small hole dug on the perimeter of the village graveyard. At one funeral a few years ago, a dear friend was eulogized by her husband and two grown children to such an extent that afterwards we co-workers shook our heads - were we at the right funeral? Did we not know her at all? Did they not know her? Their words did not reflect the person we knew and loved as only a close group of women can. The family did not talk about her, but about them.

When I think about dying, I wonder if funerals will be carried out in the same way by the time I die? Will there be the money, time, and space to celebrate a person's passing or will bodies be disposed of in as quick a way as possible? If the domino effect takes place and institutions collapse in my lifetime affecting economy, food and fuel as has been so long predicted, will cemeteries still be viable institutions? Will pollution's march force the closure of crematorium ovens, will the lack of space and shortages of fuel and food limit group gatherings? Will tradition be forced to end? If I state that I want change, and I understand that the forces of change are not going to be pretty, therefore I have to expect that any plans I leave behind for a ritual of my passing may be useless, even laughable, when the time comes.

Any words of wisdom I would like passed on at my funeral are already in my consciousness. They are already printed on any record I leave behind in the noosphere. Whether my family plays Claire de Lune or Neil Diamond, whether my body is covered with my purple cloak or naked, whether I am in a casket, a bag, or thrown in a mass grave, it will make no difference. My life will have already been disseminated in my words, my relationships, my laughter, and my support. It will make no difference how my body is disposed of - even if, heaven forbid, with no respect by marauding strangers - or what words will be said over it, or how it will be honoured, if honoured at all. I will have no control over that. None. My body will be of no use any more. My life will have been lived and will continue to live on, and the essence of 'I' will return and fill in a new space on this planet. My energy will work with the energy already here and energy yet to be generated, and will dance around for another, what we call, lifetime. This is the conscious way with which I can face my death.

When I got married in the sixties, the focus was on the wedding, the dress, the china pattern, the trousseau tea. Not much thought went into the future of the actual union itself. If I focus on my funeral, the music and readings, I am not concentrating on my actual death. I need to think of my dying process rather than the trappings, the effect on other people, the stuff that we feel is so important. It's not. It's all illusion. Marilyn Schlitz quotes Michael Bernard Beckwith as saying, 'They realize how they spent so much time worrying about a death that never happened, because death doesn't exist...when a person dies...they simply awaken to the fact that they are no longer in the physical body.' [81] Consciousness is knowing that this body as I know it will have no more use to me after my death, and accepting it.

My grandparents used to go on a Mystery Bus Tour after they retired. They would buy two tickets and get on the bus, not knowing where it would take them. Sometimes they went to the sea, sometimes a band concert in a park, or a cathedral or a museum in a city. The anticipation and surprise were simple ways of getting some excitement into their mundane lives. Of course, they always knew that they would end up back in the bus station near their house. I wonder if they looked at death as another mystery tour. After all, one buys a ticket with one's birth and gets on the bus of life in the hands of an unseen driver who plans the trip. If I am the driver of my own destiny, does the Divine plot my destination? Do I follow the schedule but take my own route? With faith and trust, one knows a surprise is ahead and eagerly anticipates it. Mystery tours are practice for reaching out into the unknown, which does not have to be painful. I think it might be like going to the dentist. If you tense up and tighten all your muscles it's harder for the dentist to poke and drill and far more painful for the patient. I have had plenty of experience with dentists over my life (old story) and have learned to purposefully relax the tautness of my muscles, and sure enough, the whole experience is almost pleasant (new story). Relaxing around the thought of death would surely make it easier.

I am not ready to leave this life yet. I doubt that most people are. I love my life for all the usual reasons. But one thing I have learned about myself is that once I say Yes, I adapt well, bend like the willow. I just need to practise saying Yes, practise adapting and bending, practise not knowing, relax into the mystery trip.

In *The Second Half of Life*, Angeles Arrien writes: '... the greatest challenge at the end is to have the courage to face whatever suffering, sadness, or pain may come during this ultimate process called dying. Here we awaken to a courage and faith unrealized before.' [82] This is the practice, the work which is a true leap of faith. After all, what's the worst that can happen? I can only die.

Spirit

I face the Centre: Welcome, Spirit, into the circle of my life.

I reach the centre ether spirit noosphere.
Her wheel turns around me never-ceasing.
I am at the beginning and the end
between life and death, dark and light, silence
breath and no-breath
and the song of the universe.

I breathe in, up from earth
up through toes and calves, belly and breasts
up the channel of my throat to nasal canals
spiral my brain, out of my skull
into beyond,

and let out my breath into the skies
to join the cosmos.
I have wings.

I breathe in, down from the heavens
down through my cheeks, larynx and lungs
twist round intestines, bowel, sliding down thighs
to the ankles, out of the soles of my feet
into beyond,

and let out my breath into the earth
to join Her soul.
I have roots.

With roots and wings
I align with spirit
I am free
I am here
I am She
We are One

Blessed Be

Story-Telling Time: Soulspirit

On Christmas Eve, 1991, a bank representative knocked at my door. This antithesis of Santa Claus informed me that my landlord had declared bankruptcy. We had to vacate our rented house within 60 days. I felt like a criminal, evicted by Scrooge, through no fault of my own. This was the fourth house we had lived in since transitioning from our comfortable corporate life nine years earlier. Moving every two years had become an uncomfortable habit; housing prices soared in the affluent '80s and every landlord was lured to sell as soon as I moved my family into their retirement-house.

Moving from #89 to #85 in a town house complex, we walked all the furniture up the road. I, the kids, their friends, carried or wheeled loads for five days, the neighbours pulling up their porch chairs to watch the show. From #85 we moved to #104, which I had found at the last minute by putting House Wanted flyers in every single mailbox in the complex. Then its owner sold too.

A week before my youngest daughter and I had to move out of #104, her siblings now in university, I was on my early morning walking meditation visualizing an available home with all the skills I could muster. Shakti Gawain had introduced me to creative visualization and I was a devotee. Eyes shut, not even aware of where I was at the time in the middle of the road, I whirled around and pointed, repeating the mantra 'We will live in that house!' Later, when I opened the local paper to House Rentals, only one was available. I phoned. Address given, I went immediately to check it out. It was the very same house I had pointed to in my visualization that morning. I could barely afford it, monthly expenses were higher, but it was available immediately, my daughter could continue at the same school. I took it, further reinforcing my strong belief in Gawain's visualizations.

And now, two years later, we had to move again. Here was familiar panic. Where to now? A friend told me about a new condo in the next town. Unable to be sold, the units were now being rented. Better still, an incentive made the rent even more affordable. The day after Christmas, my daughter and I fell in love with the apartment. Brand new, big windows, we would each have a large space to ourselves. After living with other people's problems for 10 years, it would be heaven. There was pressure to decide, said the manager, other people were looking. But as I usually don't make quick decisions, we set off to go shopping, to 'think about it.' In only a few minutes, I listened to - my inner crone? I turned off the highway to find a phone box, called the manager, and reserved an apartment. Changes ahead: new school, paring down a lifetime of houses versus new broadloom and a secure lease. Wise decision.

We carried on to the mall and after choosing sheets for my daughter's soon-to-be new bedroom I realized I had left my credit card at home. With no cash and an overdrawn bank account, I decided to go home to get my card, nervous about leaving my 11-year old daughter alone in this huge city mall. I drove the 40 minutes north like the wind. As I approached the highway ramp to return, my mind creating dramas of a mall white slave syndicate, a massive storm suddenly descended from nowhere - pitch-dark sky, thunder, lightning, rain beating down. Visibility was zero. I pulled onto the shoulder, terrified as trucks rushed by within inches of me, rain beating on the car like hail. I still couldn't see enough to be safe on the highway and called out loud for the storm to stop. Artemis! Durga! Kali! Someone!

Suddenly there was a monstrous crash of thunder and a crack of lightning at the exact same time, and across my windscreen flashed the word *Soulspirit*. I can still see the thick black-lettered script as it scrawled across the glass. In less than a milli-second, it was gone.

Soulspirit

Rain stopped, sun shone on the wet highway, I was free to go. After reaching the mall and finding my unsullied daughter, I paid for her sheets plus a quilt I felt inspired to get in the circumstances, and then I wrote down the word as I had seen it. But I did not need to. I have never forgotten how it looked, how it came and went so fast. Where did it come from? Why? What do I do with this stunning life-changing message?

Was the universe recognizing my quick decision to make a move, the efforts I had made over the past 10 years to create homes for my family after uprooting them from their comfortable existence? Was I being led to a place where I could finally relax, a 10th-floor aerie? What I didn't know was that my daughter was yet to lead me a merry dance through her teenage rebellion, yet I would have a place of peace and security, where I could write all night while waiting up for her, a lap pool where I could swim out my work stress, a nearby park for my walking meditation every morning. My spirit had been strong through so much adversity, and it would continue to be in the years to come. It gave itself a name, and that name was given to me in a storm where it knew I would notice, trapped in the car, a captive audience staring at the windscreen begging the Goddess to stop the downpour.

Trust the universe

That was the message. If I can trust in whatever it was - the Divine, my soulspirit - that gave me a feeling of support and confidence in myself when I was panicking that day, I have all the trust I need. Can I trust in this same power in the face of my death? Surely I can let go of fear, which cannot be much more than I felt in the thunderstorm. The Divine gave me a gift. She acknowledged my spirit and gave it a name. Soulspirit will remain when my body is long gone. And from that soulspirit shall birth another expression of the universe, another person that shall be called 'me.' In that way there is no death. In that way I can have no fear.

We Don't Die

Although stars are born from dust and gas, it is in their death throes that they return dust, old and new, to the cosmos in a great ritual of cosmic regeneration visible in their beautiful death shrouds, the spectacular planetary nebulae.

Jacob Berkowitz

Another day. Another memorial. And another sudden death in the community. It's going to be like this from now on. Most days bring news, either locally or from a distance. Every week another funeral or a memorial. My neighbours are around my age; why would I feel so distanced from the death passage they are moving through? The post office has a glass case that holds recent obituaries; in this hub of connection, there is suddenly disconnection. I touch the case like a reliquary whenever I mail a letter.

Today's memorial in our village Town Hall was for a man in his late 80s, well known by many of us in the last 12 years, whose eyes twinkled and whose laughter brightened any room. His writing rivaled Stephen Leacock's for village humour; his attendance at our local Open Floor group is already missed. First his feet, then shaky legs seen descending the stairs into the library basement, heralded an evening of witty feedback, wise reflection, and red wine. His life, shared this afternoon in three perspectives by his grown children, was that of a renaissance man before his time, a role model, a mentor. Family pictures, sized large, stood on a table in the middle of the room; we were watered with wine, and fed delicacies created by his son, a prominent Toronto chef. A band of friends played loud background music like Hard Day's Night. There was much love in that hall, love he expressed to everybody being re-expressed in return as a gift for his life. A gentleman, he was a gentle man.

We walked out of the hall into a snowstorm, the lake ahead of us frozen in huge ice volcanoes, and drove home past the house he and his wife vacated three years earlier to move into a care home; past the cemetery where he had lowered her ashes into a small velvet bag-sized hole; past the library where he regaled us with laughter at his own writing; past the newspaper office where his latest 'career' saw his stories printed every week, emerging into a well-launched book. He had more fun ahead of him - an animated film was to be made of his village stories by retired film-makers, itching to revive their craft. But his body was tired, it wearied of the strength it needed for the last years when he was regularly transfused with new energy. His spirit missed his wife, no matter how many women made his eyes twinkle. There were to be no more words. It was time.

So a life is over. His nursing home room is filled with another elderly person adjusting to a small space as he had to do; his table by the window of a restaurant with a lively wine cellar, halfway between the care home and the dress shop owned by a brighter than life opera singer - just the right distance to manoeuvre his walker for a lunchtime assignation with her over a dry red - now seats two strangers oblivious of sparkling conversations held there not too long ago.

And yet, is his life over? Like every person eventually, his body is no longer breathing, gone as we knew it. We call that death. Ashes now in their velvet bag, his body waits for the spring thaw to be mixed with his wife's and buried in the same small hole, with rose petals, in a simple family ceremony. Like every dead person, he is missed. Memories of him bring a sadness sometimes not quenched easily. Like all dead people, air rushes in quickly to fill the space he held on this planet for his life span; some other man's body maybe fills his suits and someone else plies his computer keyboard. But nobody chuckles at their own stories like he did, or twinkles at a pretty woman the same way, or will ever be as proud of his grown-up children.

On every day of John's almost-90 years, he touched people in ways he did or did not know; he left part of himself with people that, in some way, changed them from the people they were before they met. As we all do. It doesn't have to be anything huge, maybe just a smile, a collision of energy that brightens a day or brings forth an idea or a memory. And all the people we touch that way meet other people in their circular day who, because of that first connection, make a speck of difference in their day. Exponentially this grows to a day full of hundreds of people reverberating from the first exchange between two of them, all echoing the spark that passed from one to another to another.

Life is not just a body. Yes, that body, we, the living, miss: the sight of it, the thought of it, the comfort it brings, the familiarity, the sense of touch, the sound, the smell, the memories. I still catch my father's unique fragrance on his gloves, and my heart jumps. I am arriving at his house again, listening to him play Ave Maria on his electric organ. Pizza brings forth a memory of Kate, remembering the last one we made together with cookie crust and fruit at her summer cottage near Lake Superior, and her generous hug before I drove away. Yes, I miss Kate and all she meant to me. But her wisdom still lies within me: the Desiderata poem she sent to me in Brazil when I was depressed after leaving Jamaica; her matter-of-fact way of child rearing and cooking that taught me not to be so fussy over details; definitely her insistence that I stop saying 'It's only me' when I phoned, as if apologizing for my very existence. Her parties introduced me to Neil Diamond. She changed my life and because of that she had an influence of how I affected others, and how, in turn, they affected others in their lives. The Desiderata always hung on my classroom wall and inspired my students to become more confident. I thnk of her every time I (still) say, 'It's only me.' Every day something occurs as a result of my knowing Kate and she may, or may not, come to mind. But she doesn't have to, she's there already.

John was an original member of our writers' group that has met on First Fridays since 2001, sharing our latest writing. During the break at one of our early meetings in a local coffee shop, I saw him talking with a Grade 11 young man, who was also reading that night. The young man had shared with us his lack of esteem brought on by teasing at school because of his tender writing, his love of poetry, and maybe, I wondered, his sexuality. For 20 minutes, the oldest and the youngest members of the group sat in private, intense conversation, and I knew that from that moment the boy's life would change in some way. He would never forget John's respect and attention, if not the shared words.

John and Kate are just examples of a thousand other meetings with hundreds of other people. I can think of dozens of ways they affected my life, down to her recipes I still use and his perspective on village life that still makes me chuckle; they became part of the person I am today. So yes, they are dead, but their lives aren't over. They live on in me, and in all the people they touched in some way in their 57 and almost-90 years. 'When you're gone, your presence will continue like a ghost puppeteer in the universes of those you know.' [83] And so on for everyone we know, from those very close to us, and those we meet on the street, like the man who passed me when I was ten, who never knew that he began my 'who am I' search.

Regardless of whether one believes in reincarnation or not, or that they will meet their Maker at the pearly gates, or just that this is it, a one-off, regardless of all beliefs, I am comforted by the knowledge that we do live on in each other. Not only does our breath mingle with the breath of everyone else who ever breathed air, and our footsteps follow a trail trod by millions before us, and we daily witness the passage of the planets as humans have done since time began, but also every thought, word, and deed, reverberates, resonates, and finds a home in someone else, to continue weaving the web of oneness that we all share. No agnostic or religious belief can take that away from me.

This awareness has made me so much more conscious of the effect that we have on each other. In earlier years as a young adult, I felt that I had little importance in the big scheme of things, insignificantly casting a tiny shadow. I now know that if the lives of others live on within me, mine must live on in them. So connecting, relating, and communicating become even more important.

Finding an escape from the premise that the body is the only proof of life is necessary for me now. My body is like the car I get into to drive to the city. I keep it tuned up, clean it, fill it up with energy; I follow the rules of the road and stay aware of my surroundngs. My soul, as part of our one big soul, chose this body to live in for a certain period on this earth, this time around. The universe expresses itself through our bodies; the Divine expresses Herself through our creativity. The essence that I called John, or Kate, or Mimi, or Nora or Mary or Stella, lives on in our hearts and minds and senses and is passed down through generations. Today I am searching for a village Christmas story by John to read in his memory at an annual event; Neil Diamond is singing Stones in the background, so midnight dancing in Kate's garden floats through my head. Mimi's book Deathing sits beside me as I write and I'm seeing Nora's white horses on the lake. Nobody dies. They live on and on and on.

Love Story: fitting in

I stoop in snow, fit a mitten
on a tiny hand, count ten snowflakes
landing on his nose, warm
a freezing cheek. 'I love you Grandma'
falls into woolly layers.

What is there left to love?

A gnarling body: bending, fading,
hollow, spilling never-ending dreams
ideas laced with tears
and wasted chances, wrinkle-dances
marking years;

a mind that's saging,
plunging deep in computation,
sense-interpretation labyrinthian
with firing thoughts;
spirals strengthen when I sleep,
reflections keeping guard;

and spirit - both protection
and my ward, far from aging,
burning bright, tying knots, fusing ends,
weaving reasons for existence
in this shell I chose to use this time
and will eventually shed.

Led by spirit through every season,
if mind surrenders to the light
my body follows.
His spring day is just beginning,
my winter nights are winding down
chased by his energy.

Thumb finds thumb space easily.

He makes an angel in the snow,
limbs spinning fragile wings
to fly us home: together ageless,
laughing spirits loving all the way.

Dancing with Goats

The idea that we are continually born into this material dimension until we are able to recover the knowledge of our divine origin and begin consciously to relate to that source or ground made perfect sense.

Anne Baring

As a little girl, I would lie in the grass, look up into the clouds and try to imagine people 'up there.' All the people ever born walk through the gates, I had heard somewhere, to see God. But I could not visualize it. How did they stay up there? Did they sit on the clouds? There must be billions of millions of people. Wouldn't they be too heavy for the sky to hold them all up? Childish thoughts developed into a lifetime curiosity, fascinated by afterlife's depiction in fictional movies like *Made in Heaven*, and *City of Angels*, and real-life stories of people with Near-Death Experiences or those clearly remembering past lives. One, lost from my library long ago, was written by an Irish woman who actually met her children from a previous lifetime, all now much older than she. Witnessing her familiarity in their family home and their village, telling family stories that nobody else could possibly know, they all gracefully agreed that this was so, and they welcomed her home as their mother.

I have developed a theory about reincarnation. It involves electricity and magnetism. I am a poet, not a scientist or a quantum theorist, a biologist, or anything remotely technical. I am a writer, not a priest or a religious scholar, or a quotable philosopher. As a cultural creative, I am deeply interested in cosmology, mythology, and wisdom spirituality. My younger self would have considered herself an ordinary person. But when I heard the words 'ordinary people' spoken by someone who thought she and I were more conscious and awake than 'other' people, than 'ordinary' people, I heard them with new ears and I shuddered, so aware of how we look at 'the other' from an elitist position or as a threat. Here was an old friend including me in using consciousness as a status symbol to actually create a polarity. I spoke up as best I could. 'This is why we are in the world situation we are in; if only we could stop thinking that way about the other.' My words severed a friendship which, on reflection, had quite likely run its course, but I have been making every effort not to use the term 'ordinary person' any more. There is no 'ordinary' or no 'normal.' We can't think in those terms any more. Dualistic and judgmental thinking and acting are so insidiously built into our lives. I want to practise a non-perpetuation of dualistic thinking - though that thought brings me back to my theory as it is based on polar opposites, on attraction and repulsion.

I read everything I can get my hands on about quantum anything, though half the time I have to struggle to understand it. But this helps me to be a part of our evolution, the birth of a new world, within and without. There is much more to know, many changes to witness, to participate in. I don't want to die yet; I don't want to miss new discoveries.

As someone who has a strong spiritual life, I am surprised that with age I have developed a quasi-scientific approach to something as supposedly spiritual as reincarnation. However, I see the current merging of science and spirit as so exciting. I believe that what we call spirit is energy, which, in turn, is manifested as the electro-magnetic spark that keeps our hearts beating, keeps our systems alive, neurons jumping. My theory about reincarnation is about life after death. It explains where we go after we die, and how we 'come back.' But as I explain electro-magnetism and energy in my non-scientific way as best I know how, I am coming from spirit. My idea is a dance, a gavotte weaving back and forth.

In my lifetime, knowledge about the body has been narrowed down to such a fine degree that we now know that our tissues and organs are basically made up of trillions of sub-atomic particles, or energy. Our knowledge won't stop there. In my grandchildren's lifetime they will know so much more about the universe's place in our bodies, and about our place in the universe. Scientists and spiritual healers are veering closer together in their quantum theories, each recognizing the importance of polarities in, and out of, the body in their different perspectives. Scientists recognize energy's place in medicine and the cosmos, outer space; spiritual healers study the chakras and energy fields around us and within us, our inner space.

In the '80s, I took my children to the Ontario Science Centre. On our first trip we discovered a booth with a repeating five-minute film about our place in the universe. The film would be considered very basic now - this was before the Hubble telescope's launch in 1990 - but in spite of its simplicity, it demonstrated quantum relationships in a way that I have never forgotten. The black and white film began with a person lying on the grass in a park, the camera focusing on the back of her hand - skin, pores and tiny hairs clearly seen. Then the camera zoomed outwards into space, until the park was a speck on the globe which gradually vanished into galaxies, speeding images racing to the boundary of the heavens as we knew then, before Hubble. If I remember correctly, exponential distances flicked by on the bottom of the screen. Lingering for a minute on the edge of outer space as we knew it then, the viewer was just as rapidly returned back through the cosmos back to the woman in the park.

After pausing for a minute on her hand, the viewer's journey was then extended into the hand, through its epidermal layers, muscles, ligaments, bone, flowing blood cells in arteries and veins, the throb of pulse, the nuclei of cells, then back out to the skin layer, whereupon the hand's owner stood up, stretched, and strolled away. I returned to see the film every time we visited the centre, totally intrigued. Now reading about quantum theories, I am so grateful for that early representation, which was a visual image for me of 'as above, so below,' the spiritual concept I was also beginning to understand at that transformational time in my life. I wonder if the film has been changed to be more current in 2016, or if it remains, with its somewhat restricted information, a dated victim of diminishing science budgets.

I interpret the electricity within our bodies that keeps our hearts beating and our brains functioning as 'spirit.' It's all energy. We are all part of a huge energy field. 'Nobel Prize winning scientists have proven beyond doubt that the physical world is one large sea of energy that flashes into and out of being in milliseconds, over and over again.' [84] There are books by those who are so much more technical than I. I skim, gather facts and trivia. And I interpret from my perspective which may be skewed. The anticipation of finally writing down my theory in simple laywoman's terms makes me somewhat nervous. It seems presumptuous. There is no language for what I want to say.

So I research electromagnetism and death, to see if there is any support for my theory. I find one article written in 1987: 'Electromagnetic Radiation and the Afterlife'. A Polish scientist, Janusz Slawinski, states that 'a specific carrying electromagnetic field, capable of organizing the inanimate matter within a living system, might be a simple model of 'the life force'...spark of life... elan vital...the fundamental carrier essence of all living forms.' [85] He goes on to say that '...a living being, that is, a body-bound consciousness, and a free consciousness belong to the same reality.' [86] He speaks of the other dimensions I envision, the freedom and the spark. I am further invigorated.

Simple research tells me that at death most of our electrical energy is used up in the body's disintegration, and the rest, a minuscule amount, leaks into the atmosphere. From the Physics Department of the University of Illinois I read, 'For warm blooded creatures, some thermal energy gradually leaks into the environment.' [87] Could it be that when energy 'leaks,' it has a mission? Perhaps when we die, the electricity in our body can't just vanish into a vast sea of nothingness. Spirit ascending from the body at death is sometimes seen or sensed by witnesses - it doesn't just disappear, its purpose over. Electricity cannot die. Its magnetic characteristics of attracting and repelling don't stop; its electromagnetic qualities are not altered by death of the physical body.

The Theory of Roz is thus: when we say that the spirit leaves the body on death, it is the electro-magnetic ions that leave the body to revert back to the energy field from whence they came at the time of gestation. Swalinski writes, 'The electromagnetic essence of life, including the conscious ego, may be radiated into space at the speed of light.' [88] Like attracts like; in space, electrons are attracted to, and are attracted by, like electrons, and they cluster together. I envision it as the ever-moving dance of attraction, freedom, colour, and the beauty that people with NDE experiences describe. Producer of *Thunderbolts of the Gods*, David Talbot, writes, 'The space between stars and planets is teeming with charged particles... glowing electric filaments spanning billions of light years... formations formed by magnetic fields. Only electric currents create magnetic fields.' [89] In life, electrons carry our energetic reactions to all of our experiences, so we are still 'alive,' but now, without the earthly body, in another reality, we continue to have a purpose in an ever-moving energy field that never ends. Again Swalinski: '...the electromagnetic consciousness field enters another 'dimension' where space and time are fused into one reality...is that immortality? Immortality does not mean life everlasting for it does not last at all; it just is. From the mathematical point of view, solutions giving infinity have no physical meaning.' [90]

So how does the Theory of Roz explain reincarnation? In early foetal development, an electrical impulse stimulates the heartbeat. More precisely, it enters at six weeks into gestation, when the spinal cord begins to close, blood vessels begin to develop, simple eyes and buds of legs and arms appear, and the heart begins its steady beat. So how does my theory explain reincarnation? While the energy that enters the fetus's body is not exactly the same cluster of electrons that was released from a prior death, it is a conglomeration of electrons that were attracted to each other in the universe that becomes this baby's 'spirit,' bringing with it imprints of activities, people and places, sounds and smells, from all like energies, because like attracts like. This is a guiding factor in each unique individual. This can explain déjà vu, or a violent fear of snakes, an instinctive love of a certain food or a strong resonance to a certain place, like mine to Lyme Regis. Or an instant dislike. In Slawinski's research, he came to the conclusion that 'the electromagnetic field, produced by necrotic radiation, containing energy, internal structure, and information, may permit continuation of consciousness beyond the death of the body.' And by Jamie Trosper an article called 'The Physics of Death:' 'In death, the collection of atoms ...are repurposed. These atoms and that energy, which originated in the Big Bang, will always be around. Therefore, your 'light' – that is, the essence of your energy...will continue to echo through space until the end of time.' [91] This is basically the theory of Roz plus my ideas behind why we never die.

I offer a very simple analogy: Marigold Jones dies; her spirit leaves her body as energy, carrying with it, say, the attraction/memory of a significant red dress (one of trillions of other memories, or imprints). In the field, there will be attraction with other electrons that share a similar 'memory' of a red dress. When the cluster of electrons enters into the body of a foetus, as like is attracted to like there is a strong resonance of a 'memory' of a red dress. To continue this simple story, George is born and in his twenties he has a déjà vu experience when meeting up with a girl in a red dress; maybe it will lead to a significant relationship with its wearer. George thinks that the connection must have come from a 'past life.' It has. But not as we think in our language, the only way we know how to describe something so esoteric. We only use the images we know. As Anne Baring writes, 'We no longer have access to other levels or modes of consciousness because our rational mind has, over the last four centuries, increasingly ridiculed, disparaged, and repressed what it has been unable, so far, to accept, prove or comprehend. It has therefore cut us off from those deeper instinctive aspects of our nature that have the power to connect us with other dimensions of reality.' [92]

I look back through my life and see physical similarities in people that I have been drawn to emotionally. I see the places that call me again and again; the place I consider my soul-place and I are entwined together. A baby will look at me with instant recognition if we pass in a shopping mall and we hold eye contact. I usually whisper 'Hi, it's good to see you again.' And I 'hear' the child respond with 'I remember you.' Attraction from another space and time. I remember meeting a woman who had been described to me as a person I would really get along with, we had so much in common. I instantly felt discomfort, even attack, an urge to move away from her, a negation which never resolved itself. Later, when we re-attempted connection, it was obvious that she had the same reaction. Psychologists, sociologists, mythologists, past life therapists, would all see that meeting from their perspective. I enjoy, understand, and follow their theories. But from my crone angle, I see strong magnetic activity, millennia in the making, carrying a web of information. In her book *Death Makes Life Possible*, Marilyn Schlitz quotes Rudolph Tanzi: 'One would think that in terms of developing a web of consciousness around yourself that interacts with all the consciousness in the universe, that's information ...information can be the structure of matter. It can be how energy is configured. We believe information cannot be destroyed. So we at least know that all of the consciousness we have experienced in our lives cannot be destroyed; it is stored somewhere...When you die is everything gone? ...The consciousness you experienced over your life stays intact, I believe that... my intuition says yes, this is probably the case.' [93]

In our Hollywood Hallmark world, we interpret attraction as 'like,' deep attraction as 'love,' repulsion as 'dislike' or even 'hate.' It is much sexier to think of hearts and roses instead of electromagnetism, wealthier for the consumer industry. We need the romantic love story as a transitory passage, a mating ritual, like the cavemen's stories explaining the stars and seasons which became our myths. But I believe that there are other ways of 'knowing' each other, not only as physical bodies and souls. We have no idea what else is 'out there.' I often imagine the room in which I work to be crowded, with spirits in forms that welcome, and attract, urging me on, that 'know' me. And that, I call it love.

When my grandmother sat in her armchair, her arthritic fingers picking at the threads - . I can still hear the scratch, scratch, scratch – she was waiting to see my grandfather in heaven. Her faith gave her support in the last few years of her rather sad life. His appearance would be beyond our limited dimensions, as would hers, but there would be a knowing, an attraction. His energy would greet hers in a state of excitement - not as they knew each other in life, but in the state of magnetic attraction. And their electrons would dance and play. Yes, his energy will greet mine too, our connection in this life was very strong. His hand won't reach out to mine like he always did; that memory keeps him alive in me now so he didn't 'die' to me. But we will be together again after my death, in a state far beyond our present comprehension. Of course 'heaven' is beautiful because the colours and light that we now can see in faraway photographs of the firmaments that will embrace us are spectacular. 'Love' would be felt from the constant dance of attraction, agitation and excitement; even electrons repelled by mine will be attracted somewhere else. And because what we think of as 'we' will be finally able to see in a different way beyond our brain and five senses, beyond the physical, we will recognize each other, and we will welcome – not with open arms, as Grannie dreamed, but as energies flowing together.

Once, clouds of migrating butterflies chose to settle in our garden on their way south. I lay down flat on the grass and gazed up into hundreds of butterflies above me, fluttering and flying in constant spirals, meeting, mating, separating, partnering again, always in movement, a constant swirl of life and love in the sky. Maybe that is what it's like in the magnetic field, a constant swirl of colourful, loving life, a dance of attraction and letting go, merging, parting, gathering.

At the first Glastonbury Goddess Conference, in 1996, a new friend was imagining a small group of us women as reconnecting after many centuries. She 'remembered' us at solstice rituals in an ancient pagan community, scurrying through the dark undergrowth to standing stones, bringing bowls and platters for the feast after. 'And Roz,' she wept with emotion, 'You always forgot the bread!' I had only known her for a few days; she couldn't possibly have known that at every family meal or social pot-luck, I always forgot the bread. I'd leave it in the car, the oven, the store, or still on the shopping list. I was well-known for forgetting the bread! My belief tells me that it was a strong magnetic attraction that drew us all to each other that weekend and the energies in ancient bodies long gone had feasted together before - without the bread.

One of my granddaughters, Susie, now 18, was eight months old when my father, her maternal great-grandfather, died. She came from Calgary with my daughter and stayed in his house for a week. Susie was an active crawler, exploring every corner, and she developed an incredibly strong attraction to a few things that had been my mother's, objects I remember always being around, nothing valuable. (My mother had died eight years earlier.) Susie instantly adopted a china dog used as a doorstop at her all-fours level. It was taken back to Calgary with her. A dish towel, depicting the birds my mother loved to watch, became Susie's comfort binkie; she wouldn't go to sleep unless it was draped over her. Susie loved 'white soup.' It turned out to be Campbell's mushroom soup - my mother's favourite. When she could talk, Susie chose on her own to call me Grannie, the name I used to call my maternal grandmother.

Five or so years later, I dreamed that my mother was telling me she had been dancing with goats. I woke up with the phrase 'dancing with goats' echoing in my head, and I tried to write a poem around it, but couldn't quite get it. After a few days, an Alberta stamped postcard arrived in the mail with a six-year-old's drawing of a happy girl and a smiling, dancing animal. Scrawled above: 'Dear Grannie. Goat and me. By Susie.' The connection between the dream, the postcard, my mother, and Susie, makes it impossible for me not to believe in some kind of reincarnation, not by telling the old story of a past life where the same soul returns to another body, but by creating a new story, a story about a conglomeration of electrons that are attracted to each other in the universe and combine to imagine a new personality as they kick-start a tiny heartbeat. Susie is not my mother re-born. My mother did not return 'as Susie,' as I was later told on my first visit to a highly respectable psychic who hadn't heard any Susie stories or even knew my mother had died.

My mother had been a fearful child, and she adored the feistiness and inner fire in Susie's mother as a child. They had a very strong connection right from the beginning. The attraction between their energies created the free spirit that is Susie, the spirited child that my mother could never have been in her restricted home. As Susie's body grew, so did her energy field. Given the opportunity of her great-grandfather's funeral, she was drawn to the china dog, the bird dish towel and the mushroom soup. Susie knew that house, those simple objects. She gravitated to them, as if by a magnet. My dream confirmed my theory with the message 'goat and me.' The matrilineal line is strong. The egg that developed as Susie was carried in me; the egg that developed as her mother was carried in my mother. I believe that when Susie was six weeks in utero, the electrons that had kept her great-grandmother's heart beating, plus other electrons from so many connections, were attracted to the electrons in my daughter's body and entered her daughter Susie's foetal body. There must be a link with the electrons that keep all our hearts beating. In this way our hearts beat as one. And we are truly one.

To take the Theory of Roz further, scientists tell us that the poles are now reversing so maybe the magnetic pull is less. I wonder if that causes a weaker attraction. An uncomfortable melding of unlike energies might be occurring as maybe the repelling activity is not so strong. So maybe some of the electrical energies that enter the foetus are at odds with each other, rather than all 'liking' each other, so we now see personality disorders growing in intensity in the 21st century. But that's another amateur theory to develop.

I speak of my flawed and unproved theory in lay-woman's words but as a crone, I claim it. And as a crone I make it my own. This imaginative idea has helped me in coming to terms with respecting my body's reactions to people and places, trusting its intuition when making a choice, stuck at a crossroad. It has helped me balance science and spirituality on a very simple level. It has helped me feel more confident about reincarnation because now it seems possible.

It feels very grandiose, writing about aging as if I know all about it. 75 isn't old; I cannot expect to imagine what it would be like to be 95. When I was 15 in England, I didn't imagine 35. I doodled dress designs, dreamed of a career in fashion; I wanted twelve children (my imaginary friends?) because I was lonely and wanted a noisy home. But I had no idea that at 35 I'd have had the travelling experiences I had, be heading for divorce and the changes that come with it. I had the noisy children-filled home, but hadn't expected to be moving around the world at the stroke of an executive's pen. How could I have conceived of that?

I no more know now what it will be like to be 95. I can romantically dream of still being active, living with my lady in our sunshiny house, draping dresses and shawls gracefully over my healthy body. But that is either a drama I create in my mind, encouraged and manipulated by media images sold to me, or could be a result of creatively visualizing my future. I do imagine a person strong enough to face the future, whatever it brings, to practise listening to her heart and her gut, to be awake and aware of what is happening in the environment, the world, now.

I instinctively did that before my marriage fell apart. After my miscarriage, I listened to my inner crone when she told me to build up my body and my spirit, both drooping after the loss. On a trip to Miami, I discovered books like *Diet for a Small Planet*, *Transcendental Meditation*, and *Feel Like a Million*, theories and ideas I hadn't known existed. Stocking up on vitamins and health foods not available in Dominican stores, I inundated my trusting children with brown rice and greens, tofu and falafel. I exercised every day becoming fitter and healthier than I had ever been, providing a solid grounding for the years ahead, none of which I consciously dreamed into existence. Miraculously I birthed my long-awaited fourth child before two major hurricanes blew my marriage apart. But I was physically ready, strong enough to withstand the emotional onslaught of the years ahead, none of which I could possibly have imagined 20 years earlier.

I spoke of this to my adult students, suggesting they prepare for college or employment as if they were Olympic athletes. Working on exercise, food, sleep, meditation, visualizing success - all in readiness for winning their next event: a job or a college course. Preparing the body is as important as preparing the mind for the journey that lies ahead, while not knowing what it will entail. Change happens in a second. We see that daily with the frightening events that happen around the world.

But this isn't a checklist for growing older. I haven't walked that terrain yet, and surely anyone who writes a traveller's guidebook must take the trip before giving any advice. I can read all I can find on anti-inflammation diets, wheat bellies, electro-magnetic sensitivities, and walking as the ideal exercise, but I still know that the ultimate test is knowing one's own body and listening to its signals. Mine surprises me now by becoming more sensitive to favourite staples in my diet - sugar, chocolate, wine, Mexican food. Even toothpaste. I highly respect that and refuse to take medication to help my body digest those things. If my body doesn't need any more sugar, and it certainly has taken in a few tons through its lifetime, then I will do what I can to help it kick the habit, hard as it is. The body knows. And the spirit listens. Whether the mind interprets it or not, doesn't really matter. In fact, if we left it to the body and the spirit we might do much better. The mind can over-analyse, over-dramatize, over-intellectualize, over-rationalize, until the original message is buried under drama.

The spirit knows when the body is about to die. Before my mother went into hospital for a checkup exploring a general weakness, she wrapped up all of her diaries tightly in three or four knotted plastic bags further sealed with yards of masking tape and several of the elastic bands she kept on a huge ball. Years later, I found the only page that she had torn out: the day I was born. Her spirit knew. And her body listened to it. She must have listened to it through all the tests and the preparations for surgery on her pituitary gland, and when the surgeon touched the vagus nerve, causing the stroke that was the precursor of the one that eventually killed her, her spirit finally began to put her body to the rest it needed. Something in her knew.

Koko's spirit knew. Two and a half months before she died, tragically too young after hitting her head on a rock in a charity river raft race dressed as the Owl (of Pussycat fame) she gave me her golden priestess cloak: 'I won't be needing it.' She also gave me her mobile phone: 'I don't want that any more, I'll get another.' That summer, we said a lingering goodbye on a Glastonbury street corner, turning back several times to wave. I walked away in tears, I thought she did too. But who would have thought it was the last time? No illness, no surgery. Just a silly dress-up race on a raft that sprung a leak; it was supposed to be fun and I expect she laughed and laughed. Yet I believe somewhere deep in her body, her spirit knew, and had allowed us to share a few special moments saying goodbye before she died.

My old friend Mimi knew. Twenty years older than me, Mimi was like the older sister I never had, the wise crone friend who taught me how to age with grace and leave at the right time. After a serious fall, Mimi survived a coma and moved to the same nursing home as her husband who had been there since he too had fallen. Joel had tried so hard to make sure Mimi had a bed there, and, once she was settled, he stopped the blood transfusions that had kept him alive for years. He chose to die. Watching Joel die was a master class. He transformed from briskly walking to barely breathing, curled up and fading into the most fragile of fairy-like creatures, like a will-o-the-wisp drifting across his bed. I witnessed labour and birth in reverse. Mimi waited, practising dying from her book, *Deathing*, which she gave to me before she died. She practised consciously closing off each chakra, visualising moving up the body, squeezing energy up and out like toothpaste from a tube, until the spirit reaches the top of the head and leaves. Every afternoon, Mimi would lie on her bed, her catatonic roommate's television blaring, their door wide open to the nursing home bustle outside, and meditate. Practising deathing. Mimi had a sense of humour that exploded in deep chuckles; we had long talks about the meaning of life and she loved me unconditionally. Two days before she died she walked to the home's front porch with me and waved me out of the parking lot The next day she went to hospital with a blood infection and that night she consciously died on the one year anniversary of Joel's death. Mimi really knew.

Before a baby is born, there is usually great preparation - crib and car seat purchased, baby clothes washed, breathing exercises practised, casseroles stored in the freezer. We can also make preparations before dying. Mimi did the ultimate; she practised her deathing. I can study that, and pare down my 'stuff,' make sure my papers are in impeccable order, plan a funeral, say loving goodbyes, and like Koko, gift friends with precious things.

It is all about practice. For years, before I go to sleep I have been reciting my gratitudes of the day. Part of the ritual is remembering conflicts I might have had with others, or myself. How could they have been handled differently, reach a different out-come? How could I have been kinder and more compassionate? I forgive those who have hurt me, knowingly or unknowingly, and, in turn, forgive myself for hurting others. I do this instinctively now and if I remain conscious, I want it to be a ritual before I die when my electrons will be welcomed into the energy field by those of Koko, Mimi, and my mother. Our electrons will flow together, we will cluster, play and dance in the energy field until some feel a new pull into a warm womb, taking with them memories of a gold cloak, a nodding orchid, and dancing with goats. I find further encouragement for my developing theory when Jean Houston writes: 'After our experience of union, we return charged with multiple patterns and evolutionary fluctuations to help evolve the world and time.' [94] Spirit lives on.

If love is the force of attraction between two beings or objects, then we view a cosmos as being defined by love from its first moments - quarks rushing to one another, hydrogen atoms bonding, helium atoms fusing, stardust joining to form planetismals; all this great coming together.

Jacob Berkowitz

Story-telling Time: Counting the Days

Compared to where we ought to be, we are half awake.

William James

After my mother died, I found a small piece of paper with columns of tiny numbers penciled on both sides, beginning with 1282 down to 1, then beginning again at 168 down to 0. The numbers were crossed out until 559. I wonder what happened on Day 559. A date was written at the top: June 29, 1933. I believe that these were the days until my parents married on July 24, 1937 (maybe the added numbers indicated a change in wedding date). My mother, desperate to leave an unhappy home, saw her marriage as liberation. She fatefully began that life at number 0. From 0 she moved into the negative. 56 years minus one week after she ended that list in innocent anticipation, she died. I remember being seven and clearly witnessing depression and disillusionment beginning to cloud her vision, my sadness reflecting hers. Maybe my mother's story birthed a need in me to act on truth and authenticity without setting up false expectations. I will not count my days down to below 0 as she did. I will go forward – my days number over 27,500 by now – and unearth the real truths behind what I have learned were valuable traditions and live in an honest space until I die. So, Mr Proust, that wisdom will be the point of view from which I will come, at last, to regard the world.

Leap of Faith

Jumping into nothing becomes my peace.
        It's the lack of destination underneath
that makes the leap so safe.

        Not like hurtling off a mountain top
where crags and boulders wait
to bleed my bruising fall;
or after pitching from a bridge
lie trapped below the overpass
as wheels squeeze out my air
and tumble-dry my brain;
not even like a dive
        into an endless-bottomed pool
                liquid space as silent as the earth
before its life began
        no worth, no reference,

expect to drown and float for ever
in no-context whirls of nothingness.

When jumping into nothing I know I will be caught.
The universe will gently soothe
push me on my way alone
        whole protected loved
in tune to heal the empty space in time

        then test with yet another leap of faith
not asking what will enter in.

Spaghetti and Asparagus

Where you come from is gone, where you thought you were going to was never there, and where you are is no good unless you can get away from it. Where is there a place for you to be? No place..nothing outside can give you any place - in yourself right now is all the place you've got.

Flannery O'Connor

I am relatively healthy and can still sit cross-legged, admitting personal pleasure at the achievement. I don't think age-related problems have over-taken me yet. However, the other night at dinner I found myself saying intently and clearly, 'Pass the spaghetti please,' when the serving plate obviously held asparagus. Now, I do forget names and places the odd time. I forgot to put on my seatbelt the other day and considering I automatically snap it shut even if I am only driving into the garage, that slip was quite noticeable. At Christmas, I sprinkled cayenne on our egg-nog instead of nutmeg. I've put a hot cross bun in the refrigerator instead of the microwave and then wondered where it disappeared to who when the timer rang. I find I often cannot connect who said what to when, although I very clearly remember the what. Sometimes my partner and I end each other's sentences and chime in on each other's phone conversations so the forgetting becomes almost invisible. I have heard of couples who cover up that way. But I do have a knack of remembering trivia; useless facts lodge themselves in some part of my brain that suddenly pops them out at the right cue, with no help from me. People look my way for useless information they can't remember, and it amazes even me. If I ever lose that skill I will worry. I could never do Sudoko or Cryptics but I love tackling the New York Times' difficult crossword puzzle - in pen. And I am presently memorizing my bank account numbers and passwords when computer bill-paying. I test my memory often, as well as my yoga positions.

So when 'spaghetti' popped out instead of 'asparagus' I was shocked. This wasn't a familiar 'pass me some of - what's it called?' or just gesturing 'over there' if I couldn't remember the name of the long green skinny vegetable that grows beneath our dining room window in the spring. No, this was different. This time the brain independently by-passed a stage - a stage that would have either sent the name of the green vegetable to my speaking apparatus, or known that it couldn't remember the name and verbalized a question instead of the word 'asparagus.' But this time the brain substituted 'spaghetti' all by itself. The 'I,' that I call 'me,' had no upfront knowledge or control. Granted, the length of the food is similar, but not the colour, or method of serving, or appropriateness of eating it with that particular meal. Why would I ever confuse the two? Some tiny part of my brain may be shutting down, or did shut down for just a brief time. Old age is creeping in. Now is the time to put my practices to work.

Mary appears often through this manuscript because, through her stroke and subsequent death, I have been introduced to long term care homes, therapies, legalities, but most important, aging at its most vulnerable. So the opportunity to question 'aging consciously' was foremost on my mind. Where is consciousness when you know what you want to say even if you don't say it? Mary lost her ability to speak clearly, then not at all. At first, she said stock phrases, like 'For instance,' and 'Speaking of that,' and then reverted to mumbling again.

Sometimes she spoke a clear sentence: 'Mary wants you to go now,' and very clearly 'One hundred percent no' when refusing to go to meals or therapy. She knew people by name but could not articulate those names. It was hard to assess her capability to make decisions because while she said yes or no clearly, she then forgot what she had agreed to.

With the backdrop of Mary's struggles in communication, 'spaghetti' popping out instead of 'asparagus' at dinner time seemed very disconcerting. If my brain is going to start taking over and substituting words and information independent of my wishes, how will I communicate? Words are my lifeline.

'They' say that nouns are the first to go. That explains the confusion over names as we get older sometimes. Maybe the decline starts with proper nouns. I don't want to lose adjectives - but then again, if I know inside how I feel about a rosy sunset or a loving touch maybe the feeling is sufficient. Maybe I don't have to verbalize every feeling I own. I can use my inside voice, as I used to suggest to my students. So along with wrinkles and twinges of an old tail-bone injury, now I must be super-aware of my words, which is quite likely bad news to those who consider me 'fussy' enough already over my too-literal thinking. I can get very finicky over the right word, causing many an argument. Maybe my spaghetti/asparagus conundrum is Mother Nature's way of dealing with such pernickitude. She eliminates it from the discussion. It has only happened that once - so far. Having caught it, I feel that I have reached a milestone. And I do know now that I am not impervious to aging.

As youngsters, we thought we were infallible, immortal and infertile - until the first car crash that killed a friend, or the first Grade 11 pregnancy. They were our early transitions to waking-up to adulthood. Maybe this is the same: a waking-up call to aging. I accept these signs from the Universe. My inner crone is prompting me to be respectful of the changes in my body and my mind, and, as well as embrace them into my life, be grateful that they are as they should be. We are always in process. If I were a flower, my faded petals would be dropping off. My stem hasn't bent over yet; maybe that has yet to come.

The Divine has used me as Her instrument to document what 75 feels like and how to pave a path ahead to dying consciously. I want to keep a record of my thoughts and feelings about aging and dying as I get older. This manuscript is an effort to begin that process, to understand how I got to this point in my life. The only direction to go is forward consciously, with love and gratitude - for my life, my partner, my family and friends, my home and abilities, my body and myself.

With newborn babies, we eagerly keep up baby books, exciting notations of growth and development. Maybe I will create a crone book, or an elder book, and record my personal steps as I age further, transitioning in as conscious a way as possible. I can begin with my spaghetti/asparagus epiphany. There are already others.

There is an urgency to waking up before dying.

May it be so.

Blessed be.

Wish-bone

What's left of me
after all those years of teenage dreams
and thirty's dances   blank canvas faces
waiting for someone else's stroke of genius?

I've shifted shape   grown beyond
an aging duplicate of promise born
in bombing raids decades ago.

Missing bits of flesh torn away and left behind,
splinters healed invisibly at last
in twisted form,
earned scars and warts
too faint to see with human eye.

Unloving deeds, abandonment
or being the one who flew
all took their toll   dues paid on time
donated blind, wrapped in layers of need.

As years go by
this body's less the birthed,
its more the soul that's left behind:
the core that burgeons into fruit despite the hurricanes;
a thumb-sized agate slipped into your pocket
to be rubbed in times of stress;

the wish-bone
that coveted, brings fortune in a single snap,
still gleaming under carcass stripped
by starving minds to whom I paid the price.

The soul that held my life together
now honours all the rest
passed the test   is now the prize

End Notes

1. Smith, Charles Hugh, "Who Has the Time and Motivation?" www.oftimes.com, (16/1/14)

2. Jamail, Dahr, "On Staying Sane in a Suicidal Culture," www.truth-out.org/news/item/24083 (2014)

3. Jamail

4. Baker, Carolyn, "In the Shadow of the New Age Spirituality," Huffpost Healthy Living, www.huffingtonpost.com, (24/1/16)

5. Knapton, Sarah, "The World's First Anti-Aging Drug," www.telegraph.co.ok/news/science-news/12017 112, (29/11/15)

6. Berkowitz, Jacob, *The Stardust Revolution*, Prometheus Books, (2012), 120-121

7. Starhawk, *The Pagan Book of Living and Dying*, HarperCollins, (1997), 148

8. Stendl-Rast, David, *Music of Silence*, Ulysses Press, (2001), 64

9. Tolle, Eckhart, *A New Earth*, Penguin Books, (2005), 197

10. Kübler-Ross, Elisabeth; Kessler, David, *Life Lessons*, (2000),102

11. Bushrui, Suheil; Jenkins, Joe, "Kahlil Gibran, Man and Poet," www.nytimes.com/books/first/b/bushrui-gibran, (1998), Chap. 1, sect. 3

12. Singh, Kathleen, *The Grace in Dying: a Message of Hope, Comfort and Spiritual Transformation*, HarperCollins, (1999), 15

13. Singh, 41

14. Costello, Melanie Starr, "Conscious Aging as a Spiritual Path," Jung and Aging, Spring Journal Inc, (157)

15. Mindell, Arthur, *Quantum Mind:The Edge Between Physics and Psychology*, Deep Democracy Exchange, (2000) 222

16. Mindell, 241

17. Mindell, 241

18. Jaynes, Julian,*The Origin of Consciousness in the Breakdown of the Cameral Mind*, Mariner Books, 291

19. Jaynes, 217

20. Singh, 215

21. Scott, David, "The Secret Life of Mother Teresa," www.beliefnet.com/Faiths/Catholic/2005/03

22. Christ, Carol; Plaskow, Judith, "Thinking About Goddess and God," www.feminismandreligion.com, 24/8/15

23. Kempton, Sally, *Awakening Shakti*, Sounds True, Inc., (2013), 328

24. Walker, Barbara, *The Crone*, Harper Row, (1985), 175

25. Walker, 14

26. Myss, Caroline, *Sacred Contracts*, Bantam Books, (2002), 22

27. Jung, Carl, *Man and His Symbols*, Dell Publishing Inc., (1968), 377-378

28. Bolen, Jean Shinoda, *Goddesses in Older Women*, HarperCollins, (2001), 205

29. Mindell, 223

30. Mindell, 257

31. Simmons, Julie, *Earned Wisdom: Becoming an Elder in the Times of Chaos*, (2011), 5-6

32. Paramansa Yogananda, *Autobiography of a Yogi*, Yogoda Satsanga Society of India, (1946), 162

33. Berkowitz, 308

34. Grierson, Bruce, *What Makes Olga Run?* Random House, Canada, (2014), 178

35. Erikson, Joan; Erikson, Erik, *The Life Cycle Completed: Extended Version*, (1997), 4

36. Kathiala, Laleema, "There's a Power of Living in Awareness of Life Beyond Death," www.collectiveevolution.com, 19/2/15

37. Grierson, 178

38. Codhina, Alessandra, "Celine Unveils its Latest Poster Girl" www.vogue.com/7683419, 6/1/15

39. Marriott, Hannah, "Joan Didion and Celine," www.theguardian.com/fashion/short-cuts/2015/1/07

40. Revlon Inc, Company Profile, www.referenceforbusiness.com/history2/10/Revlon-Inc, 2010

41. Marriott

42. Freeman, Hadley, "It's Great That Celine is Celebrating Joan Didion – But to Sell Accessories?" www.theguardian.com/fashion/2015/1/12

43. Cohen, Claire, "Every Schoolgirl Needs to See This Video," www.telegraph.co.uk/women/women's-life/11335179/2015/1/9

44. Wente, Margaret, "Advice to Younger Women," www.theglobeandmail.com/globe-debate/article22383707/ 2015/1/10

45. Codhina

46. Baring, Anne, *The Dream of the Cosmos*, Archive Publishing, (2013), 529

47. Baker, Carolyn, *Love in the Age of Ecological Apocalypse*, North Atlantic Books, (2015) xxiv-xxv

48. Singh, 215

49. Thurman, Robert, Trans, *The Tibetan Book of the Dead*, Bantam Books, (1994), 134

50. Jenkinson, Stephen, *Die Wise: a Manifesto for Sanity and Soul*, North Atlantic Books, (2015), 315

51. Jenkinson, 310

52. Singh, 211

53. Kűbler-Ross; Kessler, 138-139

54. Dossey, Larry, *One Mind: How Our Individual Mind Is Part of a Greater Consciousness And Why It Matters*, Hay House Inc, (2014), 238

55. Joseph, Lawrence, "James Lovelock: Gaia's Grand Old Man", www.salon.com,/2000/08/17

56. Kashi, David, "USS Ronald Reagan Crew Members sick with cancer," www.ibtimes.com, 24/12/13

57. Jamail

58. Harris, Massimilla; Harris, Bud, *Into the Heart of Feminine*, Daphne Publications, (2014), 83

59. Lamott, Anne, *Bird by Bird: Some Instructions on Writing and Life*, Anchor Books, (1995), 28

60. Singer, Michael, *The Untethered Soul: a Journey Beyond Yourself*, New Harbinger Publications, (2007), 129

61. Weller, Francis, *Entering the Healing Ground: Grief, Ritual and the Soul of the World*, (2012), 120

62. Berry, Patricia, "Cross-cultural Perspectives on Hillman's Archetypal Psychology," online seminar, www.depthpsychologyalliance.com, 11/12/2015

63. Anzaldúa, Gloria, *Borderlands/La Frontera*, Aunt Lute Book Company, (1987), 195

64. Jamail

65. Tempest-Williams, Terry, "Survival Becomes a Spiritual Practice," www.yesmagazine.org/issues/the-debt-issue/10/5/2015

66. Tempest-Williams

67. Erikson, p. 3

68. Erikson, p. 4

69. Erikson, p. 4

70. Singh, Kathleen, *The Grace in Aging: Awaken as You Grow Older*, Wisdom Publications, (2014), 9

71. Jung, Carl, *Memories, Dreams, and Reflections*, Vintage Books, (1961), 356

72. Tempest-Williams

73. Kessler, Kűbler-Ross, 205

74. Schlitz, Marilyn, *Death Makes Life Possible*, Sounds True Publishing, (2014), 180.

75. Mindell, p. 379

76. Chodron, Pema, "The Know Yourself is to Forget Yourself," www.lionsroar.com/pema-chodron,22/1/16

77. Jung, *Memories, Dreams and Reflections*, 302

78. Macy, Joanna; Brown, Molly, *Coming Back to Life: the Updated Guide to the Work that Reconnects*, New Society Publishers, (2014), 274

79. Singh, *The Grace in Dying*, 3

80. Kathiala

81. Schlitz, 88

82. Arrien, Angeles, *The Second Half of Life: Opening the Eight Gates of Wisdom*, Sounds True Inc., (2005),174

83. Lanza, Robert, "Five Reasons You Don't Die," www.huffingtonpost.com, 20/1/2011

84. Assaraf, John, "Why You Should Be Aware of Quantum Physics," www.the-open-mind.com, 31/12/2014, 214

85. Slawinski, Janusz, "Electric Radiation and the Afterlife," Journal of Near-Death Studies, Winter 1987, 84

86. Slawinski, 91

87. Ask Van, "Life Death, Energy Conservation," Department of Physics, University of Illinois, www.van.physics.illinois.edu, 5/2/2014

88. Slawinski, 85

89. Talbot, David; Low, Gord, Thunderbolts of the Gods part 1,Tutorial, www.youtube.com/watch?x-yt-ts=1402601098, (2012)

90. Slawinski, 90

91. Trosper, Jamie, "The Physics of Death" www.futurism.com/the-physics-of-death, (2013)

92. Baring, 491

93. Schlitz, 186-187

94. Houston, Jean, "Some Thoughts on Time," www.m.facebook.com/jean.houston.oage/posts/736768443065959 (2014)

Previously published poems in *The Fireman's Child* (2012)

Mushroom Clouds

I Imagine

Salvadokathedral

Previously published poems in *Spirit of Lyme* (2003)

Sometimes, Something

Crossing the Edge

After-words: Soul on the Page

We dance around in a ring and suppose.
The Secret sits in the middle and knows.

Robert Frost

Aging Consciously, Dying Awake was included in my dissertation as a creative offering nestling within the academic requirements that finalized my Doctoral studies with the Wisdom Graduate School of Ubiquity University. One of the necessary preparations was identifying with an appropriate research methodology. This caused concern for me: I write in that in-between realm sustained by the soul that allows a poem, an essay, a story, to go beyond facts, beyond the obvious, into unexplored territory. Metaphors pave the way between personal and universal, from past to present, and open the door between now and the cosmos. I surrender to the process. Labelling a methodology was challenging for me. My writing itself became a major character in this dissertation drama where it must hold its own, speak its unique voice in its labyrinthine style. But to be true to the dissertation requisites, I had to keep one foot in the real world and befriend the one that spoke an unfamiliar language, the lead actor in the drama: Research Methodology.

At first I misinterpreted the plot and balked at introducing data and statistics, facts and figures, into my creative endeavor. Words like rules and discipline pushed triggers. But my inner crone reminded me that, as an evolutionary being, I had pledged to be flexible with change, to think outside the box. So I tried to befriend this imposed house-guest but still battled with the concept.

And then I saw the word 'sacred' on the cover of one of the many books on research I ordered: *An Organic Inquiry Reader for the Novice Researcher.* I admitted I was a reluctant researcher rather than novice, but when the book confirmed that I was already 'interacting with the liminal domain' (p.29) and I could 'hold data up to bodily senses, emotions of the heart, and intuitive resonances' (p.85), I began to feel secure in my process. The researcher can 'find connections between things that might otherwise be thought separate...' (p.7) At last! That's what I do – it exists!

Then I discovered Garance Marechal's seminal essay, 'Autoethnography'. 'A relational commitment to studying the ordinary practices of human life...makes sense of lived experience and contributes to social criticism,'(p.3) she writes. 'Anthropology has recently shown a widespread and recent interest in personal narrative, life history and autobiography, as a result of changing conceptions of self-identity and relations between self and society.' (p.1) Now my 'I' has permission to become the 'It'! I was excited. I found a fit - a methodology that named my own creative process and could integrate my writing with the more formal and required presentation of my body of knowledge.

Finally, in Robert D. Romanyshyn's *The Wounded Researcher*, I read, 'perhaps the...method of research done with the soul in mind is simply a recognition that all our acts of knowing are attempts at remembering what we once knew but have forgotten. Perhaps all our attempts at research are sacred acts whose deep motive is salvation or redemption.' (p.268) I welcomed autoethnography into my life. And my book within a book was born, accepted in the academic world, and now offered to you, the reader, with love.

Bibliography

Anderson, Rosemarie, *Transforming Self and Others Through Research*, NY: State University of New York Press, 2011.

Anderson, Sherry R., *Ripening Time: Inside Stories for Aging with Grace*, Great Britain: Changemaker Books, 2013.

Anzaldúa, Gloria, *Borderlands/la Frontera*, San Francisco: Aunt Lute Book Company, 1987.

Argüelles, Jose, *Manifesto for the Noosphere*, California: Evolver Editions, 2011.

Arrien, Angeles, *The Second Half of Life: Opening the Eight Gates of Wisdom*, Boulder, CO: Sounds True, Inc., 2005.

Baker, Carolyn, *Navigating the Coming Chaos*, United States: iUniverse, 2011.

Baker, Carolyn, *Love in the Age of Ecological Apocalypse*, California: North Atlantic Books, 2015.

Baker, Carolyn & McPherson, Guy, *Extinction Dialogues: How to Live with Death in Mind*, San Francisco: Next Revelation Press, 2014.

Baring, Anne, *The Dream of the Cosmos: A Quest for the Soul*, Dorset UK: Archive Publishing, 2013.

Berger, K. T., *Zen Driving*, New York: Ballantine Books, 1988.

Berkowitz, Jacob, *The Stardust Revolution*, New York: Prometheus Books, 2012.

Bolen, Jean Shinoda, *Goddesses in Older Women*, New York: HarperCollins Publishers, 2001.

Bolen, Jean Shinoda, *Crossing to Avalon*, New York: HarperCollins Publishers, 2004.

Bolen, Jean Shinoda, *Urgent Message from Mother*, Maine: Conari Press, 2005.

Collins, Mick, *The Unselfish Spirit: Human Evolution in a Time of Global Crisis*, Hampshire, UK: Permanent Publications, 2014.

Csikszentmihalyi, Mihaly, *Creativity: the Psychology of Discovery and Invention*, NY: HarperCollins Publishers, 1996.

Curry, Deah. & Wells, Steven, *An Organic Inquiry Primer for the Novice Researcher*, PA: Infinity Publishing.com, 2006.

Dossey, Larry, *One Mind: How our Individual Mind is Part of a Greater Consciousness and Why it Matters*, United States: Hay House, Inc., 2014.

Erikson, Joan & Erikson, Erik, *The Life Cycle Completed: Extended version*, New York: W. W. Norton & Co., Inc., 1997.

Foos-Graber, Anya, *Deathing: An Intelligent Alternative to the Final Moments of Life*, Maine: Nicolas-Hays Inc., 1989.

Fox, Matthew, *Sins of the Spirit, Blessings of the Flesh*, New York: Three Rivers Press, 1999.

Greer, Germaine, *The Change: Women, Aging and the Menopause*, USA: Ballantine Books, 1991.

Grierson, Bruce, *What Makes Olga Run?* Toronto: Random House, Canada, 2014.

Harris, Massimilla & Bud, *Into the Heart of the Feminine*, North Carolina: Daphne Publications, 2014.

Harvey, Andrew, *The Hope: a Guide to Sacred Activism*, United States: Hay House, Inc., 2009.

Hedges, Chris, *Empire of Illusion*, Canada: Vintage Canada, 2010.

Hillman, James, *The Force of Character*, New York: Random House, Inc., 1999.

Hubbard, Barbara Marx, *Conscious Evolution*, California: New World Library, 1998.

Hughes, Kristoffer, *The Journey into Spirit: A Pagan's Perspective on Death, Dying and Bereavement*, MN: Llewellyn Publications, 2014.

Jaynes, Julian, *The Origin of Consciousness in the Breakdown of the Bicameral Mind*, New York: Mariner Books, 1995.

Jenkinson, Stephen, *Die Wise: a Manifesto for Sanity and Soul*, California: North Atlantic Books. 2015.

Jones, Kathy, *Priestess of Avalon, Priestess of the Goddess*, Glastonbury UK: Ariadne Publications, 2006.

Judith, Anodea, *Wheels of Life: The User's Guide to the Chakra System*, Minnesota: Llewellyn Publications, 2002.

Judith, Anodea, *Waking the Global Heart*, California: Elite Books. 2006.

Jung, Carl G., *Memories, Dreams, and Reflections*, NY: Vintage Books, 1961.

Jung, Carl G., *Man and his Symbols*, New York: Dell Publishing Inc, 1968.

Kafatos, Menos & Nadeau, Robert, *The Conscious Universe: Parts and Wholes in Physical Reality*, (2nd ed.), New York: Springer Verlag, 2000.

Kempton, Sally, *Awakening Shakti*, Boulder CO: Sounds True Inc., 2013.

Kingsley, Peter, *In the Dark Places of Wisdom*, California: The Golden Sufi Centre, 1999.

Kübler-Ross, Elisabeth, *The Wheel of Life: a Memoir of Living and Dying*, New York: Scribner, 1997.

Kübler-Ross, Elisabeth & Kessler David, *Life Lessons: Two Experts on Death and Dying Teach Us About the Mysteries of Life and Living*, New York: Scribner, 2000.

Lammott, Anne, *Bird by Bird: Some Instructions on Writing and Life*, New York: Anchor Books, 1995.

Laszlo, Ervin, *Science and the Re-enchantment of the Cosmos*, Vermont: Inner Traditions. 2006.

Levine, Stephen, *Who Dies: An Investigation of Conscious Living and Conscious Dying*, New York: Doubleday, 1982.

Lipton, Bruce, *Biology of Belief: Unleashing the Power of Unconsciousness, Matter and Miracles*, CA: Mountain of Love/Elite Books, 2005.

Macy, Joanna & Brown, *Molly, Coming Back to Life: the Updated Guide to the Work that Reconnects*, Vancouver, Canada: New Society Publishers, 2014.

Marechal, Garance, *Autoethnography*. www.academia.edu/843133/Autoethnography. 2010.

Meade, Michael, *Fate and Destiny: the Two Agreements of the Soul*, United States: Green Fire Press, 2010.

Meade, Michael, *Why the World Doesn't End*, United States: Green Fire Press, 2012.

Meredith, Jane, *Journey to the Dark Goddess*, Great Britain: Moon Books, 2012.

Meredith, Jane, *Rituals of Celebration: Honouring the Seasons of Life through the Wheel of the Year*, MN: Llewellyn Publications, 2013.

Mindell, Arthur, *Quantum Mind: The Edge between Physics and Psychology*, Oregon: Deep Democracy Exchange, 2000.

Mumford, Dr. Jonn, *Death: Beginning or End?* Minnesota: Llewellyn Publications, 1999.

Myss, Carolyn, *Sacred Contracts*, Great Britain: Bantam Books, 2002.

Myss, Carolyn, *Defy Gravity*, United States: Hay House, 2009.

Paramahansa Yogananda, *Autobiography of a Yogi*, India: Yogoda Satsanga Society of India, 1946.

Publication Manual of the American Psychological Association (6th ed.), Washington DC: American Psychological Association. 2010.

Richmond, Lewis, *Aging as a Spiritual Practice*, New York: Penguin Group, 2012.

Roberts, Carol & Hyatt, Laura, *The Dissertation Journey*, CA: Corwin Press, 2004.

Romanyshyn, Robert D., *The Wounded Researcher*, Louisiana: Spring Journal Inc., 1997.

Sarton, May, *The House by the Sea*, New York: W.W. Norton & co., Inc., 1977.

Satprem. *Sri Aurobindo or the Adventure of Consciousness*, Canada: Institut de Recherches Évolutives, 2000.

Saul, John, *On Equilibrium*, Canada: Penguin Books, 2002.

Sawin, Leslie, Corbett, Lionel, & Carbine, Michael, Eds. *Jung and Aging: Possibilities and Potentials for the Second Half of Life*, USA: Spring Journal Inc., 2014.

Schlitz, Marilyn, *Death makes Life Possible: Revolutionary Insights on Living, Dying, and the Continuation of Consciousness*, Colorado: Sounds True Publishing, 2014.

Scott-Maxwell, Florida, *The Measure of my Days*. New York: Penguin Books, 1968.

Sheldrake, Rupert, *A New Science of Life: The Hypothesis Morphic Resonance*, Rochester, VT: Park Street Press, 1999.

Simmons, Julie, Earned Wisdom: *Becoming an Elder in Times of Chaos*, United States: Trafford Publishing, 2011.

Singer, Michael A., *The Untethered Soul: the Journey Beyond Yourself*, New York: New Harbinger Publications, Inc., 2007.

Singh, Kathlenn Dowling, *The Grace in Aging: Awaken as You Grow Older*, MA, USA: Wisdom Publications, 2014.

Singh, Kathleen Dowling, *The Grace in Dying*, NY: HarperCollins Publishers, 1999.

Slawinski, Janusz, *Electromagnetic Radiation and the Afterlife, Journal of Near-Death Studies*, Volume 6, No 2, Winter 1987. Human Sciences Press, 1987.

Starhawk, *The Pagan Book of Living and Dying*, New York: HarperCollins Publishers, 1997.

Starhawk, *The Spiral Dance*. (20th ed.), New York: HarperCollins Publishers, 1999.

Starhawk, *The Earth Path: Grounding your Spirit in the Rhythms of Nature*, New York: HarperCollins Publishers, 2004.

Swimme Brian & Berry Thomas, *The Universe Story*, New York: HarperCollins Publishers, 1992.

Thurman, Robert A. F. Trans., *The Tibetan Book of the Dead*, New York: Bantam Books, 1994.

Tolle, Eckardt, *A New Earth*, New York: Penguin Books Inc., 2005.

Van Eyk MacCain, Marian, *Elderwoman*, Scotland: Findhorn Press, 2002.

Vaughan-Lee, Lewellyn, *The Return of the Feminine and the World Soul*, California: The Golden Sufi Center, 2009

Vogler, Christopher, *The Writer's Journey: Mythic Structure for Writers* (3rd ed.), CA: Michael Wiese Productions, 2007.

Walker, Barbara, *The Crone*, United States: Harper Row, 1985.

Weller, Francis. *Entering the Healing Ground: Grief, Ritual and the Soul of the World*, CA: Wisdom Bridge Press, 2012.

Wilber, Ken, *Grace and Grit* (2nd ed.), Boston: Shambhala Publications Inc., 2000.

About the Author

Roz Bound, poet and writer, elder and crone, began her writing life at four, when her first poem was published in the local newspaper. Fifteen years of living in the tropics as a corporate wife provided valuable resources for reflection and growth, as did divorcing and moving back to Canada with four children who had never experienced any season other than summer. A retired teacher of both children and adults, Roz earned her degrees while she was teaching and parenting by searching out innovative programmes, non- and low-residential – her BA with the University of Alabama External Degree programme at 56, MFA in Creative Writing at Goddard College, Vermont at 60, and Doctor of Ministry in Wisdom Spirituality at Ubiquity University, California, at 75, all highly memorable for this eternal student. She has spoken many times in Ontario, Alberta, and at the Goddess Conference in Glastonbury England on feminine spirituality and the strength of the human spirit. For the past twenty years, Roz has loved nurturing writers in their transformational process, creating safe space when facilitating writing courses and monthly Open floor readings. Believing that writing in solitude is as necessary as writing in community, after retirement she spent sixteen months in retreat in her soulplace by the sea in England which inspired her first poetry collection, *Spirit of Lyme* (2003). *The Fireman's Child* (2012), honours a journey of forgiveness and love. Now living by Lake Ontario with her partner Vicki, Roz celebrates Mother Earth on Solstices and Equinoxes by leading community rituals, and offers meditation and healing circles, always stressing the vital importance of Goddess, myth and ritual, not only for today but also for our evolution into an uncertain future.

For Bideford Exhibition

(1) "Sails in the Sunset" Framed. Acrylic

(2) "Regatta"

For ALP online

(1) "Up and over" — on Paper, not framed, Acrylic

(2) "Jump"

(3) "Riding on the Moors"

(4) "Girl Riding a Horse" framed with Glass

Left ½ Bernie for David Jeckell on Wed 13th Nov. at Tesco Rose Lane Car Park.

~~ARCHWARD ISA NAWIDE~~

2022
875
2047

ROW